Library of Congress Cataloging in Publication Data

Bologna, Jack.
  Corporate fraud.

  Bibliography: p.
  Includes index.
  1. Fraud. 2. Fraud—Prevention. 3. Corporations—
Corrupt practices. 4. Fraud investigation. I. Title.
HV6691.B64 1984   364.1'63   84-9591
ISBN 0-409-95129-3

Butterworth Publishers
80 Montvale Avenue
Stoneham, MA 02180

10 9 8 7 6 5 4 3 2 1

Printed in the United States of America

Corporate Fraud
The Basics of Prevention and Detection

Jack Bologna

BUTTERWORTH PUBLISHERS
Boston • London
Sydney • Wellington • Durban • Toronto

Acknowledgments

I would like to extend my thanks to Greg Franklin and Elaine Cox of Butterworth Publishers for their help in the editorial and production processes of this book. I would also like to thank Linda Dziobek, who copyedited with kindness and care. Special thanks also go to my wife, Jean, who suffered quietly while I wrote the book, and to my secretary Barbara Davis, who toiled diligently trying to unscramble my syntax. You all deserve my gratitude.

Contents

Preface

The first recorded incident of fraud in Western man's literature is contained in the book of Genesis. Eve was tempted by a serpent to eat the fruit of the Tree of Conscience, or of good and evil. The serpent falsely represented that she would become godlike if she did so.

That biblical story has all the elements of fraud as we know it today:

- A wily perpetrator who knows the true state, condition, value, ownership, quantity or identity of some thing
- An innocent victim who lacks such knowledge or who cannot learn enough information, even with due diligence, to protect himself
- A willful misrepresentation of a material fact by the perpetrator that is intended to deceive the victim, or a failure to communicate a material fact when a legal or equitable duty exists to do so

For thirty years I have been involved either directly or indirectly or full time or part time in auditing and investigating frauds of an accounting or financial nature. With more than twelve years of federal experience in investigating and auditing for tax frauds, labor organization and pension fund frauds and embezzlements, and antitrust violations; twelve more years in private practice assisting attorneys and accountants in ferreting out financial frauds and employee embezzlements; and finally, with degrees in both accounting and law, I vainly thought I could easily write a definitive book on the subject of fraud, or more specifically on business and financial frauds, from an auditor's point of view—a how to do an audit for fraud textbook.

But when a major part of your life has been spent doing a particular type of work—rather than thinking about it, teaching it, or researching it—you are at a great disadvantage. That is probably why most texts on technical subjects are written by university professors. They do not need to do to survive, so they can give the subject more thought, do more thorough research, and be up to date. But university professors either in law or accounting schools do not seem to write books on fraud. (I should have remembered that my own college text on auditing had only one paragraph on fraud, which dealt with check kiting and receivables lapping. In law school, where fraud was treated more extensively in courses on criminal law, torts, and contracts, the word fraud was never defined except in very broad terms. There were types of frauds discussed in these texts such as fraud in the execution of a contract; fraud in the inducement of a contract; fraud, duress, and undue influence in making out a will; and criminal frauds, like forgery, counterfeiting, false tokens, false pretenses and willful misrepresentations of facts material to a commercial transaction.) Fraud has never been the subject of scholarly study as far as my own limited research has determined. Fraud apparently is a lot like the weather—everyone talks about it but no one does anything about it, at least not from the academic standpoint.

This book is not an academic or scientific treatment of the subject either. Lest I commit fraud on the reader, let me say that my intention is to provide a primer on the subject of fraud auditing and some useful hints and not to write a definitive work. Three years have been spent in preparing this manuscript, and full treatment of the subject might no doubt take longer than the years I have left.

Fraud deals with the seamier side of man, man at his worst—lying, cheating, stealing, exploiting, seducing, tricking, deceiving, and setting traps for the unwary and innocent victims of his schemes. This may be the reason why academics do not enjoy writing about it. We would like to believe all men are noble, trustworthy, and otherwise virtuous. Even in the field of psychology where man's inhumanity to his fellowman is explored, fraud has received little attention. Yet fraud and deceit are such common forms of human misbehavior, one might ask with good reason why psychologists and psychiatrists have written so sparingly about it.

To add to the literature of human behavior and hopefully to spark some controversy and perhaps some research interest, let me assume that man has a tendency to lie and cheat (commit fraud) whenever his economic, social, or political survival is threatened. It is almost an autonomic response and is a sign of a weakness we all share as human beings. Some people become so good at lying and cheating that they will continue to do so even when there is no need i.e., no threat to them. Since the rewards for lying and cheating in a materialist society are so great and the punishments so weak, the behavior is reinforced in every generation. Therefore, fraud and deceit may be with us for a long, long time, in fact until man realizes his full human potential to be accepted, trusted, respected, cherished, and loved for what he is not what he was or could be nor by what he owns. After this potential has been achieved, the motivation to commit fraud may be finally dispelled for most people. However, the current world of reality is that fraud in interpersonal transactions exists. The question is how to handle it until man becomes less imperfect.

Let us therefore begin this primer by admitting frankly there is no commonly accepted legal definition of fraud. But a variety of human acts have been statutorily defined and judicially construed as being tantamount to fraud. So while we have some legal precedents by which to define some types of fraud, the legal genus remains undefined except in terms of lying and cheating.

We also do not have a taxonomy of fraud, that is, a rational and coherent classification system based on clinical observations or empirical research. What we do have, for legal purposes, is a collection of precedents, i.e., this act constitutes fraud, that act is not fraud, and behaviors that are regarded as fraudulent such as counterfeiting and forgery, but we don't put all fraudulent behaviors in a definitional framework. So fraud definitions are in a continual state of evolution, along with the legal concept of what constitutes fraud. What was regarded by the courts as a merchant "puffing" his wares one hundred years ago may be regarded as consumer fraud today, i.e., false advertising.

Human experience, rather than empirical research, is the basis for law. Laws reflect past experience much more than the present or future. Laws therefore tend to be historical documents rather than living documents. So fraud like truth, honesty, justice, and beauty may never be fully defined, but, like these concepts, will continue to be transformed by human experience and new knowledge.

CHAPTER 1

History and Evolution of Fraud

FRAUD AND MAN'S NATURE

The essential quality of man which distinguishes him in the animal kingdom is his ability to reason and derive truth. But that same ability can be used by man to distort the truth as he knows it, or to contort it for his own economic, social, and political advantage if he wills to do so. While man can reason, man can also rationalize. Therefore, the possibility of fraud or deception exists in all human interactions and will no doubt continue for some time to come. But lest the reader accuse me of being a pessimist regarding human nature, let me add the following commentary.

Truth and justice are idealistic concepts or virtues for which we strive. Truth and justice are living concepts. They may change from time to time as man garners new insights from his being, his experiences, and his discoveries. They grow in social importance over time. As principles, ideals, and guidelines by which to live, however, they may be far less changeable.

The opposites of truth and justice—untruth and injustice—are therefore changeable as well. Fraud today is not fraud tomorrow. And if there is more fraud today than yesterday, it may well mean that our standards of truth and justice are greater. We expect more truth and justice than we did before. So more human conduct is labeled as fraudulent today not because man is more fraudulent, but because man expects more truth, honesty, and justice in his interactions and business transactions than ever before. Despite the peeves of some social critics of our times, man's rise up the ladder of truth and justice has been steady and consistent over the centuries.

FRAUD DEFINED AS DECEPTION

Commonly defined, fraud means deception. But deception can be self-directed (rationalization, for example) or directed against others. In the latter sense, fraud is relational. It deals with how people interact or transact business with one another, that is, whether their interactions and transactions are just and equitable.

It is in the relational context of fraud that I will concentrate. I will leave self-directed deceptions like rationalization, projection, denial, overcompensation, regression, and reaction formation to the psychological community. The "why" and "who" of fraud will not be as important as the what, when, where, and how of fraud. There will be some fleeting references to the why and who (motivations and profiles of typical defrauders) but only as obiter dictum and asides. Frankly, not much is known about why people commit fraud, i.e., lying and cheating, other than for economic, social, and political survival or for such pathological reasons as self-aggrandizement (greed and ego inflation). Honesty, as mentioned, is an ideal not a unversal trait.

If we define the word fraud, in its broadest context, as the intentional deception of another person, through means such as lying and cheating for the purpose of deriving an unjust personal, social, political, or economic advantage over that other person, we can all confess that we have been both victims of fraud and perpetrators of fraud. In that sense, fraud is the most common form of human misbehavior which exists in the world.

Most societies abhor fraud in personal and family matters, but the same standard does not hold true in business matters. Commercial transactions are not looked upon as situations which require the highest care and concern for truth, honesty, and fair dealing. Sellers of goods are expected to "puff their wares," to put their best foot forward, and to "put the best side of the meat, up." There are hundreds of words which connote or describe fraud. (See the glossary on page 201.) But there are few words to describe the opposite of fraud, i.e., truth, honor, justice, integrity, candor, honesty, fairness, or perhaps in a word, love.

FRAUD DEFINED AS LYING AND CHEATING

Fraud, as it is understood today, means an intentional deception or a willful misrepresentation of a material fact. Lying, the willful telling of an untruth, and cheating, the gaining of an unfair or unjust advantage over another, could be used to further define the word *fraud,* since these two words denote intention or willingness to deceive. But all untruths are not frauds. Untruths may be uttered or repeated innocently because of mistake, miscalculation, misinformation, misperception, or nonculpable ignorance. And an untruth may involve a matter of no personal or financial consequence (a "white lie," for example) or a matter of grave consequence, i.e., loss of money, social status, or political power.

So perhaps cheat is a better synonym for fraud for our purposes than lie, or at least less subject to confusion. If cheating is the gaining of an unfair or unjust advantage over another, there must be some underlying notion of what constitutes "fairness" or "justness" in interpersonal relationships and transactions. Otherwise, how could we judge or determine whether a given act or set of circumstances constitutes fraud?

FRAUD AND MORALITY

Fairness in interpersonal transactions involves the concept of equity or equality. Its simplest embodiment is contained in the Golden Rule: "Do unto others as you would have them do unto you." While the Golden Rule has never been enacted as a law per se, it has influenced the thinking of jurists, as well as moral philosophers, since the time of Plato and Socrates.

Before there was law there was morality and moral philosophers who tried to provide us with some guidelines for conducting human interactions. Moral philosophers gave us standards of conduct by which we should comport ourselves when dealing with others either in matters of social intercourse or in business transactions.

Socrates, for example, in defining justice (a somewhat broader term than fairness) says that justice is

- Telling the truth and rendering up what we have received
- Rendering to each his due
- Complying with the interest of the stronger, that is, of the ruling class as is expressed in law
- Minding one's own business both in external relations with others and in the internal ordering of the soul

If morality predates law, rules of morality must underlie laws that govern interpersonal relations and transactions. In Christ's gospel of love, He preaches both the Golden Rule as a general guideline and the Ten Commandments of Moses as more specific guidelines for human conduct; but He makes it clear that love of God and neighbor are the most important of the commandments. Intentionally deceiving someone you know and really love, respect, and trust is hard to imagine. Deceiving someone you do not know or whom you fear, despise, or distrust is not difficult to imagine. But Christ says that you should even love your enemies and those who despise, revile, and persecute you for God's sake. That concept of love has been the most difficult to realize or comply with for Western man. Therefore, fraud, or deception, continues to exist even in our day, although hopefully with less frequency than in the past.

Fraud can come in a number of forms but its nature never changes. It is an intentional deception of another, committed usually to derive some measure of undue economic, political, or social advantage over another. The measure of the undue advantage is what the law attempts to deal with, not the lie, the trickery, or deceit itself—and it does so from considerations of justice and equity. All lies and deceits may be immoral but not necessarily illegal. Justice and morality are not the same principles. Principles of morality do crop up in the law and do influence the law, but law can never have the literary precision for which moral theologians strive. Laws are man-made and man-derived, not divinely inspired. So, on occasion, laws may be construed as immoral by philosophers. But the need for laws as guides for human interactions, relations, and transactions has rarely been assailed by philosophers except those who propose anarchy as a way of self-governance or social control.

Laws are based on human experience rather than divine intervention. But as man seeks perfection, the law reflects changes in man's moral views, his attitudes toward others, and his social values.

In this sort of ever-changing environment, legal definitions cannot be fixed. They must be broad enough to include the changing perceptions and perspectives of mankind as well as to satisfy man's need for social order and regularity, i.e., consistency and continuity. For example, the Ten Commandments say "Thou Shalt Not Kill," "Thou Shalt Not Commit Adultery," or "Thou Shalt Not Covet Thy Neighbor's Goods." But in the law, these rules have many qualifiers. Very few substantive rules in the law are absolutes. The substantive rules are general and exceptions are far greater in number than the general rules themselves.

FRAUD AND ENGLISH COMMON LAW

Early references to fraud in English common law define it as cheating or deceit. A common law cheat was one who, by false pretenses, false tokens, or intentionally false representations, induced another to part with his real or personal property, and/or his legal or equitable rights. Common law cheating or fraud was considered both a crime (a misdemeanor as distinguished from larceny, which was a felony) and a matter for civil redress in courts of law and equity, by way of contract rescission, restoration, restitution, or recovery of damages. So fraud has a historical foothold in the English civil law as well as in its criminal law.

Since fraud will be presented mainly from the perspectives of commercial transactions and law, some comments about commerce and law may be in order. Commerce, once it passes the barter state, relies on law. Laws are social controls evolving from conventions (customs and usages) and are designed by societies to protect the rights these societies confer on their members.

The "law merchant," from which we have derived many of our legal rules of commerce, began as a set of rules of fair business conduct during the Middle Ages. Merchants, tradesmen, freight handlers, and brokers of goods had to have some way of assuring themselves that their work and products would be paid for and protected from theft or conversion. Commerce could not flourish in an environment where no trust existed between buyers and sellers. (A man's word may be his bond, but if it is reduced to writing there is a higher level of assurance that he will, in fact, make good on his word.) So rules of contract evolved, i.e., contracts of sale, of agency, of bailment, and of carriage. Since all commercial transactions could not be paid for in cash (coin) for fear of robbery, credit had to be extended. Mediums of exchange other than cash or coin had to be designed, such as drafts (guarantees of payment), bills of lading, etc. Rules on negotiable instruments were created. Banking and insurance companies were formed as intermediaries to facilitate commerce and to minimize the risk of loss from perils such as robbery and shipwreck. So rules of fairness in commercial transactions were introduced into the laws of the time and were based on human experience (customs and traditions) and not necessarily on moral principles of right conduct.

As mentioned previously, morality and the law are separate worlds. Moral principles may influence the law or enactment of laws, but laws have an existence of their own quite apart from morality. What is right and just legally may be far different from what is right and just morally. Morality is concerned more with individual virtue while law concerns itself with group and interpersonal relations from the standpoint of who has the most power to impose his will on others.

In the Middle Ages, the mercantile interests had far more power than the masses or consumers of goods and services. Therefore, the "law merchant" dealt mainly with how merchants should interact in business transactions with one another, i.e., "at arm's length," neither trusting nor distrusting completely. There were few rules governing how they should transact business with consumers other than "let the buyer beware." The idea of fairness at that time had to do with the subject of business transactions, not with the object of such transactions, i.e., with reasonable and equitable exchanges of value. Values in the medieval mind were subjective. "Whatever the traffic will bear" was the rule of thumb in setting prices for goods and services.

The fairness or reasonableness of the price charged for goods and services by a merchant or tradesman was determined at common law by the price at which an accord could be struck by a seller willing but under no compulsion to sell and a buyer willing and under no compulsion to buy. This subjective rule as to fairness in pricing articles of commerce holds generally true today. It is difficult to set precise objective limits on the value of anything. So value (the price at which goods or properties are exchanged in an arm's length transaction), will continue to be construed on a rather subjective basis, i.e., what seems to be reasonable under the circumstances; what is the going price for like or similar goods, in similar condition, in that market area at that particular time. Courts are not inclined to impose their judgment on the value of an article so long as the parties to a transaction are on a similar footing, i.e., of roughly equal intelligence, competence, and means. It is only when the value paid seems clearly unconscionable under all the circumstances of the case that a court will interject itself when the issue of value is raised.

But deceptions as to the kind, character, and condition of goods, their quantity, their quality, and their ownership have historically been grounds for judicial concern and review.

Misrepresentations as to value therefore were generally not actionable offenses in common law times. Value, like beauty, was considered to be "in the eye of the beholder." Statements about the value of goods were seen as "puffery," or as expressions of personal opinion, or as subjective judgments not objective realities. Who knew what the *value* of anything was, in an era of ignorance and illiteracy? But willful misrepresentations about such things as the quantity of the goods (weights and measures) could be determined. People could at least count, if not theorize about values. Value determinations were left to

philosophers and moral theologians to argue about. Commerce could not flourish if arguments were raised about the value or consideration paid for goods.

Unless it appears clearly unconscionable even today the value of an article
or the consideration paid for it is not generally a subject of great judicial concern
in contract litigation. And even if unconscionable, the cases turn more on the
issue of competency than adequacy—anyone paying that much must be crazy,
totally inexperienced in business, too young or too old to know better, or a victim
of duress or undue influence.

Fraud from a legal standpoint, then, can be viewed as 1) a tort, i.e., a civil
or private wrong, where recovery of an asset and/or monetary damages are
sought, 2) a contract law or Uniform Commercial Code violation, in which rescission and return of money or property are sought, and 3) a criminal offense (a
public wrong), where a fine and/or imprisonment can be imposed.

FRAUD VERSUS FAIRNESS

Judicial constructions (definitions and interpretations of statutes) of fraud, over
the years, have tended to hinge on the legal notion of "fairness." If justice is to
be accorded to the parties in a litigated matter, some criteria must be established
to facilitate the disposition of the law suit. In tort actions involving allegations
of negligence, the criteria used by judges is the so-called prudent man rule, i.e.,
what would an ordinary, reasonable prudent man have done under similar circumstances. In tort and contract actions involving an allegation of fraud, the
equivalent of the reasonable prudent man rule, exists the rule of fairness or fair
dealing. The theory of fairness has to do with "undue advantage." If the seller,
for example, in a sales transaction has superior knowledge, there may be an
obligation to disclose such information. Business transactions operate on the
legal theory that both parties, buyer and seller, are or can become equally
knowledgeable about the substance of their transaction, i.e., the value, worth, or
condition of the article or service being sold. Therefore, if an advantage lies with
the seller or buyer in terms of knowledge of value or condition that advantage
cannot be silently used to exploit the other person. Silence may be golden, as the
proverb says, but not when silence may contribute to a fraud. The transaction
must be conducted "at arm's length," i.e., "without trusting to the other's fairness or integrity and without being subject to the other's control or overmastering
influence." At arm's length means: "beyond the reach of personal influence or
control." (See *Black's Law Dictionary*. 4th ed. rev. St. Paul, Minnesota: West
Publishing Company, 1968.)

So the legal concept of fraud relates to human interactions in social and
business transactions. Social transactions may result in allegations of fraud, as in
situations that involve seduction, undue influence over a person making a will, or
a breach of promise to wed. That aspect of fraud will not be covered in this text,
nor will situations involving confidence schemes like the "pigeon drop game,"
or sleight-of-hand tricks with playing cards (Three Card Monte), or stacked or

marked decks, or loaded dice. Our primary concern in this book is with frauds in business transactions, the so-called corporate and management frauds, and more particularly those frauds involving either theft or conversion of assets by corporate personnel or financial deceptions practiced by these personnel against shareholders, creditors, and regulatory authorities. Corporate books of account and financial statements are generally part of these fraudulent schemes and our main emphasis will be on how such schemes can be detected or uncovered in the course of a fraud audit and investigation. Through a strange quirk in history, the evolution of the law of fraud began about five hundred years ago in the English common law, about the same time that double entry bookkeeping came into vogue in Italy, through the efforts of Pacioli, an Italian mathematician and Franciscan friar.

FRAUD, TRUTH, AND JUSTICE

The problem with defining fraud is that while there seem to be many definitions of types of fraud such as bank fraud, business fraud, consumer fraud, etc., there is no generic definition of the word fraud itself other than "a deliberate deception," i.e., lying and cheating. But lying about what? Cheating over what? Is all lying and cheating fraud? Or is deliberation the primary criterion that distinguishes a simple untruth from a fraudulent untruth?

Defining fraud would first require defining truth, if truth is the opposite of lying or the telling of an untruth; or defining fairness, if fairness or fair dealing is the opposite of cheating.

Truth and fair dealing are value-laden words like justice. They are ideas as well as ideals, conditions of the mind as well as of the soul, are self-directed and other-directed concepts. To be just is to do justice to oneself and to others. Unfortunately, we cannot define justice to everyone's satisfaction, nor can we so define truth nor fair dealing. We know these concepts more by their exceptions than their rules. To be just means refraining from being unjust or unfair. To be truthful means refraining from telling untruths or distorting the truth by exaggeration or hyperbole. So while justice, truth, and fairness may not be able to be defined with literary precision, we can talk about them in terms of what they represent.

Justice, for example, has been defined as

- A guide by which men direct their actions toward others—a social norm, so to speak
- Approbative; something used for evaluating men and their actions; or a quality which is ultimately desirable to realize in the conduct and social relations of men
- Obligatory or prescriptive; it imposes an obligation or duty on the members of society; i.e., a standard of what should be done in human transactions and interactions

But what is just in any situation is not always so easy to say. What is just depends on who the actors are; their personal characteristics, position, and status; their relationship; the subject of the transaction or interaction; the time and place of the transaction or interaction; the capacity and competency of the parties, their past relations, customs, and traditions. Justness or justice is highly situational. Whatever rules exist are by necessity broadly stated, so that the concept of justice will not be restricted; it is a concept man wishes to keep alive, like all his other ideals. We may not wish to define it too concretely even if we could, for it would then no longer be an ideal or a virtue. A virtue realized is no longer a virtue. It has no power to compel or control behavior.

A FRAUD TAXONOMY

While fraud can be defined simply as deception, deception can be intentional or unintentional. For our purposes then, we will define fraud as "a deliberate (intentional) deception, practiced on another to secure an unfair or unlawful gain."

One might then say more broadly that fraud is the opposite of fairness, as applied to interpersonal relations (as in seduction, duress, undue influence) and commercial transactions (buying, selling, and exchanging real and personal property, and commercial mediums and instruments, i.e., drafts, checks, notes, bills of lading, warehouse receipts, stocks, bonds, etc.)

While all frauds by our definition (intentional lying, cheating, i.e., deception) may be immoral, they are not all illegal, that is, actionable at law or prosecutable in a criminal court. Frauds can be made illegal by statutory law (civil law) or considered as illegal based on past court precedents (by common law).

Frauds that are made illegal by the civil law or the common law may be punishable in the criminal proceedings, as for example, in cases of counterfeiting, forgery, false tokens, and false pretenses, where a fine or imprisonment may be imposed, or actionable in a civil proceeding for rescission of contract, restitution of property or monetary recovery (damages).

So, as the starting of a taxonomy on fraud, we can begin by distinguishing fraud as:

- Self-directed   versus   Other-directed
- Unintentional   versus   Intentional
- Material   versus   Immaterial
- Interpersonal   versus   Commercial
- Immoral or Unethical   versus   Illegal
- Nonactionable   versus   Actionable
- Statutory   versus   Common Law
- Civil   versus   Criminal

With such a broad definition of fraud, we could include here everything from white lies to the most sophisticated schemes of imposture, everything from consumer frauds to grand deceptions, and everything from sleight-of-hand tricks to stings. Fraud as a subject of study is both wide and deep. We shall, therefore, concentrate our efforts on the class of frauds known as management frauds or corporate frauds. These we shall define as "willful misrepresentations of financial facts by management and nonmanagement personnel of business organizations." Embezzlement, since it may involve people in positions of trust in business organizations and since it may also involve the manipulation of accounting records to conceal its existence or carry it out, will also be included. Employee theft or larceny, if it involves manipulation of accounting records to conceal it or carry it out, will be included too, as will such business crimes as commercial bribery (employee corruption by outside vendors, contractors, and suppliers); in short, that class of business crimes in which a business organization may become a victim of fraud, theft, or embezzlement by insiders or outsiders.

Frauds within a business organization are sometimes intended to benefit the organization (tax and other regulatory frauds like price fixing, false weights and measures, false labeling and branding, etc.) and are also sometimes intended to benefit its officers or employees as in thefts and embezzlements of corporate assets.

To continue our fraud taxonomy, we can then say that fraud can also be distinguished as to:

- Business Fraud   versus   Non-business Fraud
- Management Frauds   versus   Non-management Frauds
- Frauds for the Company   versus   Frauds Against the Company
- Frauds Committed from within   versus   Frauds Committed from without
  an Accounting System   an Accounting System
- Internal Fraud   versus   External Fraud

CORPORATE FRAUD: THE CURRENT ERA

A 1980 survey by *Fortune* magazine disclosed that a total of 117 of America's largest and most prestigious corporations were involved in at least one federal criminal offense since 1970. The survey of 1,043 firms showed that 11% of them were either convicted of, or made pretrial settlements of, federal criminal charges. Many of the firms were repeat offenders.

The specific violations in the survey were limited to 1) antitrust charges, 2) kickbacks, bribery, and illegal payments, 3) illegal political contributions, 4) corporate tax evasion, and 5) fraud. The survey also editorialized that *all* the crimes were committed for the corporation's benefit and not for the personal benefit of its officers and executives.

The survey included crimes such as 1) fabricating financial data to arbitrarily inflate profits and deceive shareholders and lenders, 2) fabricating financial data to disguise sub rosa payments or evidence of price fixing, 3) payments to curry the favor of politicians, union leaders, and regulatory authorities, and

4) padding expenses on government contracts. One might rationalize that these actions were intended to benefit shareholders, because showing a better-than-actual profit performance or cash flow keeps the value of a corporation's stock high. But the truth may lie elsewhere.

Corporate frauds, or economic crimes if you will, are often intended to satisfy the economic needs of the officers, executives, and profit center managers of public companies, whose compensation is based largely on one measure of performance and a very short-term measure at that: *current* profitability. Rarely is compensation based on the longer term growth and development of the firm. As a consequence of this myopic view of performance criteria, the executives and officers of many public companies have a built-in incentive or motivation to play fast and loose with their firm's assets and financial data. But before we begin to cast stones at these harried executives, let us review how we got to this point in our nation's corporate history.

Since the end of World War II, the growth and development of corporations in America has been nothing short of spectacular. As a result of this phenomenal growth, shareholders have grown accustomed to things like an annual increase in dividend rate, a 20% or more annual growth rate in sales and earnings per share, and long-term capital gains. Like everyone else in America, shareholders also suffer from rising expectations. "Last year's financial performance was fine, but what are you doing for me this year?" seems to be their constant demand of executive management. "Long-term growth be darned. It's what you're doing for me *now* that counts" is another way of stating the shareholders' expectations.

A 10% return on investment for shareholders was quite respectable twenty years ago. With a 3% to 5% inflation rate, anything beating that rate was considered a worthwhile investment, whether it came in the form of common stocks (a high-risk investment), or government and corporate bonds, or real estate (a more secure investment), or even in bank savings accounts. But with higher inflation rates and the continuing rise in shareholders' expectations and their increased financial sophistication, shareholders began to demand and shop for investments which were safe and secure and which provided a good current return in the form of higher and higher dividends and high capital appreciation. Shareholders showed no more loyalty to their corporations than did their assembly line employees. Their loyalty was to the dollar and return rate. If they could do one quarter percent better in another company or another investment opportunity, they quickly sold out.

So with these high performance demands and diminished loyalty on the part of the shareholders, it isn't any wonder that professional managers began to think of their owners as something less than generous, tolerant, understanding, patient, and considerate investors. Beyond that, the typical shareholder was no longer the little old widow from Pasadena living on the dividends from stocks left to her by her hardworking and frugal husband but a multibillion dollar pension or mutual fund, or bank trust department, managed by a cold, calculating portfolio specialist whose only criterion for investment was outperforming the Dow Jones Average.

Outperforming the Dow Jones Average has become such an insidious disease that the more conservative portfolio specialists have begun to buy mutual funds invested totally in the stocks which make up the Dow Jones Average. The worst they can do, therefore, is to perform at least as well as the Dow. (Who can criticize your professional judgment when you meet or beat the standard of excellence?)

Is there another way to describe this recent phenomenon of shareholder disloyalty, executive conniving, and investment portfolio management competition? Yes, but the expression is a harsh one: economic greed or "short-term high performance mania."

Economic greed is becoming a pervasive sort of thing. With banks, fund managers, and stock brokers competing for the few dollars of savings most people have, we have transformed our society into a collection of Shylocks. While the portfolio manager struggles to beat the Dow, the saver struggles to beat the inflation rate and the nonsaver struggles to survive. In an environment like this, economic values tend to blot out social values in a sort of Gresham's Law of Social Disintegration. So truth and loyalty are out. Avarice and greed are in. In a business environment like the current one, it is not any wonder that some corporate officers view their positions from a perspective of economic self-interest. Everyone else in society seems to be doing just that.

CORPORATE FRAUD AND WHITE COLLAR CRIME STATISTICS

The social cost of white collar crime has been variously estimated to be between $400 million and $40 billion per year. Computer-related crime estimates show about the same degree of spread, i.e., between $40 million and $4 billion, or roughly 10% of all white collar crime. The wide range of estimates is due to the fact that no hard data on white collar crime is available, and more importantly, that definitions of which crimes fall into the white collar category vary a great deal.

White collar crime can be viewed in terms of losses incurred by industry as the result of employee theft, fraud, embezzlement, corruption, and sabotage and losses incurred by industry as the result of customer shoplifting, vendor, supplier, or contractor overbilling and short shipment, predatory practices by competitors, and larceny, burglary, robbery, extortion, and frauds committed against businesses by unrelated parties, i.e., outside criminals.

But businesses can be both victims of white collar crimes, as stated above, and perpetrators of white collar crimes as in crimes against consumers (false advertising, labeling and branding), against shareholders and lenders (stock frauds, misrepresentations in stock offerings and financial statements), against government (padding on contracts), or against competitors (antitrust). Whether the latter costs are included in the above estimates of white collar crimes losses is unknown.

A major problem with crime statistics of all kinds—white and blue collar, violent and nonviolent, personal and property—is that all incidents of such crimes do not get reported, nor do those which are reported get collected and tabulated by one originating source. We know from past studies that reported crimes of all types may represent no more than half of the actual number. But we cannot extrapolate, nor project, nor rationally interpret such data because the potential for statistical error is so high.

For example, the FBI's Uniform Crime Index reports show that certain crimes in the United States rose dramatically during the 1970s: rapes per 100,000 by 49%, assaults by 45%, robberies by 33%, and burglaries by 36%. But the FBI's data include only the information it gets from state and local police authorities. They in turn report only those crimes which have been reported to them. However, since 1973 the U.S. Census Bureau has been sampling the general public as to its crime victimization rate. The rates so compiled show two things. The bad news is that there were far more crimes than those reported to the FBI. The good news is that the Census Bureau's data indicate that there was no significant change in the crime trend during the 1970s, i.e., the proportion of the population that reported having been raped, assaulted, robbed, or burglarized. On the contrary, the incidence rate of these four crimes fell slightly between 1973 and 1980.

The FBI's latest (1982) crime statistics indicate less crime overall for that year than the preceding year (1981). Have we become more law abiding? I would hope so, but I would not stake my reputation on it. What is odd about the 1982 data is that it flies in the face of the "conventional wisdom" in the social sciences. Crime is supposed to go up during economic downturns. Yet the FBI's data suggest it went down—went down despite mass unemployment and police budget cuts.

Another anomaly in this area of crime statistics is in the annual survey report on security and inventory shrinkage conducted by the National Mass Retailing Institute. In 1981, despite a 14% increase in security dollar expenditures by retailers the level of inventory shrinkage remained the same as in 1980, at 2% of sales.

A final anomaly is that a social scientist (James Fox) projected a forthcoming downtrend in crime as early as 1978. Fox's studies indicated that crime was a demographic phenomenon—more crimes are committed by young people than by old people. And, as the 15-21-year-old segment of the population ballooned in the 1970s, crime rates rose. Fox prophesized in 1978 that since that segment, as a percentage of the total population, was about to shrink, crime would head downward. And it apparently did, if you can believe the data.

Crime statistics of the blue and white collar varieties never tell the real or whole story of fraud in business practices. A quick review of some of the more celebrated cases may perhaps be more insightful. Our interest in fraud is not limited, however, to the criminal type alone. Civil fraud or allegations of civil fraud may provide a better handle on the subject.

Appendix 1 at the end of the book lists incidents of civil and criminal frauds, and employee thefts, embezzlements and corruption. These were extracted from the *Corporate Fraud Digest,* edited and published by the author, during the period June 1, 1982 through May 31, 1983. This list of alleged corporate and management frauds, employee thefts and corruption, insider trading abuses, embezzlements, bribery, audit inadequacies, and misrepresentations in financial statements is large but hardly exhaustive, and is intended to show the diversity and complexity of fraud in business today, to show its extensiveness not its volume. Fraud in business transactions and relationships is pervasive. It permeates the whole business environment. Whether fraud is on the rise or not is not as important as its seriousness. Fraud in business has been taken too lightly for too long, and if it is not dealt with, there is no doubt that it will increase. Awareness of its existence is part of the solution. This book is intended to increase that level of awareness, without also causing hysteria or paranoia. Hysterical responses to frauds in business accomplish very little in the long run, and commitments to ethics in business is what we need and not mass suspicion.

ACCOUNTABILITY FOR ASSET PROTECTION

The protection and preservation of a firm's assets (human, capital, technological, and information) from the foreseeable consequences of acts of God (climatic catastrophes) and acts of the public enemy (property theft, fraud, embezzlement, sabotage, information piracy, and commercial corruption) and human errors and omissions (employee negligence, design flaw and mechanical failure) are made the peculiar responsibility of the firm's own officers, directors, and agents by a host of federal, state, and local laws, such as the Foreign Corrupt Practices Act, Occupational Safety and Health Act, EEO Act, Privacy Act, ERISA, incorporation statutes, worker's compensation laws, building and fire safety codes, product liability laws, and the general common law of contracts, agency, torts, and fiduciary responsibility. The exercise of prudent business judgment and due diligence would dictate that enlightened firms undertake from time to time a serious review of the adequacy of their asset protection measures.

Officers and directors of public companies are now more keenly and more painfully aware of these responsibilities than ever before. The point has been brought home to them not only by Securities and Exchange Commission initiated actions, but also by law suits initiated by irate stockholders and creditors, employees, environmentalists, state and local authorities, and community organizations. So officers and directors must exercise discretion, good business judgment, and due diligence in their management of the firm's assets and business operations. Any failures in exercising these standards of care may subject them to ouster by shareholders, or to law suits by damaged parties.

One way to avoid these dire consequences is for enlightened managements to provide an in-house capability for preventing and detecting internal and external fraud. This book is intended then as a training aid or instruction guide for those employees to whom a prudent management has delegated responsibility for asset preservation and protection, i.e., internal and EDP auditors, security and loss prevention specialists, and risk managers. They form the new conscience of the corporation. My advice to them is not to mistrust their colleagues, co-workers, superiors, and subordinates, but to remember P. T. Barnum's admonition: "Trust everyone, but just to be sure, cut the cards."

A CORPORATE FRAUD CLASSIFICATION SYSTEM

Corporate frauds can be classified into two broad categories: (1) those frauds or crimes that are directed *against* the company and (2) those frauds or crimes that *benefit* the company. In the former, the company is the victim, and in the latter, the company through the fraudulent actions of its officers is the beneficiary.

A rough guide to a classification system might therefore be as follows:

I.   Crimes Against the Company
    A.   Theft, Fraud, and Embezzlement
        1.   Input Scams
            a)   Cash and Petty Cash Diversions, i.e., thefts
            b)   Cash and Petty Cash Conversions, i.e., check kiting, check raising, and signature or endorsement forgeries
            c)   Receivables Manipulations, i.e., lapping, fake credit memos
            d)   Payables Manipulations, i.e., phony vendor invoices, benefit claims, and expense vouchers and overcharges by vendors, suppliers, and contractors
            e)   Payroll Manipulations, i.e., phony employees and altered time cards
            f)   Inventory Manipulations, i.e., specious reclassifications of inventories to obsolete, damaged, or sample status
        2.   Thruput Scams
            a)   Salami Slicing, Trap door, Trojan Horse, Time Bomb, and Superzap Techniques (by passing controls in systems and application programs)
        3.   Output Scams
            a)   Destroying exceptions reports and logs
            b)   Stealing files, programs, reports, and data (Customer lists, research and development results, marketing plans, etc.)
II.   Crimes For the Company
    A.   Smoothing profits (cooking the books)
        1.   Inflating sales
        2.   Understating expenses
        3.   Not recording sales returns
        4.   Inflating ending inventory
    B.   Balance sheet window dressing
        1.   Overstating assets
        2.   Not recording liabilities

   C. Price fixing
   D. Cheating customers
      1. Short weights, counts, and measures
      2. Substitution of cheaper materials
      3. False advertising
   E. Violating governmental regulations, i.e., EEO, OSHA, Environmental
      Standards, Securities and Tax Violations, etc.
   F. Corruption of customer personnel
   G. Political corruption
   H. Padding costs on government contracts

LEGAL WORDS AND PHRASES WITH FRAUD IMPLICATIONS

To the ordinary layman, the words theft, fraud, embezzlement, larceny, and defalcation can be used somewhat interchangeably. Breach of trust or fiduciary responsibility, conversion, false representation, false pretenses, false tokens, false entries, and false statements are rarely used by laymen because they sound more ominous and legalistic.

The word with the broadest connotations is theft. Most people have some sense of what the term means and implies. Even little children are wont to say and understand the implication of "You stole my toy." Translated, that means "You took my toy without my permission and are keeping it from me against my will."

Theft and stealing have become so generally understood and so commonly used that they are considered generic terms for a range of different crimes. The words themselves are rarely used in criminal statutes. The technical charge for the kind of behavior most of us think of as theft or stealing is called "larceny."

Larceny is usually defined as the "wrongful taking and carrying away of the personal property of another with intent to convert it or to deprive the owner of its use and possession." If the taking is by stealth—surreptitiously—the crime committed is larceny. If the taking is by force or fear, the crime committed is robbery. If the taking is by guile and deception, by false representation, or by concealment of that which should have been disclosed, the crime charged may be fraud.

Fraud then is any kind of artifice employed by one person to deceive another. Fraud is a generic term, too. It embraces all the multifarious means human ingenuity can conceive of to get an unfair advantage over another—surprise, trickery, cunning, false suggestion, or suppression of truth.

Because of its generic use and application, the word fraud now means behavior which may be either criminal or civil, actionable or nonactionable (Caveat Emptor: Let the buyer beware), actual or constructive (by legal construction), and in a contractual sense, fraud may be found as the inducement for a contract or in the execution of a contract.

Embezzlement, which we have not yet discussed, is a "kissing cousin" of larceny and fraud. By definition, embezzlement is the "fraudulent appropriation of property by a person to whom it has been entrusted, or to whose hands it has lawfully come." It implies a breach of trust or fiduciary responsibility.

To prove an embezzlement from a legal and linguistic point of view has always been difficult. There is a story told in most law schools—usually in criminal law courses—of an ingenious lawyer who represented a bank teller charged with the crime of embezzlement. He very skillfully convinced the jury that his client may well have been guilty of larceny but certainly not embezzlement and that technically the crime charged was incorrect and his client should therefore be found innocent of that charge. So eloquent was his plea that the jury returned a not guilty verdict.

Indignant at the loss, the prosecuting attorney then filed a complaint against the teller charging him with larceny. With a new jury and protection from the introduction of his remarks at the earlier trial, the defense laywer just as eloquently convinced the jurors that if anything his client was guilty of embezzlement, certainly not the crime of larceny.

The major distinction between larceny and embezzlement lies in the issue of the legality of custody of the article stolen. In larceny, the thief never had legal custody. He "feloniously took" the article from the owner. In embezzlement, the thief is legally authorized by the owner to take or receive the article and to possess it for a time. The formulation of intent to steal the article may occur subsequent to the time when it came into his possession or concurrently with initial possession. If initial possession and intent to steal occur simultaneously, the crime is larceny. If intent to steal occurs subsequent to initial possession, the crime is embezzlement. These hairsplitting distinctions make a prosecutor's life a mite harried and probably led to the creation of the bank teller story previously mentioned.

But, this book was not written for lawyers, or teachers of English, or even psychologists. It was written for people who have the burden of ferreting out fraud and documenting its existence—regulatory agents, policemen, detectives, internal auditors, investigators, and crime writers. What should they know about fraud, larceny, and embezzlement?

One aspect that they might want to know more about would be definitions of the species of fraud crimes. The definitions given thus far are broad, generic, and of common law type of crimes, i.e., larceny, robbery, embezzlement, and criminal fraud.

What are these species of fraud crimes and how are they defined? They are:

Deceit. A fraudulent and cheating misrepresentation, artifice, or device, used by one or more persons to deceive and trick another who is ignorant of the true facts, to the prejudice and damage of the party imposed upon. *People* v. *Chadwick,* 143, Cal. 116.

Defalcation. The act of a defaulter; misappropriation of trust funds or money held in any fiduciary capacity; failure to properly account for such funds. Usually spoken of officers of corporations or public officials. In re Butts, D.D., N.Y., 120 F 970; *Crawford* v. *Burke,* 201 Ill. 581, 66 N.E. 833.

False and Misleading Statement. Failure to state material fact made letter a "false and misleading statement" within rule of Securities and Exchange Commission. *SEC* v. *Okin,* C.C. A. N.Y., 132 F 2nd 784, 787.

False Entry. An entry in books of a bank or trust company which is intentionally made to represent what is not true or does not exist, with intent either to deceive its officers or a bank examiner or to defraud the bank or trust company. *Agnew* v. *U.S.,* 165, U.S. 36.

False Pretenses. Designed misrepresentation of existing facts or condition whereby person obtains another's money or goods. *People* v. *Gould,* 363 Ill, 348. (Example: giving a worthless check)

False Representation. A representation which is untrue, willfully made to deceive another to his injury.

False Statement. Under statutory provision, making it unlawful for officer or director of corporation to make any false statement in regard to corporation's financial condition, the phrase means something more than merely untrue or erroneous, but implies that statement is designed untrue and deceitful and made with intention to deceive person to whom false statement is made or exhibited. *State* v. *Johnston,* 149 S.C. 138.

False Token. In criminal law, a false document or sign of the existence of a fact—in general used for the purpose of fraud. (Example: counterfeit money)

Falsify. To counterfeit or forge: to make something false, to give a false appearance to anything. To make false by mutilation or addition: to tamper with; as to falsify a record or document. *Pov* v. *Ellis,* 66 Fla. 358.

Forgery. The false making or material altering; with intent to defraud, of anything in writing which if genuine, might apparently be of legal efficiency or the foundation of a legal liability. *People* v. *Routson,* 354, Ill. 573.

Fraudulent Concealment. The hiding or suppression of a material fact or circumstance which the party is legally or morally bound to disclose. *Magee* v. *Insurance Co.,* 92 U.S. 93.

Fraudulent Conversion. Receiving into possession money or property of another and fraudulently withholding, converting, or applying the same to or for one's own use and benefit, or to use and benefit of any person other than the one to whom the money or property belong. *Commonwealth* v. *Mitchneck,* 130 Pa. Super 433.

Fraudulent or Dishonest Act. One which involves bad faith, a breach of honesty, a want of integrity, or moral turpitude. *Hartford Acc. and Indemn. Co.* v. *Singer,* 185 Va 620.

Fraudulent Representation. A false statement as to material fact, made with intent that another rely thereon, which is believed by other party and on which he relies and by which he is induced to act and does act to his injury, and statement is fraudulent if speaker knows statement to be false of if it is made with utter disregard of its truth or falsity. *Osborne* v. *Simmons,* Mo. App., 23 S.W. 2d 1102.

Malfeasance.   Evil doing; ill conduct; the commission of some act which is positively unlawful; the doing of an act which is wholly wrongful and unlawful; the doing of an act which person ought not to do at all or the unjust performance of some act which the party had no right or which he had contracted not to do. Comprehensive term including any wrongful conduct that affects, interrupts or interferes with the performance of official duties. State ex. rel. *Knabb* v. *Frater,* 198 Wash. 675, 89 P. 2d 1046, 1048.

Misapplication.   Improper, illegal, wrongful, or corrupt use or application of funds, property, etc. *Jewett* v. *U.S., C.C.A. Mass.,* 100 F. 841, 41 C.C.A.88.

Misappropriation.   The act of misappropriating or turning to a wrong purpose; wrong appropriation; a term which does not necessarily mean peculation, although it may mean that. *Bannon* v. *Knauss,* 57 Ohio App. 228.

The above definitions were extracted from *Black's Law Dictionary.* 4th ed. rev., copyright © 1968 by West Publishing Company, St. Paul, Minnesota; reprinted here with permission.

Fraud as a Crime

The Michigan Criminal Law, Chapter 86, Section 1529, defines fraud as follows:

"Fraud is a generic term, and embraces all the multifarious means which human ingenuity can devise, which are resorted to by one individual, to get an advantage over another by false representations. No definite and invariable rule can be laid down as a general proposition in defining fraud, as it includes all surprise, trick, cunning and unfair ways by which another is cheated. The only boundaries defining it are those which limit human knavery.

Fraud is a term of law, applied to certain facts, as a conclusion from them, but is not in itself a fact. It has been defined as any cunning deception or artifice used to cheat or deceive another.

"Cheat and defraud," as the term is ordinarily used, means every kind of trick and deception, from false representation and intimidation to suppression and concealment of any fact and information, by which a party is induced to part with his property for less than its value or to give more than its worth for the property of another. Fraud and bad faith are often synonymous, particularly when applied to the conduct of public offenders.

"The essential elements to be established, in order to constitute an offense under most of the statutes relating to frauds and cheats, are:

1. An intent to defraud
2. The commission of a fraudulent act, and
3. The fraud accomplished

The words 'cheat and defraud' do not import any common-law offense. In the absence of statute, if punishable at all as a crime, it is only when the cheat is effected by false tokens or pretenses, or when it affects the public, such as false weights and measures. To cheat and defraud a person by false pretenses is an indictable offense. The state can punish fraud committed upon its citizens by any manner of false pretenses, but cannot punish those done under color of rights held from the United States on any different grounds from others.

A falsehood does not necessarily imply an intent to defraud, as it may be uttered to secure a right, and, however much it may be reprobated in ethics, the law does not assume to punish moral delinquencies, as such.''

Fraud as a Civil Wrong

The U.S. Supreme Court in 1887 (*Southern Development Co.* v. *Silva,* 125 U.S. 247, 8 S.C. Rep. 881, 31 L. Ed. 678) provides a definition of fraud in the civil sense as:

"The burden of proof (in civil fraud cases) is on the complainant; and unless he brings evidence sufficient to overcome the natural presumption of fair dealing and honesty, a court of equity will not be justified in setting aside a contract on the ground of fraudulent representations.'' In order to establish a charge of this character, the complainant must show by clear and decisive proof:

First   That the defendant has made a representation in regard to a material *fact;*

Second   That such representation is *false;*

Third   That such representation was not actually believed by the defendant, on reasonable grounds, to be true;

Fourth   That it was made with intent that it should be acted on;

Fifth   That it was acted on by complainant to his damage; and

Sixth   That in so acting on it the complainant was ignorant of its falsity, and reasonably believed it to be true. The first of the foregoing requisites *excludes such statements as consist merely in an expression of opinion or judgment, honesty entertained; and again, excepting in peculiar cases, it excludes statements by the owner and vendor of property in respect to its value.* (emphasis supplied)

Corporate Fraud

Corporate fraud is any fraud perpetrated by, for, or against a business corporation. Corporate frauds can be internally generated (perpetrated by agents, employees, and executives of a corporation, for or against it, or against others) and externally generated (by others against the corporation, i.e., suppliers, vendors, customers).

Management Fraud

Management fraud is the intentional overstatement of corporate or unit profits, inspired, perpetrated, or induced by employees serving in management roles who seek to benefit from such frauds in terms of coveted promotions, job stability, larger bonuses, or other economic incentives and status symbols.

Financial Fraud

Material misrepresentation of a financial fact intended to deceive another to his economic detriment.

Errors and Irregularities

Audit literature rarely contains the word fraud. In fact, the topical indices of Volumes I and II of *Accounting Standards,* the original pronouncements of the Financial Accounting Standards Board as of June 1, 1982, do not show the word *fraud* at all, preferring instead the expression "errors and irregularities" to encompass fraud. This may seem like a humane practice but much meaning gets lost when a spade is not called a spade.

Errors and irregularities sound like innocent practices or human foibles and not intentional disregard for truth, justice, fairness, and equity. A rose by any other name may still be a rose, but a fraud called an irregularity sounds more like a digestive problem than a legal, ethical, or moral problem. So let fraud be labeled or defined for what it is: intentional deception such as lying and cheating.

CHAPTER 2

Mindset: Step One in Fraud Auditing

THE FRAUD AUDITOR'S GENERAL MINDSET

There is a quaint saying in the auditing profession which suggests that "most frauds are discovered by accident," rather than by audit or accounting system design. This saying has been repeated so many times by so many accountants and auditors that it seems to be accepted by the general public as an axiom or a self-evident truth. Yet many authors have written books about fraud auditing and most of these works have found willing buyers and avid readers.

Most fraud audit books address the problem from an after-the-fact perspective. The fraud was discovered (usually by accident) and the author confirmed and corroborated it by certain methods. Discovery, not detection, is the main theme of the books. Many authors of these books attribute their genius and their discoveries of fraud to chance, luck, or happenstance, never to statistics, probabilities, or scientific method. Neither deductive nor inductive logic, nor the rigors of science, had anything to do with their success.

If fraud auditing has no scientific basis and most frauds are discovered by accident, then what value can be assigned to the books that have been written? Are they simply the memoirs and war stories of old men who stumbled or muddled through audits and got lucky? Yes, some are of that variety, but others are very enlightening and useful. They catalog some of the more ingenious techniques used by the authors to ferret out and prove fraud—techniques that by and large have worked well for them, but that have limited, not universal, application. So the search for a generally accepted methodology of fraud auditing goes on. To my knowledge there is none to date. Instead, there are collections of anecdotes, a few useful gimmicks which may work under some circumstances, a number of commonly accepted myths, and a lot of hope that the future will provide more concrete and tangible solutions for the problems of detection, audit, and investigation of fraud.

Yet, a fair reading of the fraud auditing texts does disclose a common theme, and that is that fraud is endemic and pervasive in some industries, locales, companies, and occupations, at some time. For example, railroad promoters in the 1870s raised more capital, from more uninformed investors, based on more "water" in their stocks, than ever before. Samuel Insull did the same thing in the electric utility business in the 1920s. Insull sold millions of dollars of common stock in electric utility companies to unwary investors. The stock was greatly over-priced in terms of the utilities' real assets. When the stock market collapsed in 1929, it became apparent that Insull's holding company was insolvent and had been for some time. Financial legerdemain is all that had kept it afloat. During the 1950s, more doctors were involved in more income tax frauds than ever before or since that time. Food franchisors in the late 1960s are another example of the fraud phenomenon. Some fast food franchisors sold unwary small investors on untested restaurant concepts at over-valued prices. These half-baked concepts then led to the bankruptcy of many of the franchisees. In the 1970s, more politicians were involved in corruption and fraud committed against tax-payers and more corporations were involved in political and commercial bribery than ever before. Are these events merely historical flukes? Was it media atten-tion that created them? Perhaps. Media attention may have created the original public awareness, but the frauds and corruption were there all the time. What changed was the mindset of the auditors. Nothing was taken for granted any-more. Suspicion fell on industries, professions, and varied areas of government. That undivided attention by the auditors and investigators then led to wholesale charges of fraud, theft, and corruption.

Am I saying that mindset is what brought these matters to light? Yes, I am—mindset rather than methodology. There is no commonly accepted fraud audit methodology as indicated previously. It is mindset, but what particular mindset do I address? Is it the mindset of the paranoid who trust no one or see evil everywhere? No, not that one either. The mindset I speak of is one that sug-gests several things:

1.   That fraud can be *detected,* as well as discovered by accident.
2.   That financial audit methodologies and techniques come and go but none are truly designed to ferret out fraud.
3.   That fraud detection is more of an art form than a science. It requires inno-vative and creative thinking and not only the rigors of science.
4.   That doggedness, persistence, and self-confidence are more important attri-butes for a fraud auditor to have than IQ rating or class standing.

Every fraud has its own unique wrinkles. Thieves do not all think alike. They tend to be opportunists. Given a set of circumstances within which to steal, they tend to take the easiest way. Elaborate crimes make interesting reading, but they are only committed by characters in Agatha Christie novels. In the real world of corporate fraud, the culprits leave trails and make mistakes. The auditor must learn to look for these telltale signs. What are these signs? The author hopes to provide some insight to the reader—insight into the mind and behavior patterns of fraud perpetrators and into the evidence they leave behind, from which a reconstruction of their crimes can be made.

Fraud auditing then resembles putting things together, rather than taking them apart, as is the case in classic financial auditing or the modern method of systems analysis. The process of fraud auditing is also more intuitive than deductive, although both play an important part. That is why checklists and cookbook recipes in financial auditing do not seem to work as well in fraud auditing. But there is a planning phase in fraud auditing and investigation, just as there is in financial auditing, but it comes later. Checklists, questionnaires, patterned interviews, and canned audit programs may obscure the fraud problem when used too soon. The fraud auditor's mind must learn to wander about aimlessly and restlessly early on. His curiosity should be piqued about everything. This is a new environment, with new people and new or different systems. To assume that past experience alone will solve the problem is specious reasoning. Frauds are like snowflakes—they have different sizes, shapes, and consistencies and to concentrate on one type will not help much in measuring or weighing the next one. All powers of concentration and attention must be given to the case at hand. Past experience may distract.

Sociologists tell us that criminal behavior is learned behavior, i.e., learned from others. Fraud auditing too is learned behavior but it is self-learning more than it is learning from others. So while you cannot be *taught* to become a fraud auditor, you can *learn* to become one.

Fraud auditing is not easy. It is often frustrating and grueling work. You will be up to your neck in data, documents, reports, analyses, observations, and interview notes; and times, dates, places, people, procedures, and policies to remember. The pace of the audit effort is generally frantic and the working environment is hectic. The status of the audit may even appear chaotic at any point in time to the inexperienced observer. Often, the fraud auditor does not know what he is looking for or even why other than something looks suspicious or out of place. So being overorganized when doing fraud audit work may be a handicap. You need a lot of freedom and space to let your imagination run wild. You need to poke holes into everything, including your own pet theories and biases. Do not accept anything anyone says as gospel truth. Do not assume that any document is what it purports to be. When conflicts between statements of witnesses occur, do not take sides or prejudge their veracity. Keep an open mind. The proof of fraud is rarely where and what you thought it was when you first began the audit. Preconceptions are dangerous. They invariably lead you down the wrong tracks. Do not assume the victim knows or understands what happened either. Building your own theory based on the victim's preconceptions is equally dangerous. But do not discourage the victim or the victim's personnel from talking. They probably have an answer or two that will help you in the long run, an answer that they do not believe is relevant or significant at the time.

THE FRAUD AUDITOR'S PSYCHE

I joined the Internal Revenue Service as a Special Agent in 1955, after a few years in public accounting and the banking business. One of my earliest insights gained as a budding Special Agent was detecting the notable differences among my senior colleagues. Some Special Agents had been around for twenty years and had yet to make a criminal case, while others were flushing up tax frauds with regularity and had many convictions to their credit. I initially concluded that the IRS must be like a football team—you need only a few prima donnas, and the rest of the team can be "grunts."

But I learned very quickly that the IRS was not a believer in team play. Each agent was rated on his own performance. Before long, I had decided to ally myself with the agents who were the most "productive," to learn whatever gems they might be willing to share with a rookie upstart. There were then—as now—no college courses on "how to detect fraud."

What I learned from my seniors and mentors, after I waded through all their ego-tripping "war stories" was that fraud was endemic in the tax field—it was everywhere. All you had to do was find it, and the only way to find it was to "keep digging." "Never give up" they were wont to say. "If you think the son of a bitch is guilty, the evidence will show itself." (That is not very scientific, I thought. That is nothing but blind faith in yourself and no faith in taxpayers. Worse yet, criminologists often describe criminals as having those precise low-trust characteristics.) Being the youthful sage I thought I was, I concluded the old saw was correct "It takes one to catch one."

Over the years, however, I discovered my conclusion was wrong. It does not "take one to catch one." There was a growing problem in the IRS. Many agents were going "bad," i.e., accepting favors and bribes from taxpayers and lavish entertainments from CPAs and lawyers. (Getting to be too much like a tax cheat had some real pitfalls. You might step too far over the line and become one yourself.) With a little more reflection, I discovered that what my seniors were trying to communicate was simply that you have to *think* like one to catch one not *be* like one. Well, that was a blessed relief for me since I had no great desire to spend time in jail, or embarrass my loved ones, or lose my job.

As soon as I began to think like a tax cheat, all sorts of bits and pieces of information and intelligence began to take on new significance —information not taught in college accounting or auditing courses nor in conventional courses in investigative techniques.

1.   Why would the names of a taxpayer's children change from year to year but not their number?
2.   Why would a taxpayer use the street address of a prominent hotel and not the hotel's name on his return?
3.   Why would an unknown small-time Kentucky poolroom operator be seen daily in the company of the Detroit mob's biggest layoff bookmaker?
4.   Why would a large liquor distillery send eighty cases of whiskey to a state laboratory to have its proof rating verified?

(Each of these questions led to successful prosecutions.) Good fraud auditors think differently, see things differently, and see them from a different perspective. They are quick to see things that appear "out of sync," i.e., out of pattern, priority, sequence; or out of order, too high, too low, too many, too few, too often, or not often enough.

Management Fraud: Detection and Deterrence edited by Robert K. Elliott and John J. Willingham [35], is a compilation of papers presented at a symposium on that subject sponsored by Peat, Marwick and Mitchell in 1978. Peat, Marwick, and Mitchell commissioned the papers from a group of experts in relevant academic disciplines, i.e., criminology, social psychology, auditing, and computer science. The book has a number of significant strengths and valuable insights. The chapter contributed by David R. Saunders, "Psychological Perspectives on Management Fraud," offers one gem of wisdom which good detectives and fraud auditors have known for some time, but have been unwilling to speak about in public: " . . . the ability to suspect fraud by some means that is better than pure guessing is an intuitive process, not subject to predictable forms of logical reasoning." I could not agree more. Good fraud auditors and investigators are truly a breed apart from their colleagues in auditing and law enforcement. They differ in personality, communication style, lifestyle, and beliefs and values. It is like comparing Columbo and Perry Mason:

- Mason, the articulate, clinically cold, calculating, brilliant, logical, deductive reasoner whose eternal questions are: Who did it? and Why?
- Columbo, the stumbling, bumbling, cigar chomping, eternally curious fool whose persistence and doggedness on questions like what, where, when, how many, how few, and how often always seem to end up proving the why and whom issues, too.

In simple psychological terms, Mason is a left-brain thinker, i.e., logical, sequential, orderly, linear, deductive, analytical, and intellectual. Columbo, on the other hand, is a right-brain thinker: intuitive, creative, emotional, holistic, artistic, and inductive. In short, Mason analyzes, Columbo synthesizes. Mason takes it apart—Columbo puts it all together. Mason is the brilliant pathologist, and Columbo is the phenomenologist. What happened? versus Why did it happen?

A pessimist is often described as "someone who looks both ways while crossing a one-way street." The fraud auditor/investigator fits that verbal characterization and yet is not really a pessimist. In the realm of corporate fraud prevention and detection, it just pays to look both ways, and up and down for that matter.

Auditing for fraud is therefore more of an intuitive process than it is a formal analytical methodology. It is not based on a body of knowledge and is more of an art form than it is a science. As a consequence, it is difficult to teach. Skill depends on the right mindset, thinking like a thief, i.e., probing for weaknesses, and practice. Instruction at the hands of a competent mentor is important in the early development of a good fraud auditor. But it is not his techniques you should want to master, it is his mental disposition, his behavior—doggedness and persistence, his faith in his own talents—that you should emulate. No lead, no shred of evidence is ever too small to have relevance. You draw in information like a vacuum cleaner and sift and sort out all the pieces, organize them in some meaningful way, and then see what the pattern looks like. But what patterns do you look for?

The patterns you look for are the oddities and exceptions to the rule patterns—the things that do not seem to fit into an organized scheme of things because they seem too large, too small, too frequent, too rare, too high, too low, too ordinary, too extraordinary, too many, too few, odd times, odd places, odd hours, odd people, and odd combinations. You look for the unusual rather than the usual. Then you go behind and beyond them to reconstruct what may have led to them and what followed.

CLASSIC AUDITING VERSUS FRAUD AUDITING

Most treatises on auditing deal with classic audit checklists and tests of internal accounting controls:

1. Does the company have an up-to-date organizational chart delineating its major organizational functions and hierarchical levels of authority?
2. Does it have up-to-date job descriptions which spell out in detail the functions, duties, and responsibilities of all major job roles?
3. Does it provide for separation of duties?
4. Are authorizations for the sale, transfer, or disposal of assets properly documented?
5. Are authorizations for the purchase of and payment for goods and other assets properly documented?
6. Are blank checks, purchase orders, and invoices preserially numbered and securely stored? Is their issuance under the control of one person? And so forth.

There is a fixed and orderly routine followed in the typical financial audit, that is, a set of predesigned tasks, procedures, and tests for the verification of business transactions and an evaluation of the adequacy of the accounting system to reflect fairly, accurately, and consistently the financial condition of a firm at a point in time. In essence, the financial auditor takes a snapshot of the firm and that snapshot should represent the reality of the company's financial situation at the moment. (Snapshots do not, however, always reflect reality. As in photography, a lot depends on the light, the quality of the film, the talent of the picture taker, and on the caliber of the equipment used.)

But fraud auditing is different. The approach to fraud auditing is much more heuristic (trial and error) than it is algorithmic (fixed procedures). The fraud auditor's purpose is not to photograph but to dissect and rebuild a structure by using infinite details.

FRAUD ALLEGATIONS VERSUS
DETECTED DISCREPANCY

How and when does a fraud audit or investigation begin? A fraud audit usually begins with an allegation of fraud or with the discovery of a discrepancy. If fraud is alleged to have been committed, the techniques used are those of the investigator. The immediate questions to be resolved for the fraud investigator are:

1. How credible is the source of the allegation?
   a. How did he come upon the information?
   b. Is the information firsthand or hearsay?
   c. What other evidence supports the allegation?
2. Who is the alleged culprit or culprits?
3. How was the fraud committed?
4. When was the fraud committed?
5. Where was the fraud committed?
6. What assets were affected by the fraud?
7. What is the extent or amount of the loss?
8. What was the motive of the perpetrator or perpetrators?
9. What is the motive of the source of information in reporting the fraud?
10. Will the source provide a sworn statement as to the allegation?
11. Will the source testify as a witness if needed?
12. Will the source make a credible witness on the stand?

A discrepancy, on the other hand, is a deviation from a state or condition which was expected to be but which is not. Profits are down markedly, yet no one can explain why. Inventory per books is higher than what is physically counted at year end. Cash flow is negative at a time when it is expected to be higher. Physical properties are missing. Proprietary information is missing. Records and documents are missing. Fraud auditors are called in when these conditions occur. Taking snapshots at this point will not help. So the fraud auditor begins where a loss of something of value or a suspicion of property loss exists. His preliminary inquiries deal with when, where, and how the discrepancy was discovered and by whom it was discovered. The purpose of the preliminary inquiries is to determine whether an actual loss exists and whether it was perpetrated within the accounting system or without the system.

FRAUDS WITHIN VERSUS FRAUDS WITHOUT THE
ACCOUNTING SYSTEM

In frauds within the system there is usually evidence of altered, forged, fabricated, or missing documents. In frauds without the system the questionable transactions may have bypassed the accounting system completely. No internal records may even exist. All the auditor knows is that there is less of something (usually an asset) than there should be—perhaps through outright theft by insiders, or through diversion, conversion, or theft by outsiders, or through a combination of both.

Frauds from within an accounting system are often discovered by internal or independent auditors in the course of routine audits. Some are discovered by pure chance or accident, others through audit and internal control designs. The thief often leaves some telltale sign in the accounting records which causes suspicion and further inquiry or analysis. Telltale signs are manifested by gaps in internal controls such as lack of supporting documentation, merger of duties, out-of-proper sequencing of serialized documents, or evidence of lapping, kiting, or missing canceled checks, missing vouchers, control overrides, exceeded authorization limits, etc.

Frauds from without an accounting system, by outsiders—vendors, suppliers, customers, are not usually discovered during the course of financial audits but during operational audits or are detected by managers and employees as deviations in normal patterns of trade practices, pricing formulas, product costs, demand and supply trends, etc. A steady stream of intelligence is gathered by these people in their jobs and that intelligence plus their knowledge and experience is utilized in determining what is normal or usual, and what is abnormal. Abnormality or oddity is therefore what leads to detection or provides the initial impetus for further analysis. The condition of the company's books, its records, and its accounting practices may be a minor consideration in the initial stages of a fraud from without the system.

FRAUD AUDITING VERSUS INVESTIGATION

Fraud auditing is therefore unlike financial auditing in that it proceeds from a theory that is based more on investigative notions or operational audit notions than it is on financial auditing notions. Financial auditing is not designed to ferret out frauds from without, even though some such frauds are uncovered through this method (the ones discovered by accident, I would suppose). Financial auditing lays heavy emphasis on matching sets of numbers, i.e., debits equal credits, inputs equal outputs. Financial auditing also tests for the validity of data moving through an accounting system. Validity, in this sense, means that some written or magnetically recorded document supports an entry made in any one of a company's journals, i.e., cash receipts and disbursement journals, purchases and accounts payable journals, accounts receivable and sales journals, payroll journals, etc. If transactions are authenticated through supported documents, the financial auditor's main task is concluded. The proper form of transaction entries is then tested—did the proper debits and credits go to the right accounts or were they misclassified and therefore require adjustment?

The fraud auditor is rarely presented with such mundane duties. He cannot assume that because a transaction is properly recorded and documented with supporting details, the transaction itself is legitimate. The fraud auditor should not expect that irregularities in accounting procedures would be patently observable. Criminals are rarely that careless.

SUBSTANCE VERSUS FORM

As noted previously, corporate frauds can be accomplished from within the accounting system, through falsification, fabrication, or destruction of supporting documents, or from without the accounting system through outright theft, diversion or conversion of property. So it is not form so much which occupies the fraud auditor's mind but substance, the substance of financial transactions. "Why did the event occur?" becomes a more important question to the fraud auditor than "How was it recorded?" What precedes an entry may be more important than the entry itself. What follows an entry likewise may be more important. This is what we refer to as the "preinput/postoutput" mentality of the fraud auditor, or "looking beyond and before." Who benefits most from the transaction? Who benefits most from the destruction of records? Who benefits most from the misstatements? These are the more critical issues for the fraud auditor.

Classic auditing is intended to uncover deviations and variances from accounting standards of acceptable practice. But where pretense is used to disguise a transaction or to cover it up, the auditor is not likely to become suspicious. All is "in balance," so to speak. And when all is in balance, no one seems to get concerned. This overconcern with form rather than substance in the classic auditing approach can create a false sense of security over the legitimacy of financial transactions. Looking behind, before, and beyond the transaction is what fraud auditing and investigation are all about. That perspective forces the fraud auditor to focus on substance rather than form. He can assume the form is proper, or at least acceptable.

LOOKING BEHIND AND BEYOND

What does looking "behind" and "beyond" the transaction mean? It means paying lip service to classic auditing and starting the audit with a review of the adequacy of internal controls and accounting practices, i.e., compliance testing, to become familiar with the firm, its employees, and its general operations. But after that a shift in focus takes place. Now that the auditor is comfortable and knows something about the business, he is free to explore what lies behind and beyond financial transactions. The focus of classic auditing is on the present. In fraud auditing the focuses are on the past and the future. In essence, classic auditing is thruput-oriented and fraud auditing is preinput/postoutput-oriented.

The questions the fraud auditor has uppermost in mind are not how the accounting system and internal controls stack up against American Institute of Certified Public Accountants standards, a reference to the present dimensions of time, but to the following:

1. What are the weakest links in this system's chain of controls?
2. What deviations from conventional good accounting practices are possible in this system?
3. How are off-line transactions handled and who can authorize such transactions?
4. What would be the simplest way to compromise this system?
5. What control features in the system can be bypassed or overridden by high authorities?
    a. How often has this happened or is it happening now?
    b. Who is involved?
    c. What rationale have they advanced for such variances and deviations?
    d. How generally well known are such exceptions among the organization's employees?
    e. Is morale very high or very low?
        (Either extreme may suggest a problem. If morale is very high, collusion is a possibility, as in the Equity Funding Case. If morale is very low, individual theft and fraud may be more prevalent.)

Some of the more specific issues addressed by the fraud auditor are the following trends:

1. Are cash, receivables, inventories, and payables building up or diminishing?
2. Are receivables write-offs building up?
3. Are inventory reclassifications building up? For example, reclassifications from merchandise or finished goods available for sale, to obsolete, scrap, damaged, or sample status?
4. Are the company's products and services on the wane? Are sales down markedly? Is the industry itself on the wane? How do company sales compare with its main competitors?
5. What is the past relationship between inventory and accounts receivable buildup, between sales, inventory and receivables buildup, between payables and inventory buildup? Have there been any material changes recently in these relationships?

The usual method of employee theft, fraud, and embezzlement executed within the accounting or control system involves the creation of a "fake debit," which in turn will be offset by a credit to an asset account or expensed, in the case of a faked payable or a faked claim against the company. While lapping, kiting, check raising, and signature forgeries are still possible, even in computerized systems, they are more easily detectable than the fake debit in conventional auditing.

Fake debits can be created in a number of ingenious ways. For example, fake debits are possible through the use of phony credit memos, phony invoices, phony benefit claims, phony employees added to the payroll, phony expense vouchers, phony inventory reclassifications, etc. Some other techniques used mainly to defraud or deceive stockholders or lenders are overstating assets and understating liabilities for balance sheet "window dressing," overstating sales or closing inventories to inflate profit, and understating expenses and returned sales to inflate profit. But the variations in techniques for fraud against or on the behalf of a company are limitless. The human mind, when unleashed against an accounting or internal control system, seems to be at its highest point of inventive genius. It is a game most people find fascinating, but to the avowed criminal it becomes a passion.

DEVELOPING A FRAUD SCENARIO

While it is unlikely that we will find many career criminals or members of organized crime in the environment under audit, we may indeed find a number of employees who are frustrated, bored, or disgruntled enough to attempt to compromise the system of control, either for economic, egocentric, or ideological reasons. The fraud auditor must therefore be able to identify with the reasoning processes of such people.

The first imperative of the fraud auditor is to develop a fraud scenario. This is predicated on an analysis of the system's strengths and weaknesses—considering the weaknesses, what threats and risks do they open up? Where in the chain of internal controls are the most serious weaknesses? Have these control features ever been compromised before? Who is aware of the weaknesses? What is the simplest way to exploit these system weaknesses? In this environment, given these people, these systems of control, these practices and procedures, what are the most likely outcomes? How can access to assets, accounting records, forms, and data processing systems be effected surreptitiously? How can access be fabricated through impersonation? These questions are what I call "learning to think like a crook."

Once the fraud scenario is completed, an audit plan is developed. This plan should delineate the areas of audit concentration, i.e., specific accounts to be examined, specific procedures to be tested, specific transactions to be analyzed, specific policies to be reviewed, specific people to be interviewed, and specific supporting documentation to be analyzed.

Why such a scenario? Because criminals tend to exploit human and system weaknesses. They spend most of their time scheming and looking for weaknesses. They also tend to think in simple ways. The "Raffles" type jewel thief who meticulously plans each step is the rarity among criminals not the general rule. Haste is the downfall of most criminals. While they scheme and plot a great deal of the time, they rarely prepare elaborate plans and often fail to consider the consequences of their actions in the height of their excitement. So the fraud scenario built on assessed weaknesses is the most appropriate fraud audit approach because it most nearly matches the mental disposition of the typical criminal.

But doesn't the classic audit accomplish the same end? Aren't weaknesses in controls reviewed too? Yes, they are, but from a perspective of how extensive the audit should be to confirm the reliability of data on financial statements, not to assess where the vulnerabilities to employee theft may lie. Outside auditors are not detectives or at least they do not consider themselves to be detectives. Their emphasis is on the reliability and authenticity of data that support numbers in a balance sheet or income statement. They can give no assurance that the data is not specious. When things balance and seem to be as they ought to be according to the logic of accounting and auditing authorities, their job is done. But that is precisely where the fraud auditor begins. He assumes all is in balance and appears to be stated correctly. And while financial criminals are rarely geniuses, they are rarely fools. They do take some precautions and attempt to cover their tracks and bury the evidence of their crimes. They do not normally make it easy to detect their crimes. But their greatest weakness is their tendency to develop simplistic plots because of their hurry and probable fear of apprehension. The thing that has always amazed the fraud auditor, given the utter simplicity of most fraudulent acts, is how the fraud went undetected for so long. It is this fact, so embarrassing to management, that leads them to refuse to prosecute the culprit and to keep the matter quiet. If the fraudulent technique was known more generally in the firm, it might lead to attempts to repeat the same act.

FRAUD SCENARIO BUILDING

Building fraud and theft scenarios is the real stock-in-trade of a good fraud auditor. It is the part of his trade requiring the right side of the brain rather than the left side of the brain, creativeness rather than linear and sequential logic, mindset more than methodology, trial and error versus fixed procedure, and empathy with the criminal mind. "If I were a criminal, what would I do to exploit this weakness? What would be the simplest way to do it?"

The logic of a fraud scenario is unstructured. There is no set formula or fixed procedure. It is an intuitive process rather than a thinking or rational process. Engaging the brain in such a process is accomplished by forgetting you are an auditor and pretending you are a criminal—first a clever criminal and then a stupid criminal. Shifting between both types from time to time. Theorizing about how you would set up a situation for theft or fraud and how you would then cover it up—the "beyond and before" theory. Then designing a "worst case scenario," that is, one that is planned and executed by a really clever thief. Following up that with a "best case scenario," that is, a theft involving a rather stupid thief, and finally attempting to merge the two and create a midrange scenario, that is, a thief who is neither a genius nor a dummy.

Try this situation for practice. ABC company's annual audit was just completed. The outside audit firm discovered a discrepancy between the physically counted inventory and the book inventory of $1,000,000. The weaknesses in inventory controls were identified as follows:

1. Incoming freight is verified on the basis of comparing the freight bill with an open purchase order. Cartons are counted but not weighed. Cartons are not consistently inspected for unit count or quality. The carton count procedure assumes that each skid contains forty-eight cartons but skids are not dismantled to determine whether a false stacking or "stovepiping" procedure by the vendor may have been used.
2. Truck drivers making deliveries are given free access to the unloading docks, the receiving room, and the unloading staging area. They often linger after unloading and socialize with receiving dock employees. They also help these employees to make the carton count.

Now write a worst case and a best case scenario based on these facts (clever thief versus stupid thief). Having done this, write a most likely case scenario merging elements from the worst-case and best-case scenarios.

As another example, take the case of the typical accounts payable fraud. All an employee thief needs, if controls are not tight or policed too well, is a phony service company added to the vendor master file. Getting invoices and letterheads printed for such fictitious entities is no problem. Getting a post office box number and bank account are a little more difficult but no herculean effort either. (However, lying to the post office and bank may be crimes in themselves and using the mail to send the specious invoices to the employer could also be mail fraud.)

While raw materials and merchandise coming into the company require other forms of supporting documentation, i.e., receiving reports, purchase orders, packing slips and delivery tickets, a provider of services such as a janitorial service, maintenance service, repair service, or even a consulting service does not need much in the way of documentation beyond an invoice and perhaps a service contract. A written or initialed approval for payment can then be sought from someone in authority or even forged if the thief cannot find an unwitting assistant or willing accomplice to the crime.

But how is such a crime detected by the auditor? He could review the service contract files and compare those vendors with the vendor master file to see whether any names are contained in the vendor master file that are not supported by written contracts. And he can look for oddities like vendors with post office boxes, vendors with the same address or phone number, vendors who endorse their checks with pen and ink rather than a stamped endorsement, etc. Several cases that come to mind are cases of frauds I have investigated. In one case I could not understand why a company's auto repair bills were so high when so few claims were filed with its auto insurance carrier. The reason was that the fleet manager who authorized payments for repairs was taking kickbacks from the repair shop owner for phony repairs. In another case a janitorial service was charging far more than its competitors but the quality of its work was inferior.

The reason was that a senior manager had a hidden interest in the janitorial service.

To add a phony vendor who supplies raw materials for manufacturing or merchandise for resale is a bit more difficult. If proper controls are in place, there should be an authorization procedure for adding vendor names to the master file, such as a request for a vendor number assignment issued by someone in authority in the purchasing department. An accounts payable data entry clerk should not be able to do so on his or her own order, and while the clerk can forge the authorized signature of the request form, to get an invoice through for payment would require supporting documentation by way of a signed purchase order and receiving report. If controls over these documents are poor (forms are not preserialized, blanks kept on open shelves, no permanent log of issued numbers), it is still possible for a clerk acting alone to fabricate a vendor name and all the necessary documentation to justify a payment.

Reviewing exceptions and oddities is a vital part of the art of fraud auditing. Good fraud auditors train themselves to look for the hole, not the doughnut. Everyone can see the doughnut but relatively few people can concentrate on the hole. Fraud auditors also look for the things which are out of place, rather than the things which are in place. "A place for everything and everything in its place" is more than just a proverb to a fraud auditor.

Time, place, and form utility are said by economists to add value. All business transactions have a proper sequence and timing. Events that seem to be occurring out of sequence, or at odd times, at odd places, or in odd form are "red flags" for fraud auditors. When things are out of order, the fraud auditor's antennae should pick up on that condition. There is static on the line suggesting there is some obstruction or impediment to clear communication, and the cause of that impediment must be found to remedy the static.

HOW THE FRAUD SCENARIO WORKS

How does the fraud scenario approach really work? Let us say a fraud auditor has completed review of internal controls and found the following weaknesses in a cosmetics manufacturing firm:

1. Blank sales credit memo forms were found on an open shelf in the sales department. The memos are not preserially numbered but are manually assigned a sequential number by a sales clerk who uses a typewriter to imprint the number on the form. Authorizations for the issuance of such memos are routed to her by the assistant sales manager without countersignature. The authorization form is also not preserially numbered. The clerk attaches the authorization request to the company's file copy in the sales department, then mails a copy to the customer and sends a copy to the accounts receivable section clerk, who then enters the credit to the customer's account on an on-line terminal. The sales department clerk and the

receivables section clerk who enters the credit memo are friends and often visit each others homes. What are the opportunities for fraud and whom would they involve?

2. The purchasing department's manual specifies that purchase orders are to be preserially numbered, issued only on a requisition by an authorized department head and cosigned by the director of purchasing and the specific purchasing agent who is assigned the products or services requested. Vendors of products are to be approved by the department head and director of purchasing. Such approvals are to be based on the quality of past materials purchased, pricing, timely past deliveries, and financial reliability. An annual review of all vendors who sell more than $500,000 of goods, materials, and services is also required for the purpose of updating the approved vendor file. The Quality Control department head and the director of Purchasing are assigned that responsibility.

    In the course of your review of internal controls, you have found a) a supply of blank purchase orders without preserialized numbers, b) that purchasing agents have never been rotated, c) a year-long supply contract for heating oil was not subject to competitive bids, d) the largest single vendor of critical materials for production is in receivership, and e) that vendors have not been evaluated for 3 years. What are the opportunities for fraud and whom would they involve?

3. Goods that have become obsolete are to be so designated by a committee of three people: the sales manager, director of physical distribution, and the director of disposal. Upon agreement by these three, the goods are pulled out of stock and segregated and the active inventory is relieved of their cost but a residual value is assigned to a scrap account. The director of disposal is then authorized to find the best price he can that is consistent with the assigned residual value.

    In the course of your review you learn that the year-end balance in the scrap account is zeroed out and charged against profit in an adjusting general journal entry. You also learn that the directors of disposal and physical distribution seem to be living beyond their current income level and that some of the items which were declared obsolete are finding their way into salvage houses and discount retail chains and being sold as though they were new (in their original containers and packaging.) What are the opportunities for fraud and whom would they involve?

4. Returned items are required to be inspected by a clerk in the receiving department and the goods are matched against a credit advice signed by a field sales representative and the customer. Upon matching the goods and the document, the receiving clerk routes the credit advice to the sales manager and returns the saleable items to stock, the damaged items to the trash compactor, and the obsolete items to a segregated bin area.

    On the day of your visit, shortly after the Christmas season, you observe large numbers of odd-sized boxes, stacked very poorly and very high, and in bad physical condition. Many of the boxes have been opened.

The credit advices have been removed. The receiving clerk tells you in confidence that there is no way he can validate the full receipt of returned goods at this time of year because of the sheer volume. He does the best he can by assuming the credit advices are consistent with the items in the boxes and forwards them to the sales department. He then salvages and sorts the good materials, the obsolete items, and the damaged goods and sends them to the appropriate areas. However, while he is at lunch and on break the staging area where he works is accessible to most receiving employees. What are the opportunities for fraud and whom would they involve?

If the most common motive for employee theft, fraud, and embezzlement is economic, one might assume that the best defense is to make compromising the system of internal controls so cumbersome and expensive that theft will not pay for the culprit. But building layer upon layer of controls and protection countermeasures can also get to a point of diminishing returns for the company. The cost of installing and maintaining elaborate controls and countermeasures can become prohibitive from a cost feasibility or return on investment basis. The criminal mind knows that. That is why weaknesses will always be with us. The real challenge for the fraud auditor is therefore to keep these weaknesses and their potential consequences clearly in mind at all times. While you do not have to be a thief to catch a thief, you do have to learn to think like one.

THE FRAUD AUDIT TEAM CONCEPT

Fraud audits or investigations are generally triggered by two events: the finding of an accounting discrepancy and an allegation by some person that a fraud, theft, or embezzlement has been committed. Where fraud, theft, or embezzlement is alleged, the talent or technique required is that of the investigator. Where a discrepancy is found, the talents required are those of the auditor. However, in many situations discrepancy and allegation may coexist. The allegation may be based on a preliminary assessment or evaluation of a discrepancy (a hasty conclusion that since a shortage exists it must involve *this* person or *that* condition). Or the allegation may have been received without an earlier finding of discrepancy or other accounting irregularity. In either event, fine distinctions as to what talents will be required to detect the fraud and document its existence are not what is called for. It is advisable in the beginning to field a team to look into the situation. Both audit and investigative talents will be needed to assess the situation and conclude the matter. It may be also advisable to enlist the aid of inside counsel, and if the alleged fraud or discrepancy involves computer manipulation, the aid of an expert in electronic data processing. Since the firm may ultimately file an insurance claim on its fidelity bond or other crime coverage, the firm's risk or insurance manager should also be brought on board.

In situations where fraud, theft, or embezzlement are suspected on the basis of accounting discrepancy rather than allegation, the fraud auditor will spend the bulk of his time during the initial phase of the audit determining whether a loss has in fact occurred. A mere discrepancy is not necessarily evidence of fraud. So, the immediate audit objective is to rule out, or rule in, fraud. The first step in ruling out fraud is to determine whether any logical reason, other than fraud, exists for the discrepancy. For example, can it be attributed to mathematical or human error? Or accounting system inaccuracy? Or is the discrepancy based on a specious assumption of a fixed relationship between costs and revenues, i.e., normal gross profit. In essence, could the discrepancy be attributed to managerial or accounting system weaknesses or to faulty budget assumptions?

Allegations generally involve some specific information on the nature of the crime and the likely culprit. If less than that amount of information is made available, there is not much to pursue. Rather than unleashing a major audit or investigative effort, prudence dictates a thorough debriefing of the source of the allegation, including inquiry into the source's own motives and knowledge of the alleged crime. An evaluation of the credibility and reliability of the source can then be made.

If the discrepancy or allegation is substantial and cannot be attributed to human or accounting system error or managerial incompetence, an audit and investigative plan should be developed by the fraud audit team (auditor, investigator, EDP expert) and reviewed and approved by inside counsel and the risk manager. The plan should include the specific accounts to be analyzed, accounting procedures and practices to be reviewed, and the witnesses to be interviewed.

The process described thus far is depicted below.

1. Discrepancy found or allegation received
2. Preliminary inquiries completed
    a. Discrepancy resolved/allegation is unfounded
    b. Discrepancy confirmed
    c. Allegation supported
3. Develop fraud scenario
4. Legal counsel sought
5. Insurance claim needs identified
6. Develop audit/investigative plan
    a. Accounts to be analyzed
    b. Procedures, practices, and documents to be reviewed
    c. Witnesses to be interviewed
    d. Data and documents to be collected, reconstructed, and preserved

CHAPTER 3

Corporate Fraud in the Current Environment

THE MANAGEMENT DEFRAUDER'S PSYCHE AND THE WORK ENVIRONMENT

It would be nice, and certainly easier for the fraud auditor/investigator, if psychologists could provide a profiling tool for the management defrauder—a tool that is simple, not subject to multiple interpretation, thoroughly validated, and that accurately predicts at least 90% of the time in any job environment. But there is no such tool and it is doubtful whether any will ever be developed.

In an effort to provide a practical tool for auditors to use to discover potential management fraud situations, the accounting profession has developed an analytical approach called "red flags." Red flags are descriptions of human and organizational behaviors that do not necessarily prove management fraud, but when enough of them are found they may indicate the potential presence of fraud and require a more extensive audit to rule out fraud or to document its existence. So far so good. The approach, while not wholly scientific, is better than intuition alone and for the auditor who does not have Columbo's characteristics it is certainly an improvement over the traditional audit approach of matching, batching, and balancing numbers.

However, in reviewing the contents of the red flag checklists we find some strange assessments that are to be made by auditors in the course of either internal or independent audits, assessments that are highly subjective and impressionistic and that are based on cursory observations and predicated on "pop socialpsychology." For example, one group of accounting professionals suggests the following red flag characteristics of executives to be wary of in the course of an audit:

- A person who is a wheeler-dealer
- A person without a well-defined code of ethics
- A person who is neurotic, manic-depressive, or emotionally unstable
- A person who is arrogant or egocentric
- A person with a psychopathic personality

This author seriously questions whether the typical auditor is trained, equipped, or experienced enough to make psychological diagnoses in the course of a routine audit that is performed within a tightly budgeted time schedule. What we might see then would be branding and labeling of executives in audit reports—"quickie" assessments made by amateurs that are based on highly subjective observations, little clinical data, and inference.

While this author is not challenging the whole red flags concept, he does believe that rating or evaluating the personality characteristics of top management is dangerous because it tends to be highly subjective. If we are going to use anything of practical significance to determine the probability of fraud in the corporate environment, I would rather have the auditor evaluate conditions in the work environment that are conducive to fraud or that breed or foster its development or that are symptomatic of its existence. The conditions I would focus on are determined through observation and review. A checklist for such an evaluation might resemble the following:

1. Do executives and employees have an economic reason to steal from or defraud the company?
   a. Are salaries and fringe benefits equitable and competitive with other similar firms in the same market?
   b. Are pressures for production and profitable performance so great that people are "burning out" or becoming disgruntled?
   c. Are employee evaluations and salary reviews based on fair and objective criteria?
   d. Are promotions based on merit and contribution and administered fairly, impartially, and openly?
   e. Are job-related goals and objectives "imposed" on subordinates or "negotiated" with subordinates?
2. Does the company suffer from a "we-they" syndrome: management versus non-management personnel or middle management versus top management?
3. Do conflicts abound among the top management group over issues that involve corporate philosophy, corporate purpose, corporate direction, or corporate ethics?
4. Is there evidence of spite, hate, hostility, or jealousy among the firm's top management group?
5. Do employees feel oppressed, abused, exploited, or neglected by senior management?
6. What is the company's past history with respect to:
   a. Labor-management relations?
   b. Turnover of top executives?
   c. Moonlighting and conflicts of interest by employees and executives?
   d. Vandalism, theft, and sabotage by employees?
   e. Corruption of customers?
   f. Corruption by vendors?

g. Corruption of labor leaders, regulatory authorities, and political officials?
h. Association of executives with organized crime figures?
i. "High living" by executives?
j. Lack of concern for truth in advertising or selling its products or services?
k. Convictions for business-related crimes?

Non-Management Defrauder's Profile

The classic studies on white collar crime suggest the typical white collar criminal is a trusted lower level employee of long tenure with an unresolvable personal financial problem. This profile appears to be as correct today for the typical corporate embezzler as it was thirty years ago when outlined by criminologists. We know today that the cause of much midlife aberration by "loyal, dedicated, and trusted" employees may be the normal emotional pain of growing older, which is felt more keenly by some people. Examples of midcareer crises suffered by friends, relatives, and acquaintances are known to most of us who have gone through that transition in life already. A profile of the non-management defrauder would be: A middle-aged male or female of stable employment, in a position of trust, with knowledge of controls and access to company assets, who feels abused, exploited, or rightly or wrongly neglected and who has an unresolvable financial problem due to family sickness, expensive tastes, or high living, and who can rationalize his or her act as "borrowing" rather than stealing.

Management Defrauder's Profile

Management fraud, by simple definition, is the intentional overstatement of corporate or unit profits. Profits can be manipulated by overstating revenues or understating costs. Overstating revenue can be accomplished by entering fictitious sales, recording unfinalized sales ("early booking" scam), recording consignments as sales, or recording shipments to storage facilities as sales and issuing credits, returns, or allowances for such items in the next accounting period. Costs can be manipulated by a deferral to the next accounting period or by an understatement in the current period accomplished by such ploys as overstating ending inventories of raw material, work in process, and finished goods or by understating purchases of raw materials.

In theory, each of these methods for overstating profits is detectable through traditional financial audit techniques, i.e., transaction sampling, account analysis, accounts receivable and accounts payable confirmation, physical inventory counts, eyeball and reasonableness checks, gross profit tests, internal control tests, etc. In fact, few such frauds are ever discovered in the course of financial audits, at least not in the early stages of such frauds. Early warning systems for such frauds do not exist in the classical auditor's bag. He tends to look at current numbers, not numbers from the past and not at the people who generate them. Financial auditors want to believe in the numbers they are reviewing and to trust the people for whom they are auditing. Both are laudable, if slightly unrealistic, objectives.

But management fraud of the type being discussed is peculiar in ways other than the need for some faith and trust in numbers and people. Management fraud is made possible by the fact that accounting controls can be circumvented by senior managers. Controls are designed mainly to keep lower level people from becoming dishonest. Senior managers are, in effect, trusted more since they have more authority to dispense with controls under proper circumstances. Internal and accounting controls are not barriers or limits to the possibility of fraud by senior management but of fraud by lower level managers and employees. Management frauds also tend to involve a number of people; they tend to be conspiracies. A conspiracy to commit management fraud is even more difficult to detect than an act or series of acts by any one person.

A further complication in management fraud detection is that even when discrepancies, oddities, variances, and exceptions surface, it is difficult to distinguish these occurrences from innocent errors, mistakes, and omissions. And it is difficult to distinguish acts of fraud from acts of mismanagement or incompetence. Human error and incompetence are far more frequent occurrences than fraud. Not all dumb people are crooks nor are all crooks dumb people. Some crooks are intelligent and management defrauders tend to be more in that category than in the dumb category.

Another peculiarity of management fraud is that many of the perpetrators of such frauds have shown symptoms of dishonesty in the past. They tend to amplify their experience, education, and managerial accomplishments on employment applications. Their personal background and credit files often show evidence of: chronic late payment or nonpayment of debts; considerable debt; previous skirmishes with the law or regulatory agencies; unstable employment and unusual personal habits, i.e., expensive tastes, expensive hobbies, overinvolvement in civil, social, fraternal, or political activities. They often live in the "fast lane." Their home lives are often in shambles too. Mobility is another distinguishing characteristic of management defrauders. Many have had a large number of previous positions in other firms.

While the literature of white collar crime speaks about that kind of crime as though white collar criminals are old, trusted, loyal, low level employees, those descriptions are more appropriate for classic bank teller, bookkeeper, and data entry embezzlers not for profit center or branch managers or senior executives— the type of people about whom we are speaking. Management defrauders do not usually embezzle funds or steal assets. They "fudge numbers" and "cook the books" so they can look like winners instead of losers, or they take a larger bonus home, or they get a much desired promotion.

So in management-type frauds we are dealing with people who are fairly intelligent, mobile, highly trusted, highly motivated, and loosely supervised, who act in concert with others over whom they have a measure of authority and in concert with a system of controls over which they have at least some veto power. Giving all this power to a person who may be untrustworthy or easily tempted seems the height of folly, but it happens every day in business.

INTERNAL VERSUS EXTERNAL FRAUDS

Corporate fraud can be subclassified as being *internally generated* as in fraud by the corporation's own officers, directors, agents, or employees and *externally generated* as in fraud by the corporation's vendors, suppliers, customers, or competitors. Internally generated frauds, for our purposes, will also include the crimes of larceny (theft) and embezzlement by officers, directors, agents, and employees. While not falling within our technical definition of fraud, these crimes are often associated with the fraudulent preparation, alteration, forgery, or destruction of corporate books, records, and documents and may therefore lead to unwitting misstatements of financial facts by the corporation.

FRAUDS FOR VERSUS FRAUDS AGAINST
THE COMPANY

Internally generated corporate frauds can also be subclassified as frauds committed *for* the company and frauds committed *against* the company. Frauds for the company might include corporate tax evasion, price fixing, manipulation of the company's stock price, false advertising, false labeling and branding of products, false weights and measures, political and commercial bribery, padding government contracts, or intentional violations of a host of other governmental regulations, i.e., pollution, OSHA, EEO, ERISA, wages and hours, fire and building codes, etc. These violations have an existing audit literature of their own and are detectable through operational auditing. We will not cover them extensively in this book. Our main focus will be on frauds, thefts, and embezzlement against the company by its own officers, directors, agents, and employees and frauds against the company by its vendors, suppliers, customers, and competitors.

INTERNALLY GENERATED FRAUDS COMMITTED
FOR THE COMPANY

Crimes committed for the company include intentional violations of governmental regulations. Many of these violations can be detected in a routine operational audit, i.e., OSHA violations, EEO, EPA, wages and hours, padding government contracts, etc. Others are not so easily detected, as in price fixing, corruption or compromise of customers, competitors, business regulators, union leaders, or infringements of patents and copyrights. Furtiveness is required to keep the latter crimes a secret from internal and external auditors. Evidence of these crimes is therefore not likely to be found within the accounting system. If it exists, it is contained in the nonfinancial records of the company—for example, in general correspondence files, in memoranda of meetings where sales and competitive strategies or financial plans are being formulated, in the minutes of directors' meetings, etc. As a matter of routine audit procedure, it is advisable to review these files and documents to determine whether any evidence exists of such conspiracies.

A periodic regulatory compliance audit should be made a necessary part of the company's internal audit program. Waiting for government auditors and investigators to conduct such audits is not prudent business any longer, if it ever was. With the current number of lawsuits by irate stockholders and the pressures by the Securities and Exchange Commission on matters that involve Foreign Corrupt Practices Act compliance, related party transactions, insider trading, and materially misstated financial statements, it would serve the corporation well if an independent internal audit were conducted to avoid regulatory "surprise" actions.

Business crimes that on the surface were committed for the corporation (to enhance profitability by reducing costs or inflating sales or to hide actual or contingent liabilities) in the end may cost the corporation a good deal more than the net savings to be effected through such crimes. Many companies become innocent victims in these crimes because their officers' intentions are not to hurt but to help the company—and themselves if bonuses are based on cost reductions, sales increases, or profit improvement.

Most of the crimes of the regulatory type come about as a result of competitive practices in the industry or conditions in the economy. When products are selling well at good prices, operating costs are in line, stockholders are satisfied with their return, executive compensation is equitable, and competition is fair, the temptation to fudge numbers, shortchange the customer, bluff regulators, or conspire with competitors is not so great. Regulatory violations are at a low then. But when any of these factors change for the worse, the temptation increases. Economic survival is a potent motivating force, and if survival means "shaving a few corners," corporate managers are too often willing to engage in such regulatory violations. The motivation to survive may lead to "sharp practices," shoddy merchandise, and unsafe work places. In poor economic times or when competition is keen or the company's financial future is either being threatened or is highly uncertain, it is wise for the internal auditor to be particularly alert for regulatory violations. In fact, compliance audits are probably more useful at those times than during periods of business boom. Volume solves a lot of problems and when business is good, coping with manufacturing schedules and sales delivery dates may keep managers so busy that no time is left over for scams that are intended to aid the company. The temptation to cheat or lie is therefore reduced.

But even well-managed, well-financed, and prosperous companies sometimes can fall prey to performance pressures. The celebrated price fixing scheme in the electrical industry involved several large corporations: GE, Westinghouse, Electric and Emerson. A practice or habit developed in the industry of exchanging competitive information on pricing, marketing territories, and bids on sales of electrical transformers. This "swapping" of business intelligence began in the 1930s under the auspices of the National Recovery Act and with the formation of industry councils to promote such exchanges of information. Despite the ruling of the U.S. Supreme Court that the NRA was unconstitutional, the industry continued to meet and exchange sales and marketing data. The pattern had become so entrenched that its obvious illegality made no difference. It was easier to do business that way than for all members to freely compete for new business. The meetings continued but with greater security precautions. Intelligence was exchanged at offhshore meeting sites or held within the United States on a clandestine basis.

CORRUPTION FOR THE COMPANY

The area of greatest internal audit difficulty, however, is not with regulatory violations committed for the company but with corruption for the company—corruption of customers, competitors, union officials, and government authorities. Bribery payments to such people are not likely to be paid with corporate checks issued in the regular course of business. Sub rosa payments may be made in terms of unbilled merchandise; transfer of corporate properties without fair consideration or just compensation; payments to intermediaries, i.e., brokers, consultants, and lawyers who serve as liaisons; lavish vacations paid for by the company; and a myriad of funds transfer scams, i.e., payments through foreign subsidiaries or into foreign banks for the benefit of the person so corrupted.

Occasionally some evidence will be left intact among the financial records of the firm and an alert auditor may find it. For example, there may be evidence of regular exchanges of corporate checks for cash funds when no need to do so is apparent by the nature of the business. In very large multinational corporations transfers of funds between the parent and the subsidiaries or from one subsidiary to another are commonplace. Where these transfers are intended to generate cash for illegal or improper purposes, the accounting legerdemain can be so intricate and convoluted that no audit technique is available to reconstruct what happened. Without the aid of at least one accomplice in the scheme, the auditor is at the mercy of pure chance for a coherent reconstruction. Support documents probably will not be available. If they are, they may be so cryptic that no interpretation of the transaction is possible. But if a pattern of transfers without adequate documentation is found and the same principal or principals are involved in each transaction, the auditor should seek legal guidance and investigative support if he intends to interview the suspect or suspects.

At the very outset of suspicion reporting such incidents through the proper channels is a wise thing to do. If funds are being used for fraudulent or corrupt purposes, great care and caution should be taken to preserve whatever evidence exists. And before the auditor begins to make allegations and charges, he should seek the help of superiors and company lawyers.

INTERNALLY GENERATED FRAUDS COMMITTED AGAINST THE COMPANY

Crimes by Executives

Executives and high level managers of major corporations are often wedded to compensation plans that focus on immediate profits and other short-term goals such as sales increases and cost reductions. Accomplishing these short-term goals then results in bonuses, promotions, and other perquisites. While short-term profitability is not an unworthy goal, it is, if not associated with longer-term perspectives, a serious temptation to manipulate accounting data.

The most common executive crime, which is not reported often in the media or prosecuted as such, is *performance data manipulation.* The process of auditing for executive crimes therefore should include as major categories of inquiry the following:

1. The current status of economic conditions for business in general
2. The current status of competitive conditions in the specific industry of which the firm is a member
3. The relationship between the firm and its competitors
4. The long-term outlook for the firm's products and services
5. The market share of the firm and whether that share is growing, is constant, or is declining
6. The history of the firm and the industry with respect to regulatory compliance
7. The past, current, and future profitability of the firm
8. Pending litigation and complaints against the firm by regulatory authorities, vendors, customers, creditors, and competitors
9. The compensation and incentive plans and criteria for bonuses for the senior management of the firm and its divisional managers

These findings do not constitute proof of wrongdoing, but they may provide the fraud auditor with an insight into potential motivations or dispositions toward wrongdoing. Where it appears that management is inclined to play "fast and loose" with financial or operational data and where profits and bonuses are threatened by competition or economic downturn, a more extensive audit may be in order. There are enough holes in the generally accepted accounting rules to permit questionable manipulation of profits through a variety of accounting legerdemain, and a few are as follows:

1. Booking sales that are not really finalized. (The "early booking" scam)
2. Delaying necessary repairs and maintenance
3. Not making adequate provision for doubtful accounts receivable
4. Capitalizing expenses that should have been charged to the current year
5. Acquiring another company whose current profits are high and consolidating its income with the firm's income at year's end
6. Selling an asset that has appreciated in value to enhance earnings per share
7. Accepting goods or merchandise on a consignment basis without adding the liability to the balance sheet or the goods to cost of sales

Business Week lends support to the above. (See *Business Week,* 3/17/80, p. 196, "Why Managers Cheat." See also this author's articles, "Why MBO Programs Don't Meet Their Goals," *Management Review,* December 1980 and "Corporate Creed or Corporate Greed?" *Administrative Management,* December 1980.) The *Business Week* article deals with managers who fake performance data because of pressures for quick results and short run profits. The cases of Chase-Manhattan Bank, American Can, and H.J. Heinz are cited as evidence.

Such performance fakery, however, may not be grounds for dismissal in some firms nor even grounds for the filing of a fidelity bond claim for loss, unless it continues for a period of years. Many fidelity or honesty bonds contain disclaimers on losses incurred by a company for overpayment of bonuses due to performance fakery. The first year of bonus overpayment does not constitute a provable loss. Another aspect of fidelity bonding with which the fraud auditor should become familiar is the negligence disclaimer. Where it appears that managerial negligence is a factor in the fraud, for example, through slipshod accounting controls that made fraud possible, the bonding company may refuse to pay on the loss.

But how do these cases surface? What can a fraud auditor do to determine whether performance data are phony or real? One technique that might help is to review the performance bonus criteria. What goals must be reached to achieve the bonus level? A sales increase? Profit increase? Manufacturing cost reduction? Return on investment improvement? Inventory reduction? Market share increase? Liquidity? Cash flow? And how are these criteria weighed?

A clue to a possible bonus scam is the amount of pressure on key executives being applied by senior management or by directors for results on lower levels of management. How much pressure, to whom is it directed, and on what basis or criterion? These are the questions the fraud auditor must answer. That determination then leads to the building of his or her "bonus fraud" audit program. If the main pressure concerns inventory reduction, the auditor should be alert to indications of early booking of sales, delays in recording purchases of raw materials or merchandise, i.e., understating cost of sales and liabilities, or arbitrary write-downs of inventory volume or inventory values.

If the main pressure concerns short-term profits, the auditor should look for evidence of delayed recordings of expenses, early booking of sales, arbitrary write-ups of ending inventory, and the nonrecording of accrued expenses.

Expense accruals are a favorite management technique for "smoothing profits." In good years accruals may be overstated to provide a cushion for poor years. The reverse is true in poor years. If the main pressure for results is measured by a return on investment (ROI), the auditor should be alert to evidence of leasing of equipment rather than outright purchase. Unrecorded leases are a favorite technique when ROI is the primary performance criterion. The unrecorded lease is an understatement of a contingent liability of the firm.

While the lease payments are charged to current operations as would be the depreciation of the same asset were it purchased, and while this charge to operations may not distort the immediate year's profit, ROI is enhanced by leasing because the equipment does not appear on the firm's asset list. The calculation of ROI, based as it is on the relationship between assets and stockholders' equity and long-term debt, then provides management with an artful way of "pumping up" ROI by the mechanism of leasing or other forms of off-line debt.

Another technique for smoothing profits, keeping profits growing at a steady rate of increase and avoiding wide swings up or down, is the creation of off-line reserves. The author discovered one such reserve within the records of a major division of a multinational oil company. The profit center manager's compensation was based on improving year-to-year profits by at least 10%. But the retail gasoline business in those days was subject to wide fluctuations in prices. Price wars often broke out and no one could predict who would start them nor when they would occur. As a consequence, achieving the goal of a year-to-year increase in profits of 10% or more was far from a sure thing. Some years profits increased by 20% and in other years profits increased less than 10% or not at all.

The profit center manager, a former controller of the division, found an ingenious way to guarantee himself an annual bonus by creating an off-line reserve that he named "Reserve for Price Variation." In good years, as in years when profits increased by better than 10 percent, the excess over 10 percent was set aside in the reserve account with an offset against sales. In years in which profits were unlikely to exceed the previous year's level, sales would be increased and the reserve would be decreased. The manager's rationalization was that since it was impossible to predict when gasoline price wars would break out, his only hope for showing steady growth was the creation of a cushion for his division.

Orderly growth—steady improvement—is certainly a worthwhile goal. Many investors are attracted to firms which are not subject to wide variations in profits. These are the so-called conservative investments, that is, investor risk is minimized and, of course, opportunity is minimized as well. But when orderly growth is the only goal and compensation is based on that criterion alone, there is a temptation to create special reserves of an off-line nature. Business and economic trends in the real world do fluctuate and may even fluctuate wildly. Pursuing the goal of orderly growth or steady improvement in profit is impossible for many firms. Yet most investors wish to invest in "growth stocks" that have minimal risks, i.e., stocks that outperform the Dow Jones Average or Gross National Product. To simulate such patterns of growth therefore some companies may put such heavy emphasis on orderly growth that subordinate profit center managers are tempted to fudge the numbers to achieve the goal. Smoothing profits through the preceding techniques is not unusual among divisional general managers and profit center directors. So the internal or operational auditor should be particularly alert for such evidence, especially when it appears that a single goal is the basis for performance appraisal and bonus award. It is an invitation to commit fraud.

Other crimes against the company by executives that may be detectable within the accounting system include false or fraudulent expense reimbursement and benefit claims, and theft, embezzlement, or misuse of corporate assets. These crimes can be uncovered through appropriate financial audit techniques, i.e., confirmation, verification, review of supporting documents, inventory count, testing of accounts, statistical sampling, etc. Executive crimes that may not be detectable through financial audit techniques because the evidence may be outside the accounting system include corruption by vendors, suppliers, customers, and competitors and are generally referred to as commercial bribery. But some hints or clues may be found in the accounting records that might support such crimes too. For example, invoices from vendors whose prices for goods and materials seem to be consistently higher than those of other vendors for goods of similar description, quantity, and quality.

The act of bribery may consist of cash paid under the table to purchasing executives or other executives; lavish entertainments; expensive "gifts"; home improvements made at no charge; payment by the vendor of an executive's country club dues; bar tabs or other debts; procurement of prostitutes or drugs; free use of vacation homes, resorts, or company aircraft.

Corruption by vendors can be minimized if company policy against such practices is made explicit, clear, and unmistakable and is a cause for termination of employment. Another method to avoid vendor corruption is to create a vendor evaluation team with a rotating membership. Each vendor's performance is then annually evaluated against a set of criteria such as (1) competitiveness of prices, (2) consistency of quality of goods, (3) consistency of delivery dates met, (4) technological know-how of the vendor, (5) improvements made in products, and (6) financial stability of the vendor. Corruption by customers can be found where pricing and sales terms for one customer are not consistent with the terms granted to other customers of comparable size and volume characteristics. These include higher discounts, refunds, rebates, more sales returns and advertising allowances, longer terms for payment, etc.

One crime involving executives and perhaps lower level officials may be very difficult to detect through normal financial audit techniques. That crime, also a form of commercial bribery, is the sale or disclosure of company trade secrets or proprietary information to competitors. Disclosure may be intended to sabotage the company—to hurt it financially—or to induce the competitor to later hire the executive or employee. Such crimes are seen most often today in the so-called high technology firms but are also committed in other industries. The clandestine sale of proprietary computer software to a competitor is one example, along with the sale of engineering plans or designs for new products.

In the non-high technology sector, a common crime of this type is the clandestine sale of customer lists, market research results, manufacturing technology, new product plans, corporate growth and development plans, and marketing plans. The release or disclosure of such confidential information may in some cases jeopardize the future profitability of the firm. Yet the value of the stolen document is hard to assess and this makes prosecution of such crimes difficult. If such documents have been treated and handled within the company as sensitive, that is, marked as confidential, restricted in terms of distribution, and safeguarded when not in use, it may be possible to assert legally that they are proprietary in nature and civil recovery for damages may be possible as well as the criminal prosecution of the thief. But auditing is rarely the vehicle for the discovery of such crimes. Controls over such documents are management functions and do not generally fall within the purview of accounting systems and controls. Discovery usually occurs through intelligence efforts—knowing what the competition is doing and how well they are doing, what their capacities are, and what level of technology they possess.

CRIMES BY LOWER LEVEL MANAGERS AND EMPLOYEES

Pilferage—theft of supplies, parts, small tools, and merchandise—is probably the most common form of employee crime. The best defense against this crime is tight inventory accounting controls that are monitored on a regular basis, i.e., periodic cycle counts of preselected items. A good physical security system is also important to discourage small thefts. Explicit policies against such thefts must be articulated at time of hire and then periodically reinforced through house organs, bulletin board postings, and at meetings. Pilferage that gets out of hand can cost a lot. One employee stealing one spark plug in an auto plant may not be much, but when this becomes a general practice by many employees the cost can be significant. In one situation of which the author has personal knowledge, almost 100 assembly line workers in an auto plant took to stealing 6 to 8 spark plugs a day by secreting them in cartridge belts worn inside their shirts. At a rate of 600 to 800 spark plugs a day, on three shifts, it will not take many days to accumulate a million dollar loss at manufacturer's cost. If inventory and cost of manufacturing controls had been better policed in that plant, much of the loss could have been avoided.

Another form of employee theft is the abuse of company property. That could take the form of outright sabotage of equipment, merchandise, or machinery, or the intentional waste of raw materials. These thefts most often involve blue collar workers. The white collar workers have their own pet schemes. Thefts of office supplies and equipment are not unusual, along with abuse of company telephones. And the office copier is now fair game for everyone's personal use including grandma's recipe for oatmeal cookies, knitting patterns, garden club announcements and newsletters, and the latest Charlie Brown episode in the comics page. One recent type of asset abuse is the theft of computer time by people who have access to a terminal. There are known incidents of computers being used by employees to run lotteries, to store their own Christmas card lists, and to produce Snoopy calendars, holiday greetings, and even pornographic art. Then there is the clever programmer who rents storage space in the company computer, or sells time on it to outsiders, or uses it after hours as his own private service bureau.

These so-called small crimes by blue and white collar employees probably cannot be eliminated in large organizations—in any random group of 1,000 employees a small number, at least, will be thieves. Good controls and good management may discourage even some of these thieves. But the habitual thieves will attempt to find methods to overcome the controls and if persistent enough will probably find a way to compromise the control system. That portion of the employee theft problem may be the irreducible minimum. Constant attention and concern, however, will keep the amount of the loss within the bounds of cost feasibility. Vigilance is the only effective strategy to keep this sort of theft to a minimum.

Some of the crimes enumerated in the section on executive theft also apply here:

- False claims for bonuses, benefits, or expense reimbursement
- False productivity and time and attendance reports
- Sale or disclosure of proprietary information

The previous comments and suggestions in that section have equal application here. The only difference is that small thefts by lower level white and blue collar workers tend to be less sophisticated and are easier to detect through audit. However, small thefts unattended can lead to large losses.

One might suspect that corporate frauds, thefts, and embezzlements by higher level employees are less frequent than those involving lower level employees. That proposition sounds logical because there are fewer employees at the top than there are at the bottom in any organization. But the per capita rate of crime at the top echelon compared with the lower echelon has never been determined on a scientific basis. By analogy to the research findings in criminology one might logically conclude that since crime is basically a phenomenon that involves people in the lower socio-economic classes, the incident rate of corporate or business crime is higher among lower level employees. One could with equal logic conclude that crime is "learned behavior" or a mimicking of the behavior of peers or superiors. If superiors steal or defraud, then why not their subordinates? So where should the audit emphasis be placed: on crimes at the lower level or on crimes at the higher level?

From a loss potential point of view, it would seem that more audit effort should be spent searching for potential fraud, theft, or embezzlement at the higher echelon. The possibilities for compromise of controls (bypassing, circumventing, or overriding controls) are much greater at the top. People at this level have more authority and are more knowledgeable about controls and the means and methods by which to compromise them. The dollar loss potential from any one incident is greater.

But another audit consideration is the loss potential created by computerized accounting systems versus manual and mechanical systems. The computer has made possible the threat of significant losses without the effective audit means to detect them. Effectiveness in this context means cost feasibility: time, effort, and EDP audit expertise required to ferret out the fraud. One could also add the change in the character of the audit trails in EDP that make computerized accounting systems more vulnerable to compromise, especially in environments with on-line processing of accounting data. A host of new frauds is now possible in such environments, frauds that have been given such colorful names as: data diddling; piggybacking; Trojan horses; salami slicing; trap doors; scavenging; logic bombs; and superzapping. Most of these frauds cannot be committed without a fairly extensive knowledge of systems and/or applications programming. Data diddling and piggybacking do not require a knowledge of computer programming. They are old-fashioned crimes that have assumed a new form. For example, data diddling refers to changing, or altering, input data before or during its entry into a computer. Forging or counterfeiting input documents is perhaps a simpler way to describe such a fraud. But this technique was used long before computers were invented, so the phenomenon is not new. Its form has changed. The same holds true for piggybacking, which is a form of impersonation, i.e., gaining access to a computer terminal that has not been deactivated (signed off) by its authorized user and then making false or fraudulent entries or using the computer for unauthorized purposes.

The crimes referred to as salami slicing, Trojan horses, trap doors, logic bombs and superzapping are uniquely the products of advanced technologies, that is, they are computer programming frauds committed during the thruput phase of data processing and they did not exist before the invention of computers. In terms of our present discussion, they are included to demonstrate that corporate frauds by employees have taken on a new character and form and represent a new complexity, all of which the fraud auditor must learn to deal with. This is the fundamental reason why the author suggests that a fraud audit team must now have multidisciplinary talents. No longer can the auditor act alone when doing fraud auditing. The team may require EDP audit talents, telecommunications and physical security expertise, computer programming expertise, and legal and insurance expertise.

EXTERNALLY GENERATED FRAUDS AND THE COMPETITIVE ENVIRONMENT

Vendors, Suppliers, Common Carriers, and Warehousemen

Internal accounting controls are designed primarily to protect the firm's assets from fraud, theft, and embezzlement by corporate insiders, i.e., officers, directors, agents, and employees. When properly designed and regularly monitored, these controls minimize the risk and loss from such crimes. But they also serve an added purpose. Internal controls provide a mechanism by which to protect assets from outside theft and fraud; these controls, along with physical security safeguards and countermeasures like alarm systems, closed circuit television, guards, fencing, and other surveillance tools, provide the company with a system of protection. Outside the firm defrauders include vendors, suppliers, common carriers, warehousemen, customers, competitors, and public enemies or professional criminals.

The types of incidents perpetrated by outsiders causing loss to the corporation include false weights and counts; quality misrepresentations; double billing; full billing for partial shipments; diversion by common carriers; conversion by warehousemen; intentional overpricing and pricing extension errors; corruption of corporate employees; padding charges on service contracts; false claims for refunds, rebates, and allowances by customers; predatory sales practices by competitors; information and technology thefts by competitors; and a host of other criminal acts such as robbery, hijacking of merchandise, burglary, usury, sabotage, extortion, blackmail, and terrorism.

Criminal acts against the company by public enemies should be handled by the firm's security staff. These professionals are the best equipped and best trained to deal with these situations. But vendor, customer, and competitor frauds and thefts may also require investigative input; therefore, it would be wise to add an investigator to the audit team if discrepancies are found or allegations are received that involve outsiders. Vendor frauds against the company usually consist of falsified invoices for goods, materials, and services sold. If purchasing, receiving, and quality control procedures are firmly established and regularly monitored, such crimes can be minimized. However, gaping holes in such procedures have often been found, i.e., materials received that are not regularly confirmed against purchase orders with respect to weight, count, or quality specifications.

The fraud auditor must be particularly alert to situations in which adequate controls are specified in procedures manuals but are not applied in practice. Having good controls in a written form is only the first step in an internal control system. Consistent application of control procedures is even more important. Inconsistencies between standard procedures and actual practices are evidence of internal control weaknesses and can expose the company to risk of loss. So a critical step in the fraud auditor's program should be a review of internal control procedures compared against actual practice. If gaps exist, the auditor should theorize about the likely consequences of such slipshod practices. This is what is referred to as building a fraud scenario. What compromises of internal controls are possible given these weaknesses and vulnerabilities? What are the most likely outcomes of such compromises? Who would be involved? Who could best exploit the weaknesses? How difficult would a theft or fraud be to execute under such circumstances? Would such a theft or fraud require more than one person, such as an insider with an outsider?

Customer Crimes

Shoplifting ("boosting") is the most common form of customer crime in retailing. Variations may include such practices as switching price tags on merchandise (putting a lower price tag on a higher priced garment), passing counterfeit money or bad checks to pay for goods, hiding stolen garments under clothing, in shopping bags, or in briefcases, etc. Since much has been written on this subject and since these types of theft may not involve the inventory accounting system in a direct way, customer crimes will be covered on a general basis.

The main concern of the fraud auditor working in the area of customer crimes relates to the falsification of credit worthiness, which is a control function of the credit department, and false claims for sales and advertising refunds, rebates, discounts, warranties, and allowances for damaged goods and returned items, i.e., stale, obsolete, outdated, and unsold goods. The corruption of someone inside the firm may be required to carry out the fraud, usually someone in the sales department with authority to approve returns and allowances.

When reviewing the returns and allowances account, the fraud auditor should be particularly wary of transactions outside of the normal sales pattern—more returns than usual for other customers of equal volume, more frequent refunds or allowances to one or several customers than to others of similar size and volume of sales, higher discount rates or advertising allowances that are not consistent with sales volume, free services, or unbilled merchandise allegedly for sample or review purposes, etc. A pattern of discriminatory practices favoring one or several customers over others may be a symptom of fraud or a possible regulatory problem. It should not be treated lightly. For example, one large automotive manufacturer was a victim of a large number of warranty claims by one of its dealers. The warranty claims were false and fraudulent, but the scam went on for a number of years until an internal auditor compared the dealer's warranty claims with the dealer's volume and compared that in turn against the average for dealers of similar volume. Here again, the technique used by the auditor was what is called "out-of-pattern transactions" or exceptions from the norm—too high, too low, too many, too few, etc.

Competitor Crimes

Competitor crimes against the company may take the form of predatory sales practices, i.e., selling below cost, discriminatory pricing, freebies and giveaways to selected customers. These practices may be violations of the Federal Trade Commission Act or the Robinson-Patman Act. As such they can be referred to federal authorities for investigation.

The more insidious practices of competitors today, however, consist of theft, conversion or appropriation of manufacturing technology, trade secrets, proprietary information, patents and copyrights. Evidence of these crimes is not usually found in financial audits but results from intelligence gathered in the normal course of business by the company's own engineering or marketing staffs. A weak competitor suddenly shows up with a "look-alike" product or beats the firm to introduction of a new product for which it had neither the manufacturing know-how nor the engineering or research expertise. In these circumstances the fraud audit team may be composed of investigative, research, engineering, and legal talents. Accounting talents may also be required to analyze the competitor's financial resources to determine whether its capital base could have sustained a research and development effort to produce the new product independently of data stolen, converted, or appropriated from others.

The theft of information is more prevalent in business today than the theft of physical properties. Software piracy alone is a serious problem. Stealing competitor's marketing research, marketing plans, and customer lists are close seconds. Stealing high technology employees, while perhaps not a crime in most instances, is a rather common practice in some sectors of industry and if it is not clearly illegal, it is certainly unethical. These employees are pirated away by competitors not only for their talents and skills, but also because they possess knowledge of product development plans and manufacturing and technology know-how, which has been learned at great expense to their current employers.

CORPORATE FRAUD BY COMPUTER

Computers dedicated to business applications came into general use in 1954. One of the initial sales features of computers beyond the benefits of speed and the elimination of repetitious, error-prone, manually made bookkeeping journalizations was the measure of security provided by sophisticated hardware. It was alleged that employee theft, fraud, and embezzlement would be thwarted or at least minimized because of the new complexities involved in committing these acts. And indeed it appeared for a time that complex hardware did provide such insurance. However, while the computer made it more difficult to appropriate small sums of money, it also made it possible to steal large sums with less likelihood of discovery. Worse yet, while the technology of the computer itself was exploding, the security of EDP systems continued to lag. Today, the gap between EDP technology and EDP security is bigger than at any point since 1954.

EDP Technology versus EDP Security

The current state of the art in EDP technology exceeds, by an order of magnitude, the state of the art in EDP security. This is a primary reason why independent auditors and internal auditors cannot assure top management and directors that fraud, theft, and embezzlement are nonexistent in the firm. Nor can they assure them, given all the controls presently available, that these events are not likely to occur. Qualified assurance is the best they can provide, assuming all available precautions are being taken.

But fraud, theft, and embezzlement existed long before computers were invented. Accountants and auditors were as concerned about these matters during the days of manual accounting systems as they are now. The defenses they built into manual systems were fundamentally of two varieties: the development of accountability through paper trail documentation at each point of property and currency transfer and the separation of duties between those accountable for making or recording transaction documents and those accountable for the physical handling and transfer of property and currency. While these controls were not foolproof even in manual systems, they have grown more difficult to maintain in the computer age.

Many early business applications involved entering, manipulating, and summarizing accounting data, and generating management reports. Most output produced by computers was manually reviewed for (1) correctness and/or (2) to decide what courses of action should be taken on the basis of the output report. As more complex computer processing developed, the applications became more exotic. Computers were assigned certain repetitive decision-making chores that were formerly done by clerical and technical personnel, i.e., purchasing agents, inventory control clerks, sales clerks, accounts receivable and payable clerks.

With the development of on-line order entry systems came a further dilution of paper trail controls. The substitute controls were then placed mainly in the system's specifications and in the programming. Documentation of the systems and the programming became the major defense against fraud, theft, and embezzlement. Separation of duties came to mean both the physical and functional segregation of the analyst, programmer, operations, and data entry staffs. Because of the expense involved in maintaining these separations, many smaller firms combined a number of job functions, i.e., programmer/analyst. In some small firms, three functions were combined. One person might function as a programmer, analyst, and a computer operator simultaneously. The current movement toward minicomputers has exacerbated the problem. Independent auditors are appalled by these developments which foreshadow a total breakdown in the traditional notion of internal control.

EDP and the Annual Audit

The audit approach during the embryonic period of EDP is referred to as the "audit around." Auditors merely took final account totals and verified them against basic input documents that were supposed to support the validity of entries. Later auditors began their process of review by identifying the controls built into computerized systems, i.e., organization charts, work rules, procedures, systems flow charts, and program documentation. These controls were then challenged in computer run-through tests to ensure that the controls were there and functioning according to the documentation. The quality of documentation is more critical than ever before because the records that formerly existed in written form are now stored as magnetic impulses on tapes or discs. Adequate and timely program documentation accomplishes two goals: it builds back a measure of control so that at audit time verifications can be made and it allows one programmer to follow the logic of the program of another programmer and make whatever modifications and corrections become necessary.

Decision Making Between Audits

In an ideal environment, internal control policies and procedures become guides for routine decision making and matters of standard practice. Until a policy or procedural imperative is changed by a responsible and authorized person, it is to be followed without variation. Where variances do occur between the stated policies and procedures and actual practices of the firm, the exceptions are quickly noted, logged, reviewed, and acted upon by the person responsible for the system of internal controls. Unfortunately, few firms are ideally run, and often there occur situations where quick compromises are made whenever time rather than control becomes the imperative. We pay lip service to controls but defeat them at the slightest provocation. More often than not, controls become afterthoughts— something we think about after the fact or, worse yet, after a substantial loss.

Loss prevention through adequacy of controls and the systematic monitoring thereof does not win many friends or advocates with the exception of those whose professional careers and reputations depend on it and those who most recently have been damaged by the inadequacy of internal controls.

The New Risk: Remote Terminals

As stated previously, there are no truly foolproof computer security systems. The best anyone can design is a fail-safe system composed of layers of barriers, controls, and backup positions. But there comes a time in even the best fail-safe systems when these barriers and controls become so cumbersome and expensive that the benefits they confer are outweighed by their costs in dollars and employee demotivation.

The truly dedicated intruder can always find weaknesses in the physical defenses. Even if these defenses can be made insurmountable, penetration is still possible by way of compromising an inside source. In fact, that may be the most expedient method in many cases. Insurance against loss, therefore, becomes a paramount consideration and a vital link in a total protection plan.

Until recently most computer frauds, thefts, embezzlements, and other abuses were perpetrated by people trained in the computer sciences acting alone. Because of the improvements in built-in software and hardware controls, the more recent instances involved collusion among insiders or between an insider and a nonemployee. The Equity Funding case demonstrates that a computer fraud of colossal proportions can exist among insiders. That the fraud went undetected for years is even more startling. But Equity Funding was a "securities'' fraud. The intention of the principals was not to steal or embezzle company funds but to deceive the investing public by overstating assets and profits by computer. In so doing, the principals' own stock continued to rise in value. Unfortunately, the media created the impression that wholesale thievery of company assets by employees was involved. Equity Funding does provide some insight, however, for it shows that the accepted auditing technique of the past, audit around, may not be useful when a dedicated group of insiders decides to use the computer to deceive auditing authorities and directors by generating specious output.

In the author's view, the most serious computer abuses of the future will come most likely not from EDP professionals but from the new generations of users—remote terminal users. For many years, computer professionals could rest comfortably with the notion that users were an unsophisticated lot and therefore unaware or not knowledgeable about techniques to sabotage, compromise, bypass, or override control features in hardware and software. But as remote terminal users continue to grow in numbers, the likelihood is that their sophistication will also increase.

The trend in EDP technology toward network and data base information systems, time-sharing, and distributed processing indicates the magnitude of the new security risks for EDP managers. By 1985, it is estimated that there will be 7,000,000 remote terminals in operation in the United States alone. If the proliferating use of low-cost microprocessors for dedicated or special purposes is added to that figure, the enormity of management and administration problems becomes obvious. The loss of centralized control over data processing hardware and software introduces an element of risk not seen before. One favorable aspect of centralized control has been the clear line of accountability of EDP results, i.e., quality of output, hardware, and peripheral efficiency, etc. The movement toward decentralization will obscure the lines of accountability for these results.

Also, in attempting to balance user satisfaction with adequate internal controls a serious problem will emerge between the EDP needs of users and adequate procedural security safeguards. Security controls that are too rigid and inflexible will frustrate computer users and discourage them from utilizing a valuable management tool. Inadequate controls, on the other hand, may expose the company to a variety of security vulnerabilities that include theft, embezzlement, sabotage, and information piracy. The question we must address today is: how do we balance these needs so that users can be satisfied as well as stockholders, directors, and outside auditors?

Motivational Climate and Computer Threats

The most critical threats to computer security can be broadly classified as (1) acts of God, (2) machine-made errors, and (3) human errors. Among the human errors, those of omission far exceed those of commission; however, of the errors of commission, those originating from human beings within the organization far outweigh those from human beings outside of the organization. Threats from outsiders, whether they are terrorists or predatory competitors, may be real and substantial, but they are insignificant when compared to the probability of exposure and potential damage that can be done to an organization by a disloyal or disgruntled insider.

We offer the following as a tentative rationale for employee theft, fraud, and embezzlement by computer.

I.   Opportunity Inducements
  A.   Inadequate Prevention Measures
    1.   Security Awareness
    2.   Security Planning
  B.   Inadequate Controls
    1.   Procedural Controls
    2.   Documentary Controls
    3.   Internal and Audit Controls
    4.   Physical Security Controls
    5.   Personnel Security Controls
    6.   Information Protection Controls
  C.   Inadequate Detection Measures
    1.   Logging and Monitoring Exceptions
      a)   Access and Authorization Limits
      b)   Out-of-Pattern Transactions
        (1)   Exceptionally Large
        (2)   Exceptionally Frequent
      c)   Unusual File Access Within Authorization Limits
II.   Environmental Inducements
  A.   Inadequate Rewards
    1.   Pay, fringe benefits, job security, promotional opportunities, recognition, meaningful work
  B.   Inadequate Interpersonal Relationships
    1.   Trust, level, group cohesiveness and support, morale, interpersonal and intergroup communication
  C.   Inadequate Structural Support
    1.   Clarity of organizational mission, goals, job roles, and performance expectations
  D.   Condoning Influences
    1.   Unspecified organizational values and ethical norms, tolerance for antisocial behavior, management laxity, and managerial incompetence
III.   Personal Inducements
  A.   Unresolved Personal Problems
    1.   Employee self-worth, self-identity, moral/ethical values obscurity
  B.   Unresolved Interpersonal Conflicts
    1.   Rivalry, spite, revenge, and jealousy
  C.   Unresolved Personal Economic Problems
    1.   Heavy debts, acquisitiveness, greed, high-life style

Both research and recent experience show that among all the available security safeguards, the one that bears most heavily on minimizing EDP security risks and threats is the maintenance of a highly motivated work climate. Providing a safe, friendly, challenging, and satisfying work climate is the best and often the most cost-feasible defense against employee theft, fraud, embezzlement, larceny, and inefficiency.

SUMMARY

Corporate frauds can be distinguished as follows:

- Civil   versus   Criminal
- Internally generated   versus   Externally generated
- Management   versus   Non-management personnel
- Against the company   versus   For the company
- Within the accounting system   versus   Without the accounting system
- Form   versus   Substance
- In manual accounting   versus   Automated systems

Corporate frauds can be further distinguished as to typology by the following characteristics:

I.   Internally generated corporate frauds
    A. For the company
        1. Regulatory violations
            a) OSHA, EEO, ERISA, EPA, FTC, FDA, ICC, OFCC, Wage-Hour, Antitrust, SEC, IRS, FCPA, Building and Fire Codes, State Sales, USE, Extraction and Property Taxes, Rate Regulations, Padding Government Contracts, etc.
        2. Consumer and customer frauds
            a) False labeling, branding, advertising, and packaging
            b) Short weights and counts, defective products, and substitution of inferior goods
            c) Price fixing
        3. Stockholder and creditor frauds
            a) False financial statements and representations
            b) False or forged collateral
            c) Stock manipulation, insider trading, and related party transactions
        4. Frauds against competitors
            a) Theft or compromise of competitors' trade secrets or proprietary information
            b) Predatory pricing and other forms of unfair competition
            c) Copyright and patent infringement

      5. Corruption of customers' and competitors' personnel and/or regulatory authorities or union leaders

B. Against the Company
    1. By executives
       a) False claims for bonuses, benefits, or expenses
       b) Commercial bribery by vendors
       c) Sales of proprietary information or trade secrets to competitors
       d) Theft or embezzlement of corporate assets
       e) Fabrication of operational or financial performance data
    2. By non-management employees
       a) Pilferage
       b) Sabotage of company property
       c) Theft or embezzlement of corporate assets
       d) False claims for bonuses, benefits, or expenses
       e) Intentional waste
       f) Falsifying time and attendance and productivity reports

C. Frauds from within the accounting system
    1. False input scams (creating fake debits)
       a) False or inflated claims from vendors, suppliers, benefits claimants and employees, or false refund or allowance claims by customers
       b) Lapping on receivables payments or customer bank deposits
       c) Check kiting
       d) Inventory manipulation and reclassification
         (1) Arbitrary write-ups and write-downs
         (2) Reclassification to lower value—obsolete, damaged, or "sample" status
       e) Intentional misclassification of expenditures
         (1) Operational expense versus capital expenditure
         (2) Personal expense versus business expense
       f) Fabrication of sales and cost of sales data
       g) Misapplication and misappropriation of funds and other corporate assets (theft and embezzlement)
       h) Computerized input and fraudulent access scams
         (1) Data diddling and manipulation
         (2) Impersonation and imposter terminal
         (3) Scavenging
         (4) Piggybacking
         (5) Wiretapping
         (6) Interception and destruction of input and source documents
         (7) Fabrication of batch or hash totals
         (8) Simulation and modeling fraud (fraudulent parallel systems)
       i) Forgery, counterfeiting, or altering of source documents,

authorizations, computer program documentation, or loan collateral

j)   Overstating revenues and assets

k)   Understating expenses and liabilities

l)   Creating off-line reserves

m)   Related party transactions

n)   Spurious assets and hidden liabilities

o)   "Smoothing" profits

p)   Destruction, obliteration, and alteration of supporting documents

q)   Exceeding limits of authority

2.   False Thruput Scams

a)   Salami slicing, trap doors, Trojan horse, logic bombs

b)   Designed random error during processing cycle

3.   Output Scams

a)   Scavenging through output

b)   Output destruction, obliteration

c)   Theft of output reports and logs

d)   Theft of programs, data files, and systems programming and operations documentation

D.   Frauds from without the accounting system

1.   Confidence schemes by outsiders

2.   Fraudulent misrepresentations by current and prospective vendors, suppliers, customers, and employees

II.   Externally generated corporate frauds

A.   Vendors, suppliers, common carriers, warehousemen

1.   False weights, counts, and quality representations

2.   Double billing

3.   Full billing for partial shipments

4.   Diversion and conversion

5.   Intentional overpricing and extension errors

6.   Corruption of purchasing employees

7.   Conspiring with employees to overlook shortages

B.   Customers

1.   Falsification of identity and credit worthiness

2.   False claims for refunds, discounts, returns, and allowances for damage

3.   Shoplifting

4.   Switching price tags

5.   Corrupting sales personnel

6.   Conspiring with employees to ship unbilled merchandise

C.   Competitors

1.   Predatory sales, advertising, and pricing practices

2.   Theft, conversion, or/of appropriation and technology, trade secrets, proprietary information, patents, and copyrights

    3. Employee pirating

    4. Commercial slander

D. Public enemies

    1 Robbery, larceny, and burglary of corporate assets

    2. Usury

    3. Terrorist or violent acts against the company's assets and human resources—kidnapping, sabotage, extortion, and blackmail by criminal elements and hostile foreign governments

    4. Hostile takeover by financial pirates

CHAPTER 4

Corporate Fraud Investigation in the Electronic Data Processing Era

INTRODUCTION

Investigations of common law crimes (murder, mayhem, larceny, robbery, burglary, rape, and arson) begin with a fairly definitive state of facts. Someone has just been injured physically or financially and demands justice, that is, criminal action against the offender. Even if we do not know who committed the crime, we do know that a crime was committed or at least that one was alleged to have been committed, and we often know how it was committed and upon whom it was committed.

In computer crimes (fraud, larceny, embezzlement, sabotage of equipment, or information theft), we often do not know what specific crime was committed, by whom it was committed, or worse yet how it was committed. The how factor of criminal investigations is often a matter left to forensic experts. Clues are analyzed to determine how the crime was committed in the hope that the analysis may provide some insight into who the likely culprit is.

Auditing and accounting, while not thought of as forensic sciences, are the most useful tools in the investigation of computer-related crimes, at least those involving thefts of tangible assets and instances where computers have been used as the means and instruments for the execution of the crime. Investigators of computer crimes must therefore have at least a general knowledge of accounting and auditing principles and techniques, as well as some understanding of how computers operate with respect to the recording of financial transactions and financial information.

What follows is by no means an exhaustive treatment of auditing of computerized accounting systems, but it may help to save time by directing investigative effort to the more serious internal control weaknesses of most of these systems. Control weaknesses create the conditions that lead to fraud by computer, and auditing is designed to detect where such weaknesses are most likely to occur.

There is another reason why investigators should become more familiar with accounting and auditing principles: It may save the investigator from embarrassment when, in searching for evidence of the crime, he does something really stupid. For example, an East Coast police detective who was called in to investigate a computer fraud by a company employee ordered that the computer's core memory be removed as evidence without considering the consequences. The core memory, which was in magnetic form, was not able to be read by him. What he might have ordered perhaps was a core "dump," the printing out of the information in the core memory onto paper. Then he might have had some data he could read.

In another similar situation, a police detective ordered the complete shutdown of a large bank's computer system and sequestered all tapes, files, and programs so that he could search for evidence of the crime. A teller had been accused of "lapping" deposits of customers and "borrowing" from inactive savings accounts. Needless to say, his misadventure cost the bank as much as the teller's fraud did. You can rest assured that if such employee behavior occurs again at the bank, its management will not be too interested in inviting the detective back.

So it is imperative that investigators develop some awareness and competence in electronic data processing (EDP) methods and procedures. The criminals at this point seem to be better trained in stealing by using a computer than the police authorities are in detecting and documenting such crimes.

ACCOUNTING PRINCIPLES

An accounting system consists of records that provide both detailed information of business transactions, which are called journals, and summary information of account balances, which are called ledgers. The most commonly used journals are for the recording of cash receipts and disbursements. Other journals used include those in which sales and purchases are recorded. Ledgers can be subclassified into general ledgers, which reflect the current balance in asset, liability, revenue, and expense accounts in a summary form, i.e., total debits and credits posted, and subsidiary ledgers, which reflect the specific details of transactions between the firm and its customers and suppliers, i.e., accounts receivable and accounts payable subsidiary ledgers. These subsidiary ledgers are kept on the basis of individual customer or vendor name and/or account number (see Figure 4-1).

The process of recording business transactions is called double entry bookkeeping. Each transaction is divided into two parts of equal amounts: a debit entry and a credit entry. When an asset is purchased or acquired or when an expense is incurred, a debit entry is made to the appropriate asset or expense account and an offsetting credit entry is made to a liability or revenue account. When an asset is sold or disposed of, or a liability is incurred, a credit entry is made to the appropriate revenue or liability account and an offsetting debit entry is made to an asset or expense account (see Figure 4-2).

The information recording process begins with a business transaction of one

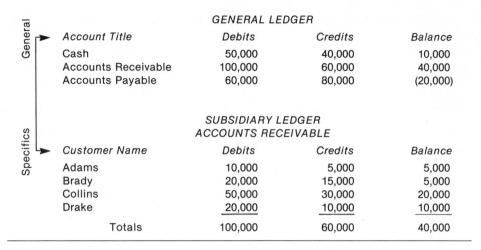

Figure 4-1 Ledgers

ASSETS	Debits	Credits		LIABILITIES	Debits	Credits
(1) Auto	$5,000			(1) Notes Payable		$5,000
(2) Accts. Rec.	1,000			(2) Accts. Payable		500
(4) Office Furn.		$250				
(4) Cash	250					

EXPENSES	Debits	Credits		REVENUE	Debits	Credits
(3) Raw Material	$500			(2) Sales		$1,000

DESCRIPTIONS OF TRANSACTIONS
(1) Purchase of company car
(2) Sales of merchandise on account
(3) Incurring of manufacturing expense
(4) Sale of old furniture for cash

Figure 4-2   Double Entry Bookkeeping

of the following types: the purchase or aquisition of an asset, or the incurring of an expense, or the sale or disposition of an asset, or the incurring of a liability. These transactions are summarized in ledgers and result in periodic statements that assess or measure the financial condition of the firm, in a balance sheet, and its degree of profitability, in a statement of income (see Figure 4-3).

ACCOUNTING SYSTEMS AND METHODS

An accounting system may be manually operated (handwritten entries), or by automated (electro-mechanical equipment entries), or by computerized (elec-

BALANCE SHEET
12/31/80

ASSETS

Cash	$10,000	Accounts Payable	$30,000
Accounts Receivable	20,000	Notes Payable	20,000
Inventory	5,000	Accrued Taxes	5,000
Land and Building	90,000	Equity	70,000
	$125,000		$125,000

STATEMENT OF INCOME
12/31/80

Sales	$500,000
Cost of Sales	250,000
Margin	250,000
Expenses	230,000
Net Income	$ 20,000

Figure 4–3   Statements

tronic equipment entries). Some accounting systems are operated with attributes of each: manual, automated, and computerized.

Computerized accounting systems are designed to expedite the speed with which repetitive business transactions are processed and recorded. Speed is accomplished in several ways:

1. By making simultaneous entries in journals, subsidiary ledgers, and general ledger control account balances, thus avoiding multiple postings.
2. By eliminating unnecessary paper flow-to-document transactions.
3. By decreasing the number of human control points and substituting programming controls, to verify accuracy and validate expenditures.

Computerized accounting systems come in two forms: batch-oriented and on-line systems. In a batch-processing system, transactions are accumulated and entered as a batch at some point in the business day or processing cycle. In on-line systems, transactions are processed as they occur. In batch processing, the controls for accuracy are composed of batch totals, item counts, and hash totals. Batch totals are the sum of all the amounts to be entered, i.e., total dollar sum of all the invoices about to be entered for accounts payable processing. Item counts are the total number of invoices to be entered. Hash totals are another form of accuracy check. They consist of adding up all the vendor identification numbers or payment voucher numbers before entering, and then comparing the sum with the

VENDOR NO.	VOUCHER NO.	VOUCHER AMOUNT
00215	1001	$1,000
00268	1002	3,500
00317	1003	7,050
00472	1004	4,250
00518	1005	500
1790 (Hash Total)	5015 (Hash Total)	$16,300 (Batch Total)

Number of Vouchers Processed = 5 (Item Count)

Figure 4-4 Input Controls

number the computer generates from the same addition while the data is being processed. If a difference exists between the original hash total computed manually and the total calculated by the computer, an investigation is made to determine why more or fewer items were processed than expected. Batch totals, item counts, and hash totals are called input controls. They are intended to ensure accuracy, but not validity, of transactions (see Figure 4-4).

Validity checks involve authorization procedures established to determine whether a payment to be made is based on a legitimate claim against the company by a vendor or supplier who has actually supplied something of corresponding value. For example, in the case of a vendor who has supplied raw material for manufacturing, the steps, or procedures, leading up to payment are as follows:

Forms Flow	Purpose of Document
Budget Document	To regulate and control the amount spent for purchases of goods
Approved Vendor List	To control with whom the company does business
Inventory Accounting Records	To determine normal consumption patterns, current stock status, and re-order points
Purchase Requisition	To limit purchasing authorities and verify needs for goods
Purchase Order	To document goods ordered, quantities, quality, cost, and time for delivery
Receiving Report	To verify receipt and condition of the ordered goods and conformity with purchase order terms
Check Voucher Request	To verify accuracy of vendor invoices (quantities, pricing, and extensions)
Check	To pay for goods actually received

DISBURSEMENT CONTROLS

As previously indicated, validity checks are designed to accomplish several goals:

1.   To separate the duties of those with property handling responsibilities and those with property recording responsibilities.
2.   To determine that a purchase has been approved (a) by someone who has the authority to commit funds for such purposes, (b) from a vendor who is approved, (c) by a person who is authorized to buy; to determine that (d) the specific goods ordered were in fact received and that (e) the proper unit price was charged and extensions stated correctly on the vendor's invoice.
3.   To provide an oversight mechanism at each step in the processing of transactions that detects errors, omissions, and improprieties in the previous step. (Division of labor and dual responsibility for related transactions, i.e., counter signature, segregation of functions, dollar authorization limits, etc.; thus forcing collusion by at least two parties to effect a fraudulent transaction.)

The above checks and controls are what auditors call the paper trail documentation flow, or simply the audit trail. In manual accounting systems, it is possible to trace back from an issued check the sequence of events through retained paper documents, to determine whether the check was authorized, accurate in amount, supported by the actual receipt of the specific goods ordered, based on actual need, and provided for in the budget.

Computerization and automation have changed the forms of these documents. Records are still retained but in electronic form (magnetic impulses on tape) or microfiche form (microfilm reduction). The human controls have been replaced by control mechanisms in computer operating systems and applications programs, i.e., parity checks, limit checks, echo checks, sequencing checks, etc.

Parity checks are controls which ensure that data initially read into a computer have been transmitted correctly to other components of the computer system. Limit checks are designed to flag transactions in which amounts or quantities are compared with predetermined limits or standards for such amounts or quantities. For example, if payroll checks rarely exceed $500, the payroll system can be programmed to flag any check exceeding that amount for managerial attention.

Echo checks are computer messages that play back a transmission to its original source for comparison. The echo check tells the transmitter of data that the data transmitted has been received as originally transmitted. Sequencing checks are designed to determine whether any gap in sequencing has occurred between transmissions or processing cycles of prenumbered documents such as checks, invoices, purchase orders, etc.

But as you can see these new controls are mainly intended to assure management that the computer is processing the information, as fed into it, correctly. If incorrect data are fed in, the controls are designed to flag the transaction, or order retransmission, or instruct the person transmitting how to transmit properly, or to log those items that seem exceptional and report them to management. However, if fraudulent messages are transmitted in proper form and amount, the above controls will not detect them. The same was true in manual accounting systems; fraudulent or forged documents were no more discernible than they are now in computerized systems. Good controls discourage fraud, but they cannot prevent it.

The "separation of duties" principle and the audit trail requirement were the main defenses against employee fraud in manual systems, and they persist in a new form today. Separation now means segregating the work efforts of computer operators from systems analysts (who design systems), from programmers (who write instructions so that the systems will operate efficiently and correctly as designed), and from people who enter data into the system. The audit trail now consists of history files, programs, flowcharts, and procedures and not of supporting documents, i.e., stock requisitions, purchase orders, receiving reports or invoices.

AUDIT TRAILS

In a manual system, the audit trail is made up of paper documents that support each step in a regular business transaction (purchase, sale of goods, or services), i.e., from requisition to purchase, to receipt of goods, and to payment; or from billing a customer to receipt of his payment on account, and to its deposit in the bank. These paper documents are date- and time-stamped, calculations are reviewed and approved by supervisors, and authorized for processing in the next step of the transaction. Copies of the documents are kept and filed at each step in the transaction. The audit trail in a manual system is therefore quite visible.

In computerized systems, particularly in on-line systems, the audit trail is somewhat invisible. Authorizations of a transaction or a processing step may consist of a supervisor turning on a computer terminal key or a data entry clerk entering a password or code at the terminal. Signatures, time stamps, and initials no longer exist on source documents to prove authorization. However, in a manual system, paperwork accompanies a transaction from its point of origin to its end point. The paperwork literally travels with the product, whereas in on-line systems, it is the system that moves the product to its end point, with very little human intervention.

An auditor in an on-line environment tends to audit systems and applications programs and their documentation much more than he tests individual transactions by flow of paperwork. The procedures reviewed in these audits are more often data entry and file retention procedures and not those regarding how documents are physically prepared, handled, and stored away. The documentation required in computerized accounting systems includes operator instructions, systems and program flowcharts, sample layouts for input and output records, program listings in high-level assembly languages, and a listing of the internal controls built into the system. This form of documentation defines the new audit trail for computerized systems.

The audit trail is used by auditors to test transactions and thereby determine whether the built-in controls are providing the checks necessary to maintain proper internal control. An effective audit trail is one that provides an auditor with the opportunity to trace or reconstruct any given transaction backward or forward from an original source of the transaction to a final total. (A transaction can be traced through its entire processing cycle to see if it was entered correctly at its inception and processed correctly to arrive at its result.)

WEAKNESS OR ABSENCE OF CONTROLS

Audit techniques involving computers are called *audit around* and *audit through.* The audit around technique provides checks to determine whether data entering the computer (input) matches data leaving the computer (output). Here batch totals and hash totals are compared at both input and output stages. If they agree, the auditor assumes no mistake has occurred. But data can be manipulated while it is running through the computer as well as being manipulated at the time of entry. So the more acceptable technique for auditing computerized accounting systems is the audit through technique, which requires that programming logic be understood by the auditor. For example, in the audit around approach, the auditor would know that what went into the computer in terms of totals came out with equal totals. But if the payroll program is written so that small sums are withdrawn from each employee's check, accumulated, and added to the programmer's own salary check, the auditor would not know that. The total payroll amount has not changed nor has the total number of payroll checks issued. This form of fraud is referred to as salami slicing, i.e., slicing a little off each check will not arouse anyone's curiosity and is generally undetectable if the audit around approach is used. Therefore, the need exists to conduct audits through the computer. It is just as important to see what is happening inside the black box as it is to see what is happening outside the box.

The logic built into accounting application programs is based on a chain of events that take place in a normal business transaction. The system of logic used in such programs is based on general rules and standard operating procedures or policies. In a well-organized, well-managed and stable organizational environment, these standard rules or "SOPs" account for the large majority of transactions. Exceptions or deviations are rare. In environments where crisis and chaos abound—unstable conditions, poor management, poor organization of work—transactions are handled on an ad hoc basis. Everything is an exception. There are no general rules and in such unstable environments, opportunities for theft, fraud, and embezzlement abound. Internal controls, if they exist at all, are there for pretense purposes: to give the appearance or illusion of control. Absence of controls more often leads to fraud than failure of controls.

But even in reasonably well-managed firms, exceptions are bound to occur.

Human error alone will account for a large number of these exceptions. Corrections are then made and things continue as planned for, or as usual.

In environments in which computers are utilized for accounting, and particularly in on-line and distributed systems, the chance or probability for error is magnified by the complexity of the systems. Accommodations for regular errors are provided for in the system's programming, i.e., suspense accounts, unresolved differences, unclassified expenditures, unknown vendors, unknown payees, payables suspense accounts, receivables suspense accounts, inventory variation accounts, etc. In such environments data can be processed much faster than the human mind can take corrective action for past processing errors. So there are always large amounts of money represented by assets either bought, sold, or disposed of which cannot be fully accounted for at any given time.

Now enter the thief. In such chaos (chaos is a relative term here, denoting many items moving through the system that cannot be correctly classified yet as to account title, i.e., expense or revenue category, asset or liability category) even a semiliterate thief can have a field day. "Patching" and "plugging holes" keeps the data processing department so busy that an ultimate system of controls is never developed. A patchwork or pastiche of controls is the best that can be designed.

With such looseness in internal controls, our semiliterate thief does not need to have much imagination to exploit weaknesses. If inventory postings are already running two weeks behind, no one will be the wiser if a stevedore on the loading dock validates a shipment as fully received, when in fact it is short one or two boxes, one or two skids, or one or two barrels. Such sloppiness in work habits can then lead to an even more serious problem: why not take a box home or share the loot with a confederate, i.e., a truck driver, receiving dock supervisor, or work colleague? So the auditor in analyzing accounts and receiving transactions must be keenly aware that the danger of fraud lies not with normal transactions, but with the exceptions, the deviations from the norm, if such exists in the environment being audited.

Investigators too must become acutely aware of what is normal and abnormal in accounting systems and internal controls. These deviations from the usual course of business events represent the greatest potential threat for employee fraud because they permit easy overrides and bypasses of controls. If you cannot fabricate an entire transaction, you can always fabricate an emergency or create a distraction to justify a deviation at some intermediate step in the transaction processing.

THE MOST COMMON COMPUTER CRIMES

The most common computer crimes are those that involve the computer as a means or an instrument for effecting the crime (fraud and embezzlement) and those in which the computer is the victim (theft of information files, records, lists, and reports, and sabotage against the computer).

Looked at from another perspective, computer crimes can be classified as:

1. Input scams—where false, forged, and altered transactions are added to the stream of data being processed, i.e., false invoices for services or merchandise, false payroll claims, or false benefits claims
2. Thruput scams—where computer programming is intentionally designed to contain hidden weaknesses, i.e., trap doors, salami slicing, Trojan horses, etc.
3. Output scams—where output documents, reports, files, listings, and exceptions logs are destroyed, obliterated, suppressed, altered, or stolen

Of the three categories, most reported computer crimes to date, i.e., more than 50%, have been of the first type—input scams—and mainly involve the submission and entry of false and fraudulent vendor invoices, expense claims, salary claims, and benefit claims for payment. In that sense, nothing new is occurring in the world of crime. Historically, most accounting frauds have fallen into that category.

The easiest way to beat an accounting system is through the creation of a fake debit by way of a phony claim from an alleged vendor, customer, employee, or benefit claimant. The claimant is usually spurious or nonexistent, or real but not entitled to payment. Phony expense claims are for real claimants, but they are either completely fabricated or overinflated. What is different about this form of crime today is the increasing unavailability of the phony paper documents to use as proof of the crime. The evidence now consists of electronic impulses on magnetic tape and if the investigator is unaware of computing systems, he may overlook the electronic evidence of the crime. The tendency of the untrained investigator is to either sequester more electronic data than is humanly possible to review or to disregard the data completely and hope to gain a confession from a suspect.

But even if the suspect confesses, corroboration is required under criminal law. A theory of the crime—how it was effected—is still necessary. A broad statement of confession ("I took the money") is not enough. The investigator must reconstruct the crime from information supplied by the alleged culprit and determine whether the method outlined by the suspect is a possible rationale for how the crime was effected. Supporting documentation can then be sought, i.e., increases in the culprit's bank account balances at the specific times when false claims were submitted and paid, copies of any false invoices, payroll or time cards and benefit claims, copies of the canceled checks bearing the culprit's signature or false endorsements, etc. While computers have made fraud detection and reconstruction more difficult, such crimes are far from impossible to prove to a court's satisfaction when a confession is made.

When you must start from scratch (there are no known suspects, only the loss is known), you have a much more difficult situation. Here you must rely on professional assistance—a qualified audit and data processing expert—to aid in the conduct of the investigation, It saves time and potential embarrassment, and strengthens the case.

RULES OF EVIDENCE AND CRIMINAL STATUTES
INVOLVED IN ACCOUNTING CRIMES

The "rules of evidence" relate to the manner in which testimony and documents are presented in a court of law and to the types and acceptability of offered proofs. Establishing the guilt of the accused beyond a reasonable doubt is the burden placed on prosecuting authorities in criminal trials. In civil matters, the degree of proof required is by a "preponderance of evidence"; somewhat less than that required in criminal proceedings.

The immediate burden placed upon a prosecutor is to produce evidence to establish a prima facie case such as will suffice until contradicted and overcome by other evidence. If this does not happen, then a finding of guilt is possible.

In manual accounting systems, the nature of the proof in a criminal prosecution for theft, fraud, and embezzlement consists of business records such as journals and ledgers and business documents such as invoices, purchase orders, receiving reports, claim vouchers, check vouchers, and canceled checks that are kept in the regular course of business. In computerized accounting systems, the nature of the proof for such crimes tends to consist mainly of microfiched source documents, magnetic tapes, coding sheets, printout reports, and logs. In manual accounting systems, the evidence tends to be tangible and understandable on its face value; in computerized accounting systems, the evidence tends to be unintelligible without supporting explanation. Without a strong foundation (usually the testimony of an expert witness in computerized accounting systems), it is much more difficult to establish a prima facie case. Even to determine the "best evidence" is more difficult in computerized fraud cases. The best evidence rule in this context means primary evidence, not secondary; original as distinguished from substitutional; the highest evidence to which the nature of the case is susceptible, i.e.,

> "A written instrument is itself always regarded as the primary or best possible evidence of its existence and contents; a copy or the recollection of a witness would be secondary evidence." *Manhattan Malting Company* v. *Swetland,* 14 Mont. 269, 36 P. 84.

> "Contents of a document must be proved by producing the document itself." *Nunan* v. *Timberlake,* 85F, 2nd 407, 66 App. D.C. 150.

The best evidence rule is but one of many legal rules with which the computer crime investigator must become familiar. The best evidence rule has evolved over a long period of time. Unfortunately, the case law on the rule does not reflect the current mode of doing business by computer. Whether a transcription of a magnetic tape's contents, printed on paper in user language, is an acceptable substitute under the best evidence rule has not been judicially determined by appellate court decision. Such transcriptions have, however, been allowed into evidence at the trial court stage, as have source document reproductions on microfiche, where microfiche is the regular method of retaining and maintaining business records.

The other rules of evidence that computer crime investigators must become familiar with are:

1.   The rule pertaining to relevance, materiality, and competence
2.   Exceptions to the "hearsay" rule and the hearsay rule itself
3.   Search and seizure of evidence rule
4.   Collection and preservation of evidence rule
     • Marking of evidence and chain of custody

Evidence itself can be defined as "Any species of proof, or probative matter, *legally* presented at the trial of an issue by the act of the parties and through the medium of witnesses, records, documents, concrete objects, etc., for the purpose of inducing belief in the minds of the court or jury, as to their contention." *Hotchkiss* v. *Newton,* 10 GA. 567.

The word legally used above then takes us to the next step in our explanation. "Legally presented" means the evidence or proofs offered must be relevant, material, and competent.

"Relevancy of evidence does not depend upon the conclusiveness of the testimony offered, but upon its legitimate tendency to establish a controverted fact." *ICC* v. *Baird,* 24 S, CT. 563, 194 U.S. 25, 48 L, Ed. 860.

Some of the evidence considered relevant, and therefore admissible, include:

1.   The motive for the crime
2.   The ability of the defendant to commit the crime
3.   The opportunity to commit the crime
4.   Threats or expressions of ill will by the accused
5.   The means of committing the offence (possession of a weapon, tools, or skills used in committing the crime)
6.   Physical evidence at the scene linking the accused to the crime
7.   The suspect's conduct and comments at the time of arrest
8.   The attempt to conceal identity
9.   The attempt to destroy evidence
10. Valid confessions

The "materiality" rule requires that evidence must have an important value to a case or prove a point in question. Unimportant details only extend the period of time for trial. Accordingly, a trial court judge may rule against the introduction of evidence that is repetitive or additive, that is, evidence that merely proves the same point in another way, or evidence that tends to be remote, even though relevant. Materiality then is the degree of relevancy. The court cannot become preoccupied with trifles or unnecessary details. For example, the physical presence of a suspect in the computer room, or in the tape library, or near a terminal on a day in which a spurious transaction was generated may be relevant and material. His or her physical presence in a non-computer–related area of the building may be relevant but immaterial.

"Competency" of evidence means that which is adequately sufficient, reliable, and relevant to the case and presented by a qualified and capable witness, i.e., the presence of those characteristics, or the absence of those disabilities, which render a witness legally fit and qualified to give testimony in a court, also applied to documents or other forms of written evidence. But competency differs from credibility. The former refers to a question that arises before considering the evidence given by a witness; the latter refers to the degree of credit to be given to a witness's testimony. The former denotes the personal qualifications of a witness; the latter, his or her veracity. Competency is for the judge to determine; credibility is for the jury to decide.

The competency rule also dictates that conclusions or opinions of a non-expert witness on matters requiring technical expertise be excluded. For example, testimony by an investigating officer on the cause of death may not be appropriate or competent in a trial for murder or wrongful death, because he is not qualified by education and experience to make such an assessment. Testifying that there were no visible signs of life when the body was found may be acceptable, however.

When an expert witness is called upon to testify, a foundation must be laid before his testimony is accepted or allowed. Laying a foundation means that the witness's expertise must be established before the opinion is rendered. To qualify as an expert witness means demonstrating to the judge's satisfaction that by education, study, and work experience the witness is knowledgeable about the topic upon which his testimony will bear.

In computer crime cases, there is often a need for technical experts: experts in EDP auditing and accounting, EDP systems design and programming, computer operation, computer science, and information processing. The prosecution often fails or succeeds in such cases because of the degree of technical competence of expert witnesses and their demeanor on the witness stand. So selection of highly qualified computer experts is an absolute must in computer crime cases. Their expertise should be sought from the very beginning.

The hearsay rule is based on the theory that testimony that repeats what some other person said should not be admitted because of the possibility of distortion or misunderstanding. Furthermore, the person who made the statement is unavailable for cross-examination and has not been sworn in as a witness. But there are occasions—exceptions—when hearsay evidence is admissible. These include dying declarations, either verbal or written; valid confessions; tacit admissions; public records that do not require an opinion, i.e., they speak for themselves; res gestae statements, i.e., spontaneous explanations, if they are spoken as part of the criminal act or immediately following the commission of a criminal act; former testimony given under oath; business entries that were made in the regular course of doing business.

Because of the newness of crimes in which computers have been used as the means and instruments of the crime or in which they have been victims of the crime, case law tends to be unsettled. We are breaking new ground. Legal definitions of crimes and evidentiary rules that worked well in the days of manual systems need to be updated. The updating process may be occasioned by appellate court redefinitions or legislative action. In the current vacuum of legal precedents, however, we face some rather insurmountable tasks as investigators.

Case planning and preparation by police authorities must begin at the outset of a computer crime investigation. Securing legal counsel from prosecuting authorities should begin almost immediately because there are serious differences between gathering evidence by way of search warrants and by grand jury subpoena for records. Search warrants must specifically describe the area or areas to be searched and the evidence being sought therein. Grand jury subpoenas, on the other hand, may be challenged by motion to quash. Which is the right way to go? We frankly do not know at this point. That is why the police investigator must seek both EDP and legal expertise to determine what specific records will be needed and how they should best be collected for evidence, where the search should be conducted and by whom, and when the evidence should be collected. To reiterate, such expertise should be sought very early in the investigation, probably right after the complaint has been received and the allegations therein confirmed by preliminary investigation.

If the investigation is to be pursued by way of search warrant, the investigator should remember that such warrants must be based on probable cause and should describe with particularity the place or places to be searched and the property to be seized, i.e., (1) tools, means, and instruments of the crime, including books, records, documents, and other writings, magnetic tapes, photo reductions (microfiched documents), listings, coding sheets, and output reports; (2) fruits of the crime, i.e., money, negotiable instruments (checks, stocks, bonds, letters of credit), and tangible property (products, tape files, equipment, and supplies that were stolen); (3) contraband (articles that are illegal to possess such as controlled drugs, unregistered firearms, etc.); and (4) goods on which an excise tax is due.

A search can be made without a warrant but only with the consent of the person to be searched or the proprietor of the premises to be searched. Consent given by the landlord of premises he has leased or rented out, however, is legally questionable. To qualify as legal, a search without a warrant must be made as an incident of arrest and must be reasonable as to extent (the area searched must be proximate to the place of arrest, i.e., the room in which the defendant was arrested). With an informed consent by the defendent, it may also be possible to search adjacent rooms. Duress or coercion cannot be used to effect consent. Here no waiver of the defendant's constitutional rights is possible. There is also no waiver of constitutional rights when consent is obtained by stealth or pretense— you cannot be a thief to catch a thief and you cannot be a con man to catch a con man. Evidence obtained by illegal search, even if relevant, is no longer admissible in state or federal courts. (*Mapp* v. *Ohio*)

Evidence that has been properly seized should be marked for identification, cataloged, and preserved until needed for trial, i.e., investigator's initials, badge, or I.D. number, the date, and case number, marked on a sealed container to hold the article, then entered in an evidence log and stored safely until needed for further examination by forensic experts or for the trial. Care must be exercised in this sequence of events. Any interruptions of, or gaps in, procedures such as loss of possession or control over the article can be challenged by defense attorneys, because the authenticity of the article (its freedom from alteration, deletion, or addition) has been placed in doubt. A documented chain of possession must be established before an article is admitted into evidence.

Photocopies of original documents and other writings and printed matter are often made to preserve evidence. These are used by the investigator so that original records needed to run a business are not removed and to ensure that, in the event of an inadvertent destruction of such originals, a certified copy of the document is still available as proof. The certified copy may also be used by the investigator to document his case report. At the trial, however, the original document, if still available, is the best evidence and must be presented.

Specific crimes committed where a computer has been used as a means or an instrument to execute the crime generally involve the following:

1. Under state criminal statutes
    a. Theft or larceny of property and trade secrets
    b. Fraud and false pretenses
    c. Embezzlement
2. Under federal criminal statutes
    a. Mail Fraud (18 U.S.C., 1341, 1976)
    b. Fraud by Wire (18 U.S.C., 1343, 1976)
    c. Interstate Transport of Stolen Property (18 U.S.C., 2314, 1976)
    d. Bank Fraud (17 U.S.C., 656, 1976)

Another federal statute which may be applicable to computer crimes is the Federal Communications Act, which prohibits the interception of data transmitted over telecommunication lines (telephone tapping). At this time there is no specific federal statute on computer crimes; however, several states now have criminal statutes prohibiting certain forms of computer abuse, i.e., theft, fraud, embezzlement, and information piracy and sabotage against computers. These states include Arizona, Virginia, Florida, California, Colorado, Illinois, Michigan, New Mexico, North Carolina, Rhode Island, and Utah. Other states now considering such legislation are Hawaii, Alaska, Maryland, Massachusetts, Minnesota, Missouri, New Jersey, Pennsylvania, South Dakota, and Tennessee.

Federal legislation regarding computer crimes has been introduced but as of this writing there appears to be no strong sentiment for its adoption except in Electronic Funds Transfer (EFT) fraud cases. However, the fraud by wire statute provides a vehicle for the prosecution of such crimes, so it appears doubtful that specific federal legislation on computer crimes will be forthcoming—at least, not in the near future.

One of the more serious legal problems posed by computer crimes in states without a computer crime law is that criminal statutes, which are derived from English common law, tend to make distinctions as to the nature of a criminal act based on who had the right to title and possession of the specific article or thing stolen and its legal classification as property, i.e., real property versus personal property versus tangible property. These variables then affect the choice of the criminal statute used for prosecution: larceny versus embezzlement versus false pretenses, etc. The nature of the proof required to make a prima facie case will therefore vary and the investigation itself must accommodate these variables. Again it is suggested that a close working relationship be established between the investigator and the legal staff of the prosecution from the very beginning of the investigation. This may not only save time but may save the case as well.

CHAPTER 5

Defenses Against Corporate Fraud, Theft, and Embezzlement

THE MOMM TAXONOMY

The literature of white collar crime is replete with theft motivation rationales. Unfortunately, most of the rationales are supported by nothing but anecdotal data or the author's own bias. Worse yet, the theft motivation rationales that are offered are neither categorized nor classified.

In the hope to provide professionals in the field of crime detection, audit, investigation and prosecution with a systematic look at theft, fraud, and embezzlement causation rationales and to effect some uniformity in nomenclature, this author will propose a classification system for employee-related theft: motivation, opportunities, means, and methods (MOMM taxonomy). External theft will not be covered. Aside from that, the problem of internal employee theft is by far the more common occurrence.

In the broadest context possible, we can distinguish or classify employee thefts as having their genesis from two major areas: personal and environmental. The foundation for these distinctions is the assumption that the seeds of theft are either inherent in the nature of man, or the environment in which he must work, or in both. There are validated arguments to support each of these ideas;

1. Man can think and make choices. He can therefore discriminate between right and wrong and make moral judgments about his own behavior.
2. Man has an inherent evil quality, which he can elect to suppress or give in to.
3. Man is by nature neither good nor evil but is conditioned by heredity and/or environmental influences to behave in socially acceptable or socially unapproved ways.
4. Man is adaptable. If given proper social conditioning, training and opportunity for growth and development, he will invariably opt for socially approved behavior.
5. Man is a victim of his own time, place, and circumstances. Changes in any of these conditions can affect his behavior.

Whatever your own bias to any of these schools of thought, what rings true to human experience is that:

- Some people seem to steal or violate other criminal laws on a continuing basis (organized or professional criminals).
- Some people steal or violate criminal laws only under certain circumstances (situational crime).
- Some people never seem to steal or violate laws at any time.

What characteristics, traits, values, beliefs, or attitudes distinguish these people? Rather than surveying the whole field of criminal acts, let us mainly focus on employees who steal.

If we say thefts are either personally induced, environmentally induced, or a combination of both, how can we classify these inducements? They can be classified as follows:

- Economic
- Ideological
- Egocentric
- Psychotic

Examples of each personal inducement include:

1. Economic
   a. Some people steal because they are either in a state of actual economic need or feel or believe they are. Under these circumstances, family survival or self-preservation needs provide the motivation for theft.
   b. Some people steal because they have freely chosen that method to provide their economic sustenance. They have opted to live in a socially unacceptable way because they feel or believe the gains outweigh the risks of apprehension or the physical effort required to earn an honest living. Sloth, greed, and acquisitiveness may be their primary motivations.
2. Ideological
   a. Some people steal to wreak revenge against others with whom they have ideological differences or from whom they have suffered ideologically predicated oppression, abuse, or neglect. Spite, hate, and anger tend to be their motivations for theft.
3. Egocentric
   a. Some people steal to prove they are clever and knowledgeable or because they have an extravagant sense of self-importance—megalomania, exhibitionism. Their motivations tend to be based on jealousy, envy, or excessive pride.
4. Psychotic
   a. Some people steal out of a distorted sense of reality, i.e., misperceptions, misconceptions, delusions of persecution.

The internal environmental aspects of employee theft can be classified by the following inadequacies in the work environment. These provide the *opportunities* for theft:

A. Systems Controls
    1. Inadequacies in internal accounting controls
    2. Inadequate access controls to computers, terminals, and other information, telecommunication, and data processing equipment or facilities.
B. Management Controls
    1. Inadequate reward system
        a) Recognition, challenging work, opportunities for personal and professional growth
    2. Inadequate ethical climate
        a) Unspecified behavior or conduct expectations or approval of unethical practices or behavior
    3. Inadequate climate for interpersonal trust
        a) Excessive interpersonal rivalry or competitiveness
        b) Punitiveness
        c) Unequal or biased treatment of personnel

We have thus far discussed the motivational and opportunity aspects of theft. But effecting a theft requires (1) motivations, (2) opportunities, and (3) *means.* How can we classify the latter?

Means and opportunities tend to be interrelated with conditions in the work environment, e.g., inadequacies of accounting, access, and management controls. So the means for committing a theft involves the exploitation of weaknesses in the following categories of environmental conditions:

1. Compromising controls
    a) Exploiting weaknesses in accounting, access, or management controls
        (1) Bypassing or overriding controls
        (2) Counterfeiting or destroying data input or output documents
2. Compromising personnel
    a) Enlisting other employees in a theft conspiracy
    b) Bribery

THEFT AND FRAUD BY COMPUTER

The means for effecting a computer-related theft by employees can also be subclassified by the processing stage at which the theft was initiated, e.g., an input scam, a thruput scam, or an output scam.

Most computer-related thefts begin with the creation of a false or fake debit. Ultimately, a credit to cash or a property account must be accomplished to carry out the theft. The usual technique is to create a specious employee or vendor and then to fabricate a payroll or accounts payable voucher and make a disbursement. Variations on that theme can be accomplished by creating fake accounts receivable credits for returned merchandise or discounts and by reclassifying inventory available for sale to sample merchandise, damaged merchandise, or obsolete merchandise. These are the so-called input scams. They usually involve data entry personnel.

Thruput scams are harder to detect and require a knowledge of programming techniques. The data is manipulated while running *through* the computer rather than before the run. The salami slicing technique is an example. Here the culprit writes into a program an instruction that causes the computer to accumulate small sums of money from various accounts, i.e., interest on savings accounts or withheld income tax on employee paychecks, and then to transfer the total to his own savings account or paycheck.

Output scams involve the generation of counterfeit reports, the destruction of exceptions reports to delay the discovering of data tampering, or the theft of legitimate reports for personal gain, e.g., customer lists that are sold to outsiders.

Internal theft then arises when 1) motivations exist, 2) opportunities exist, and 3) sufficient knowledge and skills (means) exist to effect a theft. The variables here are motivations and means. Opportunities are the least variable because there are no foolproof controls systems. All accounting systems have weaknesses that can be compromised. That reality existed in the days of manual and mechanical accounting systems, too. Lest we forget, there was employee theft, fraud, and embezzlement then also. The phenomenon is not new nor was it brought about by the computer. At this point, since there are no comparison data we cannot even say whether there is as much, more of, or less theft. However, a few things are certain. Documenting and detecting an internal theft is far more difficult today. Prosecuting such theft is also more difficult. And the willingness of management to prosecute such thefts has decreased.

WHY EMPLOYEES STEAL, EMBEZZLE, AND COMMIT FRAUD

What causes employees to steal or embezzle from their employers? There may be a million reasons. But since it is a problem many clients face, they have often raised the issue with us and a generic response is not what they want in reply.

So, a few years ago I began to collect data on the motivations for, and theories of, white collar crime as advanced by the authorities in criminology, socialpsychology, law enforcement, and industrial security, as well as the media.

I discovered several things in the course of my research. There are indeed many reasons advanced by authorities as to the cause of white collar crime and their rationales were often in conflict with one another.

One school of thought held to the traditional notion of original sin as a condition which predisposed man to crime and then suggested that man could overcome that predisposition by the exercise of his free will, which seemed like a contradiction in terms. The authorities who subscribed to that philosophy were mainly religious and theological fundamentalists.

One modern school of sociology held that man is a product of his heredity and environment and that given certain socioeconomic conditions of birth and personal development, certain men might well be disposed to the commission of crime, which these philosophers viewed mainly as a lower class phenomenon, and the existence or nonexistence of free will had little to do with it.

The early psychiatrists had an array of rationales for criminal behaviors, i.e., repression, reaction formation, rationalization, projection, regression, denial, overcompensation, displacement, and fantasy, to say nothing of compulsion, obsession, frustration, anxiety, and depression. In short, stealing is a sickness that affects certain people, i.e., kleptomaniacs.

Some of the more avant-garde schools even suggest that stealing is a vindication for past neglect, personal slight or deprivation suffered at the hands of others with authority over the culprit, or a rebellion against society as a whole, or a rebellion against specific institutions which have grown stale, cold, and heartless toward the needs of their client populations.

With that much material you can imagine what fun it was to extract from each school of thought a statement or two synthesizing its position on crime motives or crime causes as applied to white collar thievery.

Over a period of time we eliminated the repeated items and the theories of causation that lacked a substantial support base and narrowed the list to the twenty-five items shown in the survey tabulation following.

We then used the tool to collect data from two seemingly disparate groups: one hundred Michigan CPAs at a morning professional training session on white collar crime in Detroit and ninety attendees at a Honeywell Information Systems conference on computer security and privacy in Phoenix, Arizona. The CPA group was composed of accountants in public practice, in industry, and in government positions. The Honeywell group was composed mainly of data processing professionals of middle to higher management, with a sprinkling of EDP auditors, security, and law enforcement officers. The results of that survey follow:

	100 Michigan CPAs		90 Honeywell Symposium Attendees	
As a general rule, employees steal or embezzle from their employers because	Strongly agree or tend to agree	Tend to disagree or strongly disagree	Strongly agree or tend to agree	Tend to disagree or strongly disagree
1. They feel they can get away with it and not be caught.	90%	10%	90%	10%
2. They think they desperately need, want, or desire the money or articles stolen.	47	53	43	57
3. They feel frustrated or dissatisfied about some aspect of their job.	63	37	75	25
4. They feel frustrated or dissatisfied about some aspect of their personal life that is not job-related.	48	52	68*	32

As a general rule, employees steal or embezzle from their employers because	100 Michigan CPAs		90 Honeywell Symposium Attendees	
	Strongly agree or tend to agree	Tend to disagree or strongly disagree	Strongly agree or tend to agree	Tend to disagree or strongly disagree
5. They feel abused by their employers and want to get even.	63	37	66	34
6. They fail to consider the consequences of being caught.	65	35	60	40
7. They think, Everybody else is stealing; so why not me?	61	39	51	49
8. They think, Stealing a little from a big company won't hurt it.	87	13	81	19
9. They don't know how to manage their own money, so they are always "broke" and ready to steal.	26	74	21	79
10. They feel that "beating" the company is a challenge and not a matter of economic gain alone.	57	43	70*	30
11. They were economically, socially, or culturally deprived during their childhood.	14	86	15	85
12. They are compensating for a personal void they feel in their own lives, e.g., love, affection, friendship.	34	66	33	67
13. They have no self-control. They steal out of compulsion.	22	78	14	86
14. They feel a friend at work has been subjected to humiliation or abuse or has been treated unfairly.	15	85	10	90
15. They are just plain lazy and won't work hard to earn enough to buy what they want, need, or desire.	14	86	12	88
16. The company's internal controls are so lax that everyone is tempted to steal.	58	42	57	43
17. No one has ever been prosecuted for stealing company property.	42	58	26	74*
18. Most employee thieves are caught by accident rather than by audit or design. Therefore, fear of being caught is not a deterrent to theft.	70	30	78	22
19. Employees aren't encouraged to discuss personal or financial problems at work or to seek management's advice and counsel on such matters. Besides, it might be embarrassing, an invasion of employee privacy, or could even jeopardize one's career to talk about such things at work.	58	42	56	44
20. Each theft has its own preceding conditions and each thief has his own motives, so there is no general rule as to why employees steal. It is a situational phenomenon. Therefore, there are many factors which lead an employee to steal, not just a single factor.	84	16	79	21

As a general rule, employees steal or embezzle from their employers because	100 Michigan CPAs		90 Honeywell Symposium Attendees	
	Strongly agree or tend to agree	Tend to disagree or strongly disagree	Strongly agree or tend to agree	Tend to disagree or strongly disagree
21. Employees steal for any reason the human mind and imagination can conjure up.	68	32	62	38
22. Employees never go to jail or get a harsh sentence for stealing, defrauding, or embezzling from their employers.	47	53	34	66*
23. Man is weak and prone to sin, particularly the sins of pride, lust, envy, anger, covetousness, gluttony, and sloth, all of which may lead to or become motives for theft.	31	69	39	61
24. Employees today are morally, ethically, and spiritually bankrupt.	15	85	18	82
25. Employees tend to imitate their bosses. If their bosses steal or cheat, then they are likely to do it also.	57	43	65	25

*Most significant variations in response between Michigan CPAs and Honeywell Symposium attendees.

Questions that drew the most support from the CPAs and Honeywell Symposium attendees were as follows:

% of Respondents Who Strongly Agreed
or Tended to Agree

Question No.	CPA Rank %	Honeywell Rank %
1	(1) 90%	(1) 90%
8	(2) 87	(2) 81
20	(3) 84	(3) 79
18	(4) 70	(4) 78
21	(5) 68	(10) 62
6	(6) 65	(11) 60
3	(7) 63	(5) 75
5	(7) 63	(8) 66
7	(8) 61	*
10	(9) 57	(6) 70
25	(9) 57	(9) 65
4	*	(7) 68

*Not among the top ten in other group's ranking.

It was interesting to note that in rank ordering both groups' responses, the top four items were the same, that is, employees steal or embezzle from their employers because:

1.   They feel they can get away with it and not be caught. (Item 1)
2.   They think, Stealing a little from a big company won't hurt it. (Item 8)
3.   Each theft has its own preceding conditions and each thief has his own motives, so there is no general rule, etc. (Item 20)
4.   Most employee thieves are caught by accident rather than by audit or design. Therefore, fear of being caught is not a deterrent to theft. (Item 18)

It is also interesting to note that item 18 was supported 70% to 30% among the CPAs and 78% to 22% by the Honeywell attendees. The oddity here is the apparent lack of faith on the part of professional accountants/auditors and systems designers/programmers in their own creations, i.e., internal accounting controls, audit trails, systems and programming documentation, and internal auditing.

THEFT REDUCTION AND THE MOTIVATIONAL CLIMATE OF THE FIRM

The classic approaches to the reduction of employee theft are

1.   The *Directive* approach: "Don't steal. If you do and we catch you, you'll be fired."
2.   The *Prevention* approach: screen out the probable thieves by 1) using background checks, i.e., employment verification, criminal record, credit, and reference checks, 2) polygraph examination, and 3) psychological testing for honesty and integrity.
3.   The *Detection* approach: set up accounting controls and internal audit procedures to periodically verify the legitimacy of transactions and to confirm the existence of assets.
4.   The *Observation* approach: monitor employee conduct, the level of stocks of valuable and portable goods, and inspect outgoing parcels.
5.   The *Investigation* approach: follow-up all allegations of theft and variances in inventories of goods, tools, materials, and supplies to determine the nature and extent of the loss and the likely culprits.
6.   The *Insurance* approach: buy enough fidelity insurance to cover the firm against substantial loss. (While this does not reduce employee theft, it softens the blow when losses occur.)

But even by adopting all the so-called classic approaches, employee theft may continue on a large scale. That seems to be the experience of many firms today. So what other options are available? What can we do to minimize the incidence rate and amount of loss from employee thievery? Should we throw up our hands in frustration and attribute it to uncontrollable societal factors, i.e., decline in morality? No. A new look at the phenomenon of employee theft is in order. If classic approaches are not working, it may be that the problem is no longer of a classic type.

To be sure, changes have occurred in our society, changes that have had dynamic impacts on the employment scene. But it would be simplistic to suggest that the so-called decline in morality has caused these changes.

What has changed in the work environment are the following:

1. Employees today desire and even demand more participation in decisions affecting their job roles.
2. They demand fair and equitable treatment and opportunities for promotion.
3. They demand important and meaningful work—freedom from drudgery.
4. They demand a safe and healthy work environment.
5. They want to be informed and even consulted about issues that may affect their employment status.
6. They pine for inclusion in the work group.
7. They pine for interpersonal trust.
8. They demand respect and recognition.

Fifty years ago the largest segment of the labor force tended to be male, relatively uneducated, economically dependent, immigrant, blue collar workers in manufacturing environments. Today the labor force is mostly white collar, better educated, more secure economically, composed of almost as many women as men, and employed mainly in the service industry. We can see therefore that both the nature of work and the workers' values have gone through substantial changes. And yet we keep applying an outdated rationale to deal with a current social phenomenon.

The classic approaches to reducing employee theft, previously discussed, were designed to increase the *probability of discovery* and are based on Theory X orientation, i.e., people are going to steal under any employment circumstances so the only alternative or choice is to place obstacles, constraints, and controls in their way to discourage, impede, or deter them from theft.

But what if we assumed that employee theft could be controlled or reduced by a Theory Y approach: decrease the *probability of commission?* Are there any data to support the notion that in job environments where people are sufficiently trusted, challenged, informed, rewarded for good work, are involved in decision making, have opportunities for promotion, and are treated equitably they tend to steal less? No, not in a direct cause-and-effect sense.

But there are anecdotal data suggesting that the most likely thief on the job tends to be highly disgruntled or dissatisfied. We might therefore by analogy apply Fred Herzberg's theory and say that where job-related motivators are inadequate, employees may tend to steal more, and that accounting, audit, and access controls and physical and personnel security safeguards are merely "hygiene" factors. They must be there to maintain, contain, or minimize theft, but even if they are present at sufficient levels of adequacy, they will not reduce theft.

Dr. Herzberg of the University of Utah is a noted authority on job-related motivations (See "One More Time: How Do You Motivate Employees?" *Harvard Business Review,* January-February 1968). Herzberg's theory is that certain conditions in the work environment create employment-related satisfactions—motivations. The motivational factors are:

- Achievement
- Recognition
- Work itself
- Responsibility
- Advancement
- Growth

These factors, according to Herzberg, contribute to psychological growth on the job and provide a longer term effect in employee attitudes.

Herzberg's theory also suggests that certain other employment factors, if not met, may lead to extreme dissatisfaction. Those factors he calls hygiene factors and they are extrinsic to the job. They include:

- Company policy and administration
- Supervision
- Relationship with supervisor
- Work conditions
- Salary
- Relationship with peers
- Personal life
- Relationship with subordinates
- Status
- Security

These hygiene factors may lead to higher turnover and decreases in productivity, or, in essence, demotivations. But even if the factors exist at adequate levels in the firm, they do not provide long-term satisfaction. They merely satisfy basic survival needs.

Unfortunately, Herzberg's research is too often viewed in terms of the generalization that "money does not motivate" employees. While that may be a fair but simple representation of his position regarding motivation, he has said much more on the subject that needs to be understood.

Herzberg's main contribution to management literature is that employees in a job environment which creates opportunities for success, i.e., achievement, recognition, advancement, responsibility, challenging work, and personal growth are much less likely to quit and are more likely to work at higher levels of productivity. But beyond the issue of productivity, it is logical to conclude, by extending Herzberg's theory, that in job environments where the motivators and the hygiene factors are inadequate, employee "goldbricking," thievery, and sabotage may abound. Even without a research base to support that conclusion, many people now believe in it as an article of faith. With this assumption, a depiction of the employee theft prevention process is illustrated in Figure 5-1.

The implications of this new look at employee theft and the theft prevention process are simply these:

1. Most prevention efforts concentrate or focus on building more accounting and access controls or physical security controls.
2. We are approaching the limits of technology in those fields or at least are unable to match the rate of growth of EDP technology with the rate of improvements in protection mechanisms.
3. Our only hope in securing company assets is to shift the concentration of effort and cost to decreasing the probability of commission. The technique for executing that strategy is to improve the motivational and ethical climate and the climate for interpersonal trust in the firm.

The author proposes that what we have traditionally done to thwart internal theft flows logically from the goal of reducing the opportunities for such thefts by increasing the probability of discovery, i.e., establishing internal accounting and access controls, patrolling, observing, leaving audit trails, and standardizing procedures.

These methods were provided by professionals in the fields of accounting, auditing, systems design, risk management, and industrial security. We owe them much for their contributions to the loss prevention process.

The point is that there is a limit to the effectiveness of conventional controls (accounting and access), cost feasibility being but one. Of even greater importance is the limitation on effectiveness resulting from the creation of a police state mentality among employees: of being watched at every turn, every minute of the work day. Such a work environment requires a higher ratio of supervisors to workers, more security hardware and software, more audits, inspections, and patrols. In a word, such an environment lacks "trust" and, therefore, may invite more theft, sabotage, "featherbedding," goldbricking, and other forms of inefficiency to retaliate against the feeling of oppression generated by the low trust level. That sort of work environment also shrinks the "bottom line" because it becomes very expensive to maintain. (Watching the watchers is a large part of that expense.)

The simple, plain, and unvarnished truth is that in environments in which a high level of trust can be established between the laboring and managerial classes of employees, there is a diminished need for accounting, access, and management controls. Self-control becomes the dominant ethic rather than imposed controls.

FRAUD REDUCTION AND THE
CONTROL ENVIRONMENT OF THE FIRM

As a result of the Foreign Corrupt Practices Act of 1977 and the SEC's implementing regulations in 1979, many public companies have seen fit to review

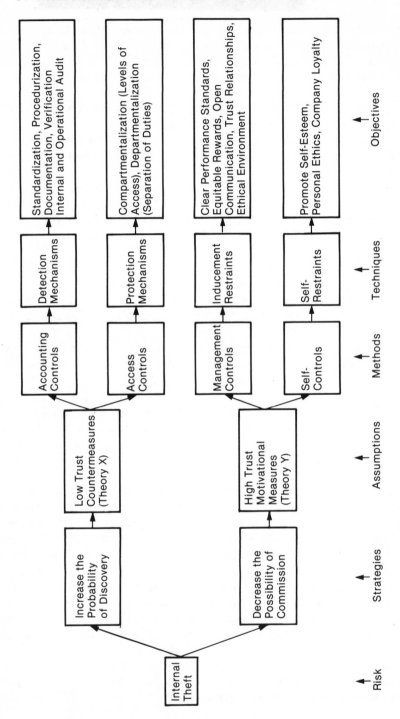

Figure 5-1   An Internal Fraud Prevention Schema

their internal accounting controls and the environment of their firms regarding "internal control consciousness" among their employees. The Act contains two features of concern to industry. The first is an antibribery provision which creates criminal liability to *any* American citizen or business enterprise who offers a bribe to a foreign official, foreign political party, party official, or candidate for foreign political office for assisting or obtaining, retaining or directing business.

The Act also establishes certain standards with respect to a company's books and records, and of significant importance, the system of internal accounting controls. But these standards apply solely to companies subject to the reporting requirements of the Securities Exchange Act of 1934, whereas the bribery provision applies to all American citizens or business enterprises.

Among other things, the FCPA requires that issuers subject to the registration and reporting provisions of the Securities Exchange Act of 1934 devise and maintain a system of internal accounting control sufficient to provide reasonable assurances that:

1. Transactions are executed in accordance with management's general or specific authorization.
2. Transactions are recorded as necessary a) to permit preparation of financial statements in conformity with generally accepted accounting principles or any other criteria applicable to such statements, and b) to maintain accountability for assets.
3. Access to assets is permitted only in accordance with management's general or specific authorization.
4. The *recorded accountability* for assets is compared with the *existing assets* at reasonable intervals and appropriate action is taken with respect to any differences.

The SEC states in its Securities Release No. 34-13185 (January 19, 1977): "The establishment and maintenance of a system of internal controls is an important management obligation. A fundamental aspect of management's stewardship responsibility is to provide shareholders with reasonable assurance that the business is adequately controlled . . . *an adequate system of internal accounting controls* is necessary to management's discharge of these obligations." (emphasis supplied)

On February 16, 1978 the SEC published Accounting Series Release No. 242 which states: "It is important that issuers . . . review their accounting procedures, systems of internal accounting controls and business practices in order that they may take actions necessary to comply . . . with the FCPA."

The *Federal Register* of May 4, 1979 contains a proposed rule issued by the SEC which cites, at p. 26704, the tentative report of the Special Advisory Committee on Internal Controls of the AICPA dated September 15, 1978. It reads as follows:

The internal accounting control *environment* established by management has a significant impact on the selection and effectiveness of a company's accounting control procedures and techniques.

The *control environment* is shaped by several factors. Some are clearly visible, like a formal corporate conduct policy statement or an internal audit function. Some are intangible, like the *competence* and *integrity* of personnel. Some, like organizational structure and the way in which management communicates, enforces and reinforces policy, vary so widely among companies that they can be contrasted more easily than they can be compared.

Although it is difficult to measure the significance of each factor, it is generally possible to make an *overall* evaluation. The committee believes that an *overall evaluation of a company's internal accounting control environment is a necessary prelude* to the evaluation of control procedures and techniques. (emphasis supplied)

The control environment in our schema is composed of accounting controls, internal controls, management controls, and administrative controls. While these words are not precisely defined in the literature of auditing, they should perhaps be given some meaning or distinction for the purposes of clarity and consistency in this book, but not for the purpose of setting policy for auditors.

When we speak of accounting controls here, we are speaking mainly of forms, procedures, and authorizations utilized in authenticating, recording, and processing routine business transactions like sales of merchandise and finished goods, and purchases of merchandise, raw materials, supplies, human, and other services.

Internal controls on the other hand include all those practices and measures applied within a company to assure, among other things, accurate and reliable accounting data. Internal controls include, but are not exclusive of, the accounting controls described and also include other things such as provisions for the formal (written) documentation of business transactions and computerized accounting systems programs (audit trails), and the separation of duties between those persons responsible for recording transactions and those persons responsible for handling and transferring assets.

As originally used by accountants and others, the term internal control described procedures designed 1) to assist in avoiding unintentional mistakes in recording, summarizing, and reporting business transactions, and 2) to reveal on a timely basis any irregularities perpetrated by employees. Internal control was intended to discourage and/or overcome the effect of intentional and unintentional personnel failure—but *not at the highest levels in the company.* In addition to assuring accurate accounting data, internal control was intended to hold accountable those employees who had access to or responsibility for cash balances, cash transactions, securities, inventories, and any other valuable portable assets; it was never intended to monitor the purposes for which management could disburse the company funds.

Provisions for protection of the organization's assets are important and desirable. Internal control is a good device and worthy of much attention. However, it is not and cannot be made infallible even at low levels, and the closer one gets to the top of the organization, the restraint offered by internal controls is weaker. In the final analysis, deliberate improprieties at the top of any large organization are restrained only by the standards and integrity of those who lead, dominate, or otherwise control that organization and not by a series of internal control measures alone.

Generally speaking, most internal controls of the types set forth previously can be bypassed or overrriden by senior management. Defending against top management fraud therefore depends more on their character (honesty) and their beliefs, attitudes, and values (ethical standards) than it does on "adequate" internal and accounting controls. We refer to the character of top management and their ethical standards as *management controls.* Based on the psychological notion of role modeling, these management controls result in a climate which can either foster fraudulent behavior or discourage it. (Where management role models are honest, upright, and otherwise ethical by conventional standards, we would generally expect to find less fraudulent behavior both on the part of top management and their subordinates.)

Administrative controls are subsets of internal and accounting controls. They include such functions and procedures as planning, scheduling, budgeting, delegating, and monitoring performance. The purpose of administrative controls is to affix accountability for individual job roles, tasks, and results, so that corporate goals and objectives can be achieved efficiently.

So the control environment would, in our opinion, include all the above measures, practices, procedures, and policies. Taken together as a whole, they might create an organizational climate where fraud is less likely to occur.

Formal versus Informal Controls

An adequate management control system is one that efficiently provides management with the means to direct, regulate, monitor, and evaluate the flow of resources (inputs) and activities (thruputs) toward predetermined goals (outputs).

Planning is the process for predetermining such goals. Budgeting is the process for allocating the resources (inputs). Scheduling is the process for assigning the timing of activities and the responsibility for their execution (thruputs).

Planning consists of weighing the opportunities for growth and development of an organization against risks. Opportunities consist of new products, new markets, and new services. Risks can be 1) *internal,* i.e., weaknesses in human, capital, informational, and technological resources; and 2) *external,* i.e., economic, competitive, social, demographic, political, regulatory, ecological, and technological threats. Planning tends to be defensive and reactive by its nature. But in another sense, planning can be responsive and proactive, i.e., responsive to change in the external environment—changes in customer needs, wants, demands, and desires, changes in general economic conditions, changes in the thrust of technology, changes in public values, attitudes and beliefs, etc.

Budgeting consists of assigning dollar values and priorities to opportunities for growth and development and to the expected return on investment from such expenditures. Budgeting may include forecasts of revenue and expenses incidental to the exploitation of such opportunities.

Scheduling is a method of programming the resources (manpower, time, money and materials) and activities (work-doing, making, creating, selling, distributing, servicing) toward goals (results).

In a systems context therefore we can depict a management control system as follows:

INPUTS →	THRUPUTS →	OUTPUTS
Resources	*Activities*	*Results*
Human Capital Informational Technological	Work – Doing, Making, Creating, Selling, Distributing, Servicing, Monitoring	Goals *Achieved* Value Added
Planning Budgeting Scheduling		Profit Reinvested

But management is more of an art than a science and management controls can therefore be formal (as depicted above) or informal.

Informal controls consist of self-control (inner control) and other control (outer control). Inner controls consist of personal values, aspirations, attitudes, and beliefs. Outer controls consist of organizational or group values, attitudes, and beliefs (cultural controls). Informal controls are far cheaper and easier to administer than formal (written, documented, mechanical, imposed) controls. So efficient management controls are a mixture of both formal and informal controls, with the emphasis on the informal type.

Imposed (formalized) controls discount the human aspects of control, and yet management controls are intended mainly to impact on human activity. For controls to be adequate they should be both efficient and effective. Imposed controls may be efficient but are not as effective as informal controls. Imposed controls say, or at least suggest, that management has little or no faith in the basic honesty and integrity of employees. Yet imposed controls can never really be fully adequate. It is commitment to controls that management wants so dearly, and commitment is not won from employees when they are neither involved in the design of controls nor allowed to monitor their own performance against the controls.

Self-control is the cheapest form of social control. Self-control derives from feelings of security and self-worth. Rigid, inflexible, imposed (formalized) controls, i.e., rules, regulations, and laws tend to demean the individual or make him feel not trusted, intruded upon, or constantly under surveillance. They can provoke feelings of insecurity, of self-doubt, or of diminished self-worth. So there is a limit on the effectiveness of imposed controls, yet they are the convention rather than the exception. Managements tend to utilize imposed controls far more than their utilitarian value suggests as reasonable. Managements try to solve human problems by proclamation or procrastination and to solve machine problems with tender, loving care and preventive maintenance. Machines are far less often overtaxed than are humans. Machine breakdowns cause production flow problems. Human breakdowns? Well, humans are expendable. "No one is indispensable." But a machine? "You can't do without the right machine."

In a cultural mindset like the one just described, one can readily see why the Japanese are knocking our socks off. The Japanese have a different cultural mindset. The machine is venerated for its contribution. But the people who make it are celebrated. People are priorities numbers 1, 2, and 3. The machine is important but is a distant fourth. After all people conceived it, designed it, and made it. And if it works well, it is only because people cared for its maintenance and properly used it. So people are the main element of control—the intended beneficiaries of controls—and the designers and implementers of controls. Formal controls (rules, regulations, policies, procedures, hardware, software, CCTV, badges, guards, fences, etc.) are there to remind us of the need to be vigilant and careful—not to become paranoid over losses but to become aware of the need to exercise prudent business judgment. Informal controls like shared purposes, directions, and values, interpersonal trust, and a common vision of the future are better adhesives to bind an organization together than all the policy and procedures manuals ever written—far better than the best physical security system ever designed.

The primary objective of security is said to be protection and preservation of corporate assets from anticipated risks. Assets are defined as 1) human, 2) capital, i.e., cash, securities, accounts receivable, inventories, land, buildings, equipment, tools, fixtures and supplies, investments, and goodwill, 3) information, i.e., data, documents, files, research reports and the processes for their preparation, entry, storage, retrieval and accessing, and 4) technological, i.e., patents, copyrights, trademarks, and trade secrets. Risks include potential losses from internal and external sources. Internal risks consist of theft, fraud, embezzlement, sabotage, waste, abuse, information piracy, industrial accidents, negligence, errors, and omissions. External risks include 1) acts of God, i.e., climatic disasters and 2) acts of public enemies, i.e., robbery, burglary, larceny, terrorism, etc.

If security is intended to protect and preserve corporate assets, its nature is defense. So we install barriers against intrusion, prepare response plans for discrete events should they occur, establish policies for recruitment of candidates for employment, and set standards for integrity. Accountants design internal controls to thwart theft, fraud, and embezzlement. Risk managers secure insurance coverage for losses beyond the capacity to insure. EDP management provides defenses against unauthorized access of information systems. Internal auditors spot-check transactions and operations to assure compliance with standards and controls. Safety engineers identify industrial hazards and provide defenses and countermeasures. These formal processes add up to a substantial amount of money, even in companies of relatively small size.

But security also comes in two varieties: formal and informal. Formalized security is visible, tangible, documented, and expensive. Informal security, which is harder to define and see, feel, or hear, is also a critical aspect of security. Informal security deals with such intangibles as employee attitudes, values, and beliefs, i.e., loyalty, honesty, and productivity—which distinguished from formal controls cannot be bought with money alone. Loyalty, honesty, and productivity are part of the culture of the firm, and culture is tradition, shared values, role models, and peer pressure.

In the last analysis, the culture of the firm is more critical to effective security (minimizing risk) than the formal controls imposed by top management. A company with a tradition of poor management, i.e., poor relationships between management and non-management personnel, low interpersonal trust, low productivity, large losses from operations or internal theft, etc., will more quickly select more formal controls than it will change its fundamental beliefs and attitudes toward its employees, customers, suppliers, and stockholders. That is the great conundrum in security today. More money gets spent for formal controls than for informal controls, but money spent for formal controls provides less and less real protection.

PROBABILITY OF FRAUD OCCURRING VERSUS PROBABILITY OF ITS BEING DETECTED

Fraud in a corporate environment is the product of two sets of interacting opposites, i.e., 1) factors that enhance the probability of its occurrence versus 2) factors that enhance the probability of its discovery or detection. When these factors are kept in reasonable balance, the probability of fraud is kept at minimum. These factors are as follows:

I. Factors that enhance the probability of the commission of internal theft, fraud, embezzlement, and corruption
    A. Motivational environment
        1. Inadequate rewards
            a) Pay, fringe benefits, bonuses, incentives, perquisites, job security, meaningful work, promotional opportunities
        2. Inadequate management controls
            a) Failure to articulate and/or communicate expected minimum standards or job-related performance and on-the-job personal behaviors
            b) Ambiguity or lack of clarity in job roles, relationships, responsibilities, and areas of accountability

3.   Inadequate reinforcement and performance feedback mechanisms
    a)   Lack of recognition for good work, loyalty, longevity, and effort
    b)   Lack of recognition for truly outstanding performances
    c)   Delayed feedback or no feedback at all on
       (1)   performance inadequacies
       (2)   unacceptable on-the-job behaviors
    d)   Failure to counsel when performance levels or personal behaviors fall below acceptable levels
    e)   Lack of challenging job-related goals and objectives—acceptance of mediocre performance as the standard
4.   Inadequate support
    a)   Lack of adequate resources to meet mandated standards, e.g., complete tasks within quantity, quality, and cost parameters, and within time frames for completion
5.   Inadequate operational reviews
    a)   Lack of timely or periodic audits, inspections, and follow-through to assure compliance with company goals, priorities, policies, procedures, and governmental regulations
6.   Condoning influences
    a)   Unspecific or ambiguous corporate social values and ethical norms
    b)   Tolerance or indifference toward antisocial behavior
7.   Fostering hostility
    a)   Promoting or permitting destructive interpersonal and/or interdepartmental competitiveness
    b)   Promotion of a low interpersonal trust philosophy (Theory X orientation)
    c)   Bias or unfairness in selection, promotion, compensation, or appraisal

B.   Personal and personnel inducements
1.   Inadequate legally maintained standards of recruitment and selection
2.   Inadequate orientation and training on security matters and company policies with respect to sanctions for security breaches
3.   Unresolved personal financial problems and status needs
4.   Failure to screen applicants for sensitive positions before appointment
    a)   Employment verification
    b)   Educational verification
    c)   Financial reliability
    d)   Character
5.   General job-related stress or anxiety

II.   Factors that enhance the probability of discovery of internal theft, fraud, embezzlement, and corruption

A. Prevention measures
  1. Internal accounting controls
    a) Separation of duties
    b) Rotation of duties
    c) Periodic internal audits and surprise inspections
    d) Development and documentation of policies, procedures, systems, programs, and program modifications
    e) Establishment of dual signature authorities, dollar authorization limits per signatory, expiration date, and check amount limits
    f) Off-line entry controls and limits
    g) Batch totals, hash totals
  2. Computer access controls
    a) Identification defenses
      (1) Key or card inserts
      (2) Passwords and code numbers
      (3) Exclusion—repeated error lockout
      (4) Time activator/deactivator
      (5) Periodic code and password changes
    b) Authentication defenses
      (1) Random personal data
      (2) Voice, fingerprint, or palm geometry recognition
      (3) Callbacks
    c) Establishment of authorizations by levels of authority or levels of security (compartmentalization and "need to know")
B. Detection measures
  1. Exceptions in logging systems
    a) Out of sequence, out of priority, and aborted runs and entries
    b) Out-of-pattern transactions: too high, too low, too many, too often, too few, unusual file access (odd times and odd places)
    c) Attempted access beyond authorization level
    d) Repeated attempts to gain access improperly—wrong password, entry code, etc.
    e) Parity and redundancy checks
  2. Management information system
    a) Monitoring operational performance levels for
      (1) the variations from plans and standards
      (2) deviations from accepted or mandated policies, procedures, and practices
      (3) deviations from past quantitative relationships, i.e., ratios, proportions, percentages, trends, past performance levels, indices, etc.
  3. Intelligence gathering
    a) Monitoring employee attitudes, values, and job satisfaction level

b) Soliciting random feedback from or surveying customers, vendors, and suppliers for evidence of dissatisfaction, inefficiency, inconsistency with policies, corruption, or dishonesty by employees

The preceding theory is predicated on the following rationale:

- When prevention measures are inadequate, *and* when
- Detection measures are inadequate, *and* when
- The environment of the firm does not provide a sense of personal and job-related fulfillment, *and* when
- An employee in a position of trust with access, and the proper skills and knowledge to override or bypass controls, develops a nonshareable financial problem and realizes the problem can be secretly resolved by violation of his position of trust, *and* rationalizes his illegal behavior is justified, uncontrollable, or noncriminal, e.g., "I'm borrowing, not stealing," *and* when all the conditions stated above come together at the same point in time, a case of theft, fraud, embezzlement, or employee corruption is most likely to occur.

FRAUD DETECTION AND EXTERNAL AUDITOR RESPONSIBILITIES

Frauds in books of account have been with us since Pacioli invented double entry bookkeeping five hundred years ago. Internal and external financial audits are intended for a number of purposes, one of which is to deter fraud but not necessarily to detect fraud. Even a diligently executed financial audit is not a guarantee that fraud does not exist in the firm being audited.

Financial audits are necessarily performed on a sampling basis. *Selective* testing of transactions (representative sampling) is the usual financial audit method; otherwise the cost of the audit might become prohibitive. The statement on Auditing Standards No. 16 (paragraph 5) indicates that an independent auditor's standard report implicitly indicates his belief that the financial statements taken as a whole are not materially misstated as a result of errors or irregularities (fraud?).

The public accountant's liability to clients and third parties for failure to detect materially misstated financial statements is derived from the common law of contracts and torts and more recently from the federal securities laws. Auditors under common law decisions must exercise "due care" in performing audits. Failure to exercise due care (ordinary negligence) subjects them to civil liability by clients who have been damaged in a contractual or negligent sense and to third parties who have relied on their certified statements for investment and credit purposes. Auditor negligence for our purposes usually means a failure to conduct an audit in accordance with generally accepted auditing standards.

Auditors are not normally held to a standard of care higher than that recognized by their own profession. Since audit standards of public accountants do not address the issue of fraud detection as a paramount purpose of financial auditing, nondetection of fraud is rarely the only basis for a suit. The law suits brought against public accountants usually deal with failures to comply with certain minimum professional standards (those which are generally accepted). And since public accountants generally do not accept responsibility for detecting fraud as part of their audit purpose, they are generally not held liable on that ground alone.

You cannot fault public accountants for being sensitive about fraud detection. As said, it is tough to detect in most routine audits. Furthermore, where frauds have been committed by top management personnel of their client firms, puplic accountants are placed in the unenviable position of biting the hand that feeds them, that is, *if* they uncover any evidence of fraud by top management. So most frauds uncovered by public accountants during routine audits tend to involve lower level officials and to be the type which is patently discoverable—the easy and simple ones, i.e., kiting and lapping schemes, and gross over and understatements of assets, liabilities, revenues, and expenses.

However, despite their legal protestations more and more public accountants are becoming unwitting parties to law suits by stockholders, lenders, and regulatory authorities in cases where financial statement misrepresentations by corporate insiders have been committed and have been undetected by outside auditors.

Watergate, Equity Funding, and overseas bribery payments may have been the triggering mechanisms for the current rash of law suits. Perhaps the general public, because of its current disenchantment with all authorities and their human failures, is responsible. And perhaps the general public is trying to tell us to "clean up our act" or to develop higher standards of professional ethics and competence. Whatever the causes, public accountants find themselves in the awkward position of fending off attacks by their critics without a strategy by which to respond with the exception of buying peace by making out-of-court settlements. Fighting the charges is expensive and takes much time, during which media exposure is ever present. The temptation to "cave in" is great. Who needs the notoriety? But hasty settlements may also invite more law suits.

From 1971 through 1982, big public accounting firms (the top ten: Arthur Andersen, Arthur Young, Coopers & Lybrand, Deloitte Haskins and Sells, Ernst & Whinney, Alexander Grant, Price Waterhouse, Peat, Marwick and Mitchell, Seidman & Seidman, and Touche Ross) have been named as parties defendant in law suits brought by shareholders, lenders, and others no less than seventy-five times. Most of these suits were mainly directed at the managements and directors of client firms for whom the accountants provided audit services. The allegations and charges were most frequently of fraud and false representations by management in accounting records and financial statements upon which the investors and lenders relied.

A number of the suits were later found to be without legal merit by the courts. Many, however, were sustained against the management defendants.

Fewer were sustained against the public accountants. However, full hearings of the facts were present in but a few cases. Managements and accountants (thereby conceding at least some tacit liability) offered settlements through the courts, before trial on the merits. The typical public response by the big ten firms after settlement was that to pursue a case through the judicial system was cost prohibitive so "discretion being the better part of valor," they settled for cash without admitting fault.

Of the fifty-two stockholder-initiated suits, twenty-eight are still pending or have been dismissed for lack of progress.

Where allegations of management fraud were the main points of contention and a trial was held, the attorneys for the public accountants argued that the independent auditors were victims of these frauds too, or that the purpose of an independent audit is not to ferret out or detect fraud but to assure investors and lenders that financial statements fairly present the condition of the company at the time of the audit. That in turn is a product of adequate internal controls and the application of generally accepted accounting principles by the company. Where guile is used to deceive auditors, they cannot be held responsible. Public accountants have no way of knowing the true financial state of a company when management sets out to deceive them.

The good news for public accountants, based on our study, seems to be that the trend for shareholder-initiated law suits is down. Our study shows there were at least thirty-two such suits from 1971 to 1975, and about sixteen from 1976 to 1980. (Two each in 1981 and 1982).

The bad news is that more regulatory actions against public accountants for audit inadequacies are being initiated by the SEC, bankruptcy court trustees, state insurance departments, and state corporation commissions. Also, banks and other lenders, and clients themselves, seem to be more inclined to sue public accountants for audit shortcomings. (Twenty-three such suits from 1975 through 1982).

FRAUD DETECTION AND INTERNAL AUDITOR RESPONSIBILITIES

Frauds uncovered during internal audits tend to involve lower level officials of the company. Frauds by senior management are difficult to find and document. Senior management personnel can override and bypass controls so that evidence of their wrongdoings is difficult to come by unless someone confesses or informs. Moreover, internal auditors, unless they report directly to an audit committee of independent directors, are part of the political system which they are forced to audit. It does not pay for them to bite the hands that feed them either.

But if fraud has been with us since the days of old, one might think that its detection has been assigned as a specific responsibility of some functional group in organized society: the police perhaps, if the fraud is of a criminal nature. But law enforcement agencies do not profess to have much expertise for detecting accounting fraud, except perhaps for the IRS on tax matters, the FBI on bank embezzlements, and the SEC on financial statements of public companies that contain material misrepresentations of facts.

Who then is accountable for detecting frauds in corporate books of account other than law enforcement and regulatory agencies? That question has plagued auditing authorities for years. Neither public accountants nor internal auditors seem to want that distinction. Fraud auditing and detection is a function few are qualified to perform and fewer yet are eager to be held accountable for. If an independent auditor admits an expertise in the field of fraud auditing, the courts may impose a higher standard of care in performing his routine financial audits. So, in a legal sense, ignorance has been bliss until recently.

Courts are now beginning to impose sanctions on outside audit firms who fail to detect frauds while conducting financial audits, despite their (auditors') protestations that fraud detection is not part of their audit purpose. While the issue of outside auditor responsibility for fraud detection has not been fully settled by the courts, the trend seems to be moving in that direction. Certainly the lay public has come to believe that outside auditors share that responsibility with top management and internal audit resources within public companies. Many major public accountants have recently been joined as parties defendant in shareholder suits against management when management frauds have been alleged. Public accountants have been quick to settle for fear that a shattering and more costly precedent might be made on the entire public accounting profession.

But the question of who is accountable for ferreting out corporate frauds is still in legal and professional limbo.

Public accountants would like to confer that honor on internal auditors who know the firm better in the day-to-day sense and who understand its accounting systems and practices better than an outside auditor might. Internal auditors see the matter differently. Their audit purpose, so they say, is not to detect fraud either but to discover it incidentally, if it exists in an obvious way. Reality lies elsewhere, for if you are not looking for fraud as a major audit objective, you are not likely to find it. Accounting frauds are not easy to uncover. The minds generating such schemes may be simple, but rarely are their schemes simple. There is an element of creative genius in most accounting frauds which the untrained or unaware auditor may never find. The old axiom that most frauds are discovered by accident rather than by accounting system design or audit techniques may have some merit. You are not likely to find a needle in a haystack if your purpose if to count a few representative straws and then extrapolate the weight of the pile. So the argument within the auditing profession regarding who has the secondary responsibility to detect fraud (primary responsibility seems to be with management) will not be resolved any time soon, unless the public or the courts settle it for us.

In the meantime, it may behoove us to learn a little more about the subject of accounting types of frauds. If we are perceived as accountable by the public already, we should begin to pursue the knowledge that will make us professionally more responsible. Reasonable people should take reasonable precautions.

CORPORATE FRAUDS IN THE 1980s AND 1990s

In view of the scarcity of hard data on white collar crime, in corporate fraud specifically, the author recently undertook a limited survey of his own. While it is premature to do anything more than speculate, the survey respondents—forty members of the Toledo Personnel Management Association—would seem reasonably knowledgeable about white collar crime and perhaps more knowledgeable than the average man on the street. So, for whatever value the results of the survey may have, the opinions of the personnel managers follow.

Based on the white collar crimes listed in the survey, rank order in terms of seriousness, frequency of occurrence, and index weight are:

Rank	Crime Type	Weight
1.	Bribing political leaders (tie)	5.57
1.	Padding the bill on government contracts	5.57
2.	Employee theft, fraud, and embezzlement	5.20
3.	Polluting the environment	4.69
4.	Pilfering small tools and supplies	4.47
5.	Computer-related crimes	4.22
6.	Bribing union leaders	4.18
7.	Expense account padding	4.05
8.	Corporate income tax evasion	4.03
9.	Stock frauds and manipulations	3.90
10.	Falsifying time and attendance reports	3.84
11.	False advertising	3.80
12.	Selling mechanically defective products	3.70
13.	Providing unsafe and unhealthy working conditions	3.61
14.	Bribing purchasing agents (tie)	3.57
14.	Making illegal campaign contributions	3.57
15.	Selling contaminated or adulterated drugs	3.51
16.	Falsifying productivity reports	3.40
17.	Falsifying company financial statements	3.39
18.	Mail fraud	3.37
19.	Bribing foreign officials	3.19
20.	Selling contaminated or adulterated foodstuffs	3.12
21.	Sabotaging company property	3.08
22.	Price fixing	3.05
23.	Falsifying profitability reports	2.97
24.	Selling useless drugs	2.85

The surprise, of course, was that personnel managers rated such typical top management frauds as falsifying company financial statements and falsifying profitability reports so low (17th and 23rd, respectively) in contrast to employee theft, fraud, and embezzlement (2nd), after a tie for first place of political bribery and padding government contracts. Does that suggest a dual standard of integrity between higher level and lower level employees?

In terms of white collar crimes to occur with greater frequency in the future, the rank ordering and percentage of respondents agreeing are as follows:

Rank	Crime Type	Weight
1.	Computer-related crimes	67.5%
2.	Bribing political leaders	52.5%
3.	Expense account padding	50.0%
4.	Bribing union leaders	40.0%
5.	Employee theft, fraud, and embezzlement	37.5%
6.	Falsifying productivity reports	35.0%
7.	Padding the bill on government contracts (tie)	35.0%
8.	Corporate income tax evasion	32.5%
9.	Bribing foreign officials (tie)	32.5%
10.	Stock frauds and manipulations	30.0%
11.	Polluting the environment (tie)	30.0%

SUMMARY

I began this book by suggesting as a general theory that fraud (lying, cheating, and other forms of deception in human interactions and business transactions) is generally committed when man's economic, social, or political survival is threatened.

Our main focus has been on corporate fraud (management and non-management) and more particularly on 1) top management frauds involving financial misstatements (overstated corporate assets and revenues and understated corporate liabilities and expenses) and 2) frauds that may involve thefts and embezzlements of corporate assets.

Misstatements of financial facts by top management are generally intended to deceive 1) shareholders, as to the profits of the firm, and 2) creditors, as to the financial soundness of the firm.

It was also postulated that corporate frauds are perpetrated for economic, egocentric, ideological, and psychotic motives and that their execution is the result of opportunities existing in 1) a firm's control environment (weaknesses in internal and accounting controls and in management and administrative controls) and 2) its work environment, i.e., reward system, ethical standards, interpersonal trust. The methods used to carry out corporate frauds consist of compromising controls (bypassing and overriding them) and corrupting personnel (see Figure 5–2).

It was also said that the best defense against corporate fraud (after establishing adequate and cost feasible controls) is the creation of a positive motiva-

MOTIVATIONS	OPPORTUNITIES	METHODS	MEANS
1. Economic 2. Egocentric 3. Ideological 4. Psychotic	1. Internal Environment a. Weaknesses in internal, accounting, management, and administrative controls b. Weaknesses in motivational climate 　1) reward system 　2) ethical standards 　3) interpersonal trust 2. External Environment a. Economic, competitive, political, regulatory, ecological	1. Compromising Controls a. Overriding, bypassing, and defeating internal and accounting controls 2. Compromising Personnel a. Corruption, bribery, and conspiracy 3. Compromising Systems Technology a. Input scams b. Thruput scams c. Output scams	1. Overstating Assets and Revenues 2. Understating Liabilities and Expenses 3. Creating Fake Debits 4. Falsifying Performance Data 5. Lapping 6. Kiting 7. Forgery 8. Destruction of Records 9. Counterfeiting Data 10. False Claims for Payment, Benefits, Expenses 11. Theft and Embezzlement of Assets 12. Corrupting Customers, Labor Leaders, and Political Authorities

Figure 5–2   The Corporate Fraud Matrix

tional climate in the firm, i.e., fair and just rewards and promotion policies, high standards of personal and business ethics, interpersonal trust. These would then tend to minimize the threat to the economic, social, and political survival of the people within the firm.

But there is another environment that impacts on the firm and that can precipitate corporate fraud: the environment external to the firm, that is, the competitive, economic, political, regulatory, ecological, and technological environments. Threats from any of these external environments may also cause or induce fraudulent behavior within the firm. When business and economic times are poor, when competition is keen, when regulatory or political action is threatened by governmental authorities, etc., the temptation to commit corporate fraud is heightened. Here again, the survival instinct takes over and clouds prudent business judgment. (It is better to be a victimizer and survive than a victim and fail, or so we rationalize.)

We have also theorized that fraud, like other forms of human misbehavior, is a product of:

1.   Hereditary factors and significant influences on our early lives—inherited traits, parents, and close relatives.
2.   Conditioning factors and influences in the cultures and subcultures in which we were raised—the norms of our ethnic, racial, religious, or neighborhood groups and the broader community in which we live, and the values, beliefs, and attitudes of our parents, teachers, friends, and other role models.
3.   The mores of the times and of the places in which we are employed, i.e., the currently accepted practices, customs, and usages of the work group that are regarded as essential to the group's welfare and survival, and the practices in the industry to which we belong.
4.   Our own deliberations and perceptions as derived from inherited, adopted, and self-determined values, beliefs, and attitudes. (This is the most critical factor of the four.)

If the problem of corporate fraud is ever to be resolved, reduced, or minimized, changes will first be required in our own attitudes, values, and beliefs, and secondly, in those of our corporate work environments.

Truth, honesty, justice, and fair dealing, as stated in chapter 1, are ideals. If we pay them no heed, our standards of behavior will not improve nor will our behavior itself. If we elect to strengthen these concepts and commit ourselves to them, we may some day arrive at a point where self-controls can replace legal, social, accounting, and bureaucratic controls. Until that time, however, we must remain vigilant and take at least ordinary precautions against corporate fraud.

To summarize, we can postulate that corporate fraud motivations (personal causations) consist of the following:

- Economic
- Ideological
- Egocentric
- Psychotic

We can further postulate that opportunities to commit corporate fraud (environmental causations) are provided by:

- Inadequate internal controls
- Inadequate management controls
- Inadequate administrative controls

The methods for effecting corporate frauds consist of compromising controls and personnel.

The means for effecting corporate frauds consist of bypassing or overriding controls and corruption of personnel.

These considerations can be further summarized in a formulation or acronym we call MOMM, which stands for 1) motivations, 2) opportunities, 3) methods, and 4) means.

CHAPTER 6

Auditing for Inventory Shrinkage in Manufacturing Organizations

INTERIM INVENTORY ACCOUNTING

Next to stealing cash or securities or fabricating vendor invoicing, expense, and benefit claims against the company, the most frequent other business crime is the inventory scam. Inventory scams can be internally generated, as in theft, fraud, or embezzlement by employees, or externally generated by vendors or intruders. Inventory scams are perhaps the most difficult to discover and are generally the most difficult of all business crimes to prove.

The main reason why inventory scams are difficult to prove is that by the nature of most interim accounting systems, the inventory account is relieved or added to by supposition rather than by actual fact. For example, when materials are ordered, the journal entry is:

> Debit: Purchases
> Credit: Accounts Payable

When materials are paid for, the entry is:

> Debit: Accounts Payable
> Credit: Cash

When the finished article is sold, the entry is:

> Debit: Accounts Receivable
> Credit: Sales

And when the customer pays for the goods, the entry is:

> Debit: Cash
> Credit: Accounts Receivable

But no entry has been made to the general ledger inventory account. What some accountants euphemistically call "perpetual inventory records" are more often subsidiaries to the main accounting system. The interim details of inventory are therefore kept in memorandum form. Real inventory is whatever is on hand and not necessarily what the subsidiary records may reflect.

To keep these subsidiary records reasonably correct during the year so that decisions about availability of stock, order backlogs, and the need to reorder can be made, there may be times when "cycle counts" are taken of a limited number of inventory items. If discrepancies show up, the subsidiary records are adjusted upward or downward to correspond to whatever the cycle count shows the current status to be. These adjustments are often not individually authorized by senior management as would be the adjustments of journal entries of general ledger inventory account balances. The balance in the general ledger inventory account during the year is therefore what it was when the year first began.

Very often in manufacturing organizations, temporary or working paper adjustments are made to the inventory account in order to facilitate monthly financial statements. A credit is entered against inventory and a debit is made to cost of sales, based on an assumed percentage relationship between sales and cost of sales and normal inventory turnover patterns. In the year-end income statement, however, gross profit or margin is determined by subtracting actual cost of sales from net sales. The cost of sales is determined by adding the beginning inventory dollar amount to purchases of materials during the period and then subtracting the actual ending inventory for the period. During the interim accounting periods, i.e., monthly or quarterly, inventory is estimated; the estimate is based on periodic relief of the inventory account by memorandum entry for items sold. The working paper entry that relieves inventory for items sold is a supposition. The books and records of the firm, unless a true perpetual inventory system is being used, do not reflect all specific inventory items bought, made, or shipped nor their actual cost of production.

INVENTORY AND COST ACCOUNTING ASSUMPTIONS

Cost of production or goods manufactured is also based on certain assumptions (standards) or predetermined cost allocation formulas for raw materials, labor, and overhead during the year. In a job cost accounting system, the direct cost of raw materials and labor are tracked for each job order and an overhead factor is then applied. The selling price of the order is then based on a markup factor which is designed to recover actual material and labor costs, overhead (heat, light, power, water, depreciation, rent, taxes, interest, etc.), general administrative and selling costs, and a reasonable profit on the order. As you can see, the selling price is based on cost assumptions too, not actual costs. It would be economically unfeasible to design a cost accounting system so foolproof and perfect that actual costs on a job-by-job or item-by-item basis could be determined. A depiction of the process follows:

Sales for the month		$100,000
Less Cost of Sales		
Beginning Inventory	$30,000	
Purchases	40,000	
	$70,000	
Ending Inventory	20,000*	50,000
Gross Profit (Margin)		$ 50,000

---

*Estimate based on subsidiary cost accounting records, not on a physical count.

But if the inventory at the end of the month was in fact $30,000, rather than the $20,000 shown, cost of sales would have been $40,000 and gross profit would have been $60,000. On the other hand, if the ending inventory in fact had been worth $10,000, cost of sales would have been $60,000 and gross profit would have been $40,000.

To add a little more confusion, the ending inventory shown is composed of raw materials, work in process, and finished goods, and to determine the cost of goods manufactured the following formula is used:

Direct Material	$15,000*
Direct Labor	25,000*
Manufacturing Overhead	5,000**
	$45,000
Less: Beginning Work in Process	5,000
	$40,000
Plus: Ending Work in Process	10,000***
Cost of Goods Manufactured	$50,000

---

* Based on predetermined standards of unit costs.

** Based on an allocation formula of assumed costs of heat, light, power, rent, depreciation, etc.

*** Estimate based on subsidiary cost accounting records, not on a physical count.

If the accounting system is designed correctly and is being managed properly, the variance between actual costs and assumed costs is reflected as a deviation from the cost standards. This is referred to as management by exception. During the year if the gross profit variance grows to substantial proportions, something is amiss; the sales markup may be inadequate (too low: competition may have forced the company to sell at prices which do not provide an adequate profit), or costs of raw materials and labor have gone up beyond the level anticipated, or labor is inefficient, or overhead expenses are more than anticipated, or someone is stealing or wasting too much material. Whatever the reason, all that is known for certain is that a discrepancy exists between an expected or desired level of performance and an actual level of profit performance.

If the cost accounting system is sophisticated enough, we may be able to isolate the most probable causes for the deviation, i.e., too much scrap and wastage; too much nonproductive time (machine breakdowns, waiting for materials, reworking defective materials); too many returns and allowances; too many sales giveaways; increases in utility charges; inferior grades of material being received (quality control failures); spurious cost assumptions and allocation formulas, etc. But, again, these determinations of probable cause can be made only where cost accounting systems are well-designed and well-maintained on a current and accurate basis. Otherwise, we have a GIGO (garbage in, garbage out) problem.

What is the world of business reality? Are cost accounting systems well-designed? Are they well-managed? Do they supply timely, relevant, meaningful, and accurate information? The author's experience has been that most cost accounting systems are not well-designed. Many were adopted fifty years ago and have had minor updatings since that time. The information they generate for management is often inaccurate or untimely and therefore unreliable for decision making, problem solving, or control purposes. For production planning and scheduling purposes, these systems also leave a lot to be desired. For inventory management purposes, many cost accounting systems are almost disastrous. In many cases inventory levels during the year cannot be measured within a tolerance of plus or minus 10 percent. Even in the computer age, cost accounting systems have been found lacking. You can get more garbage out faster with computers than you could before, but that is about it.

Cost accounting is a field that has been left in the Dark Ages of management technology. Innovations and real breakthroughs have been rare. Advances in quantitative analysis and operations research have raised the state of the art in cost accounting somewhat. But we are still dealing with a theory base that was developed almost one hundred years ago, and except for grinding out more numbers faster today, the state of the art is still turn-of-the-century.

INVENTORY SHRINKAGE CAUSES

But returning to the issue at hand, what happens when the independent auditors determine that a gross discrepancy exists between the inventory the books say should be on hand and what the auditors determine to be actually on hand? Is that proof of theft? Hardly. No fidelity insurance claim could be submitted on such paucity of proof of loss. Insurance companies were not born yesterday. They are well aware of the shortcomings of accounting systems, and without some specific proof of who, when, and how the loss occurred, they will not accept the discrepancy alone as proof of loss.

The auditors on the other hand, once they have deduced that a discrepancy exists, are more likely to assure themselves that their audit techniques and calculations are correct than they are to make an effort to determine causative factors. The cause or causes of the loss, or *shrinkage,* becomes a management concern and not the concern of the auditors. The financial statements they certify will show the value of inventory at the lesser figure, after they adjust it downward. Their job is completed at that point except for an audit footnote reference or some recommendations regarding tightening internal controls. Now management has the problem: to elect to do nothing where the shrinkage is substantial is imprudent and to revise and revamp the accounting system will be time consuming and expensive. Where to go for help? Sometimes corporate management will ask its own internal auditors to look into the matter. If theft is suspected, management may even enlist the aid of its security personnel. But where do they start?

Inventory loss, or shrinkage, can be attributed to a host of possibilities, including:

1. Internal theft committed at the purchasing, receiving, processing, storage, shipping, or selling stages
2. External theft resulting from vendor shortage, common carrier diversion, outside intruders (burglars), buyers of manufacturing waste who short weight the scrap, warehousemen who store materials or finished goods for the firm and convert the goods to their own use, etc.
3. Accounting errors in posting quantities of stock, double payment of vendors, payment for full shipments when only partial shipments were received, costing allocations against the wrong jobs or wrong lots, incorrect intracompany or interdepartmental transfers of goods, etc.
4. Excessive wastage or scrap
5. Arbitrary write-downs of inventory values
6. Arbitrary write-ups of inventory to enhance profitability

The fraud auditor should be particularly alert to the latter, i.e., arbitrary write-ups of inventory value during interim accounting periods. This is the simplest and most expedient method available to plant management to inflate interim profitability. In organizations calculating profitability bonuses on a quarterly or semiannual basis, it is the technique most often used to "pump up profits." By year's end, however, when a clean inventory is taken and supervised by outside auditors, the discrepancy shows up. And, as often as not, local management will allege that the shrinkage is due to theft, probably by insiders such as receiving, warehousing, or shipping personnel, the blue collar types. (These people do look like prime suspects. Because of their lower socioeconomic class, many are habitually short of money, or have family problems, or have had run-ins with law enforcement authorities, or are being sued by creditors, or have filed for personal bankruptcy, or have had home foreclosures, or have been ousted for rent payment arrearages, etc. But there are usually so many of them versus the number of line and staff managers that a thorough investigation of all of them would cost an enormous amount of money. So the inventory discrepancy is charged off against the year's operations. The managers keep their bonuses and the blue collar workers are admonished not to steal anymore lest they be fired, when in fact, the only theft committed was by those who earned bonuses when none were justified.)

As can be seen, the inventory account is a marvel that can do many things for management. It can be used to cushion bad times by arbitrary write-ups or it can create a reserve in good times by arbitrary write-downs.

The inventory account is usually accurate twice a year, if then. The rest of the time the account can be easily manipulated for statement presentation purposes to fool the "big boss," if the company is a subsidiary or profit center for a larger organization. If you operate a subsidiary or profit center, you can manipulate inventory to enhance profitability and gain fame as a winner, or to gain some fortune, i.e., qualify for a raise, for a larger bonus or share of the profits, or even perhaps for a promotion to a bigger unit.

This lesson is not lost on some line and profit center managers. There are hundreds of inventory scams of the kind described going on at all times. And the record for detection of these scams is not particularly good. Unless the culprit gets greedy and shows a constant buildup in ending inventory when sales volume stays flat, the arbitrary inflation of inventory is not likely to cause much consternation. Even if the independent auditors detect the inflated value and force a write-down, the profit center manager's bonus is not taken back if it was awarded during an interim accounting period.

Hundreds of possible excuses for inventory being overstated at year's end exist. Some were enumerated previously: accounting errors by clerks, vendor short shipments, outdated accounting systems and cost formulas, etc. So proving fraud, theft, or embezzlement will not be a simple task. Unless the profit center manager actively attempts to deceive the auditors by forging supportive documents, fabricating inventory tags, or double-counting stock, it is virtually impossible to place the blame for the shortage squarely on his shoulders.

INVESTIGATING SHRINKAGE

So how does a fraud auditor proceed? Where does he start when a discrepancy of large proportions shows up? First, he must assure himself that the inventory count by the outside auditors has proceeded properly. A thorough review of the inventory audit working papers is in order. If the inventory taking and audit procedures appear correct, it can then be concluded that a loss of some amount exists. But review of the working papers is not intended to critique the audit, but to give the fraud auditor a "feel" for the environment of the firm and its people, some understanding of the business and organization of the firm, some knowledge of the audit done so as not to duplicate those efforts, and some familiarity with the general and cost accounting systems.

Next, he must tour the facilities and meet the local management. To go in under cover is usually not productive, and if caught in the lie the fraud auditor's effectiveness is destroyed. I generally identify myself as a consultant in inventory shrinkage problems. I am not there to accuse anyone of anything. My mission is simply to determine whether a loss did in fact occur, and if so, what factors and conditions may have led to the loss. I am not interested in who (at the moment), but in when, where, how, and how much was lost. If theft is determined as the cause of the shrinkage, who and why are matters of importance to the police or prosecuting authorities. My role is simply to challenge systems, procedures, practices, and controls; are there any weaknesses in the system? I attempt to project a pleasant and trusting demeanor because at this stage in the audit I have no reason to believe that anything but loose controls may exist. I have the chief executive on site introduce me to his staff and ask that they provide cooperation and some accommodations—a private office where I can work, paper, pencils, a telephone, and some records to review.

I then deliver a list of documents I wish to review to the chief financial officer, which can be randomly selected from the files. Such a list might read as follows:

- Fifty used inventory tags, receiving reports, purchase orders, vendor invoices, freight bills, work orders, stock withdrawal orders, shipping orders, customer invoices, credit memos, salvage and scrap reports, and inventory cards for the highest volume items
- The shipping and receiving logs for the beginning and ending months of the fiscal year and one other month in between (the highest volume month)
- All off-line (manually generated) canceled checks
- Canceled checks issued to vendors for three months, including the highest purchasing volume month
- Open purchase order file for the last month in the accounting year
- General journal entries made during the year impacting on inventory or cost of sales
- Copies of monthly profit and loss statements
- Comparisons of customer and vendor volumes in the year under review with the preceding year
- Inventory obsolescence and reclassification policies and procedures

The purpose of reviewing these documents is not to redo the work of the auditors but to detect the departures from the usual, i.e., items that seem too high, too low, too often, too rare, odd times, odd places, odd reasons, odd combinations, odd endorsements, etc. You might say the search is for the oddities: that which seems ''out of sync'' with normal patterns of business and accounting. The eternal question during this review is, What normal patterns changed during the year, if any? What is different? Were there new vendors, new customers, new employees, new systems adopted, new procedures, practices, or policies, new pricing and costing formulas, new equipment, new management, new information systems, new sales strategies, or new products? What logical and legitimate reasons can be advanced for the shortage? Was it simply a matter of accounting system inadequacy, managerial inadequacy, or employee incompetency? At this point in our analysis we are looking for gross explanations for the loss. We may even be mixing surface causes, and perhaps root causes.

A depiction of the problem-solving process follows:

Expected level of inventory (Inventory per books)	=	X
Actual level of inventory (Inventory per count)	=	$-Y$
Difference (the problem)	=	Z

Probable causes:

1. Accounting system inadequacies
   (a) Cost accounting assumptions, i.e., standards for raw materials and direct labor and overhead allocation formulas
2. Human errors and omissions in recording transactions
   (a) Posting errors, i.e., wrong amounts, wrong accounts, wrong lots, or wrong jobs
3. Internal theft
   (a) Overriding or bypassing purchasing, receiving, storing, or shipping controls
   (b) Employee pilferage
   (c) False journal entries and false documentation to support inventory entries
4. External theft
   (a) Vendor short shipments
   (b) Common carrier and warehousemen's diversions
   (c) After-hours intruders
5. Audit inadequacies
   (a) Improper cutoff and tagging procedures
   (b) Errors in counting, weighing, lot identification, and quality specifications
   (c) Tabulating, pricing, and extension errors, and inconsistency in inventory valuation methodology

If no discernible patterns of variance from what is the norm are found, it can be assumed that the accounting system and the document flow will not help to isolate the shrinkage problem. If theft exists, the thief or thieves have been clever enough not to directly compromise the accounting system. The theft was off-line and probably occurred during off-hours when no observers were there to see what was happening. If no consistent pattern of irregularity in journal entries, or gaps in document preparation and flow, or many posting errors and adjustments, or duplicate rather than original documents, or out-of-serial order patterns in the documentation exists, there is another kind of problem. A theft may have been committed within the accounting system and perpetrated during normal working hours, probably by a number of employees acting together.

If it appears that the shrinkage occurred without direct compromise of the accounting or costing systems, the next step is to review the plant's physical security system for weaknesses. Is the plant guarded? By whom? During what hours? Is after-hours access to the plant logged? Which employees have made after-hours plant visits? What was their alleged purpose? How often did they enter? How long did they stay? Were alarm systems tripped? When? By whom? Is the alarm system in good working order? Have there been any reports during the interim accounting period of missing inventory, tools, parts, or equipment? When? Who reported these events? What action was taken?

If it appears that the accounting and/or cost accounting systems have been compromised, a more extensive review of record keeping and documentation should be undertaken to determine whether a pattern of deviation from good practice exists and where the weakest links in the chain of internal and accounting controls are. Are the weakest links in purchasing, receiving, storing, shipping, or inventory accounting? This review should isolate, localize, or identify the most probable causes of the loss so that the audit effort can be concentrated on those areas from then on. At this point in the audit you may wish to begin building a fraud scenario, which is predicated on the theory that fraud is a product or result of certain motivations, opportunities, means, and methods (see Figure 6–1).

MOTIVATIONS	OPPORTUNITIES	MEANS	METHODS
1. Economic	Inadequacies in internal controls and physical security	Compromising internal and accounting controls	Falsifying, altering, or destroying inventory transaction data or inventory count data
2. Ideological	Inadequacies in cost accounting and interim reporting systems	Conspiracy between vendors, carriers, customers, warehousemen, and employees	Arbitrary inventory reclassification to lower or higher value
3. Egocentric	Incompetencies of management accounting personnel	Conspiracy between fellow employees	Pilferage
4. Psychotic		Surreptitious access and theft	Burglary
			Bribery
			Short weights and counts
			Overpricing
			Grade quality substitution

Figure 6–1   Inventory Fraud Scenario

BULDING AN INVENTORY FRAUD SCENARIO

The inventory fraud scenario is intended to reduce further the scope of the fraud audit by eliminating causative possibilities. If everyone is a suspect, the audit may go on forever. The questions uppermost in the auditor's mind are: Who are the most likely suspects and where are the weakest links in controls? Other questions to ask are: Why would they steal, what would they steal, how would they steal, and how would they profit from the theft?

A typical fraud scenario might read as follows:

I.   FACTS
     ABC Company is a manufacturer of electronic components, including integrated circuits, designed for use in large system computer mainframes. Its business is international and has been highly profitable in the past. Current competition in the industry is keen and profits have been falling of late. Discrepancies were found in its most recent audit pertaining to its supplies of integrated circuits ($200,000 at manufacturer's cost) and its supplies of gold and platinum ($150,000 at cost).

Its inventory accounting system seems adequate for its size and complexity of operations. Physical security over raw materials and finished goods consists of caged rooms that are inaccessible except through locked doors, which limit access to certain authorized employees with magnetic cards only. Withdrawal orders from these stocks must be in writing on a pre-serialized stock-withdrawal form and approved by any one of three shift production superintendents.

A quantity of gold was withdrawn on July 27, 1981, worth $27,500. The withdrawal order contained the forged signature of the night production superintendent. Any one of five night foremen delivered the forged withdrawal to the stores department night manager. He has no recollection regarding who may have presented the withdrawal to him but production scheduling records show that only three of the night foremen were supervising component assemblies requiring stocks of gold.

Store clerks are searched by metal detectors when they leave the storesroom. Nonclerks who have magnetic card access to the storesroom include the plant security chief, the director of internal audit, and the three superintendents. They too are searched upon leaving.

A log is kept of all cards presented for entry into the storesroom. On July 26, 1981, the only entries logged are those of the stores clerks.

Each night foreman working on the evening of July 27, 1981, has been with the firm for at least ten years. Each is trusted and highly regarded by management. The clerk on duty that night is also a veteran employee, and his performance has been excellent. But his brother-in-law, an assembler in the plant on the day shift, was fired for insubordination two months before the alleged theft took place.

II. SUSPECTS

Thus far, the suspects include the night shift foremen and the stores clerk. But there is no guarantee that the theft was committed on the night shift. It may have been perpetrated at any time on July 27, 1981, because the stock requisitions are only date-stamped, not date- and time-stamped. Therefore, day and afternoon foremen and stores clerks cannot be ruled out.

III. MOTIVATIONS

The night shift stores clerk seems to be a prime suspect at the moment. His brother-in-law's termination may have caused him to lash out at the company. But to have accomplished the theft himself, he would have had to:

a. Gain access to blank stores requisition forms, fabricate the withdrawal data, and forge the night superintendent's signature

b. Bypass the metal detector to get the gold out of the cage

IV. MEANS AND METHODS

If that be the case, it is possible that the theft was accomplished by collusion with one of the night foremen (who do not pass through the detector and who have access to blank stores requisitions), or with the plant guard who operates the detection equipment, or with both the foreman and guard as coconspirators.

The next step after the preliminary scenario is in place is to develop an audit and investigation plan (see Figure 6-2). Such a plan, based on the preceding facts and analysis, might be constructed as follows:

A. Stores Requisition Controls

1. Determine how stores requisitions are ordered: from whom and by whom

2. Determine how stores requisitions are issued: by whom, when, under what conditions, and with whose authorization

3. Determine how stores requisitions are kept, maintained, and physically controlled (both blanks and completed copies) at the production scheduling level

B. Stores Withdrawal Controls

1. Determine how stores withdrawals are made from inventory: by whom, when, under what conditions, and with whose authorization

2. Determine how stores withdrawals are recorded: on what documents, at what times, and by whom

3. Determine what normal stock levels (by quantity and/or dollar amount) should be kept, i.e., automatic reorder points

4. Determine how and by whom reorders are placed with the purchasing department

5. Determine how often stockouts occur; on which shift do they occur most frequently?

In theory, with high value inventory items and a perpetual inventory system, stockouts should not occur very often. Maintaining too high an inventory is

MOTIVES	OPPORTUNITIES	MEANS	METHODS	REVIEW
A. Economic	1. Weaknesses in Physical Security • Perimiter • Plant protection • Property protection	a. Access to premises b. Knowledge of internal and accounting controls	1) Removal of contents at odd hours 2) Unrecorded sales	(a) Access and exceptions logs (b) Sales documents
B. Ideological	2. Weaknesses in Internal and Accounting Controls • Paper Trail Documentation • Separation of Duties • Access to Transaction Documents	c. Authority to override controls d. Access to accounting system e. Access to accounting documents	3) Fabricated purchases 4) Diverted purchases 5) Inflated inventories 6) Inventory reclassification 7) Vendor short shipments	(c) Delivery documents (d) Purchase documents (e) Receiving documents (f) Freight bills (g) Vendor list (h) Customer list (i) Receivables and payables files
C. Egocentric	3. Authority to Override Controls	f. Access by confederates • Internal • External g. Counterfeiting transactions and documents	8) Vendor duplicate billings 9) Vendor overpricing 10) Delayed recording and suspense account entries	(j) Cycle counts (k) General journal adjusting entries (l) Canceled checks
D. Psychotic	4. Weaknesses in Management Controls • Reward System • Climate for Motivation, Trust, and Ethics	h. Feigned exceptions and emergencies i. Pretense of authority j. Impersonation	11) Created chaos 12) Off-line transactions and checks 13) Control overrides	(m)Physical security (n) Internal controls (o) Job description (p) Climate

Figure 6-2   Inventory Loss Scenario Matrix and Fraud Audit Plan (Copyright 1980, Jack Bologna)

expensive because of the carrying cost involved, i.e., it ties up working capital. Maintaining too low an inventory can disrupt production schedules and may cause loss of quantity discounts on purchases. Frequent stockouts may signal poor accounting procedures—inventory updating is too slow, postings are inaccurate, optimum inventory level needs to be adjusted upward; poor service from vendors—delivery dates are not being met; fraud—withdrawals are not being recorded for stolen items.

In the case at hand, our first real clue as to who the culprit was developed when we found a pattern of stockouts on the night shift. That fact, along with an inordinate number of purchase order requisitions being issued by the night clerk for items that hit the reorder point after his thefts, led us to interview him and present these anomalies for some answers. His initial response was that the day and afternoon shift stores clerks were lazy and left the reordering for him to do because he had more time at night. But shift production schedules did not support his contention: the work load was spread somewhat equally on all three shifts. The one document we had at that point, the stores requisition with the forged signature, led us to review all the other retained copies. There we found several other forgeries, all on his shift as well. Handwriting analysis led us to one of the foremen, who it turned out was the clerk's coconspirator and the mastermind of the scheme. The higher cost of goods manufactured on the night shift was further evidence. Unit costs of parts and components, which contained gold and platinum, tended to be lower on the day and afternoon shifts. The night foreman claimed that was occurring because of the shift differential in the hourly rate of night employees. But the cost accounting system was accurate enough to show that while labor costs were higher raw material costs were also higher, substantially higher than on the other shifts.

CHAPTER 7

Fraud Case Studies

INTRODUCTION

In theory at least, accounts payable frauds should be the least concern of internal auditors and top management. In fact, however, such frauds occur with greater frequency than other celebrated accounting system irregularities such as receivables manipulation (lapping), check kiting, cash and petty cash diversions, inventory frauds (overstatements), expense account padding, and the classic "bottom line" financial misstatements such as overstatements of revenue and understatements of expenses.

False claims for payment, i.e., fabricated or duplicated vendor invoices, specious benefit and expense claims, and fraudulent warranty and sales refund claims probably constitute at least half or more of all accounting frauds. And yet many auditors and audit programs fail to address the problem with any high degree of consistency or comprehensiveness.

The classic internal controls built into the accounts payable process are the ideas of separation of duties and paper trail documentation. Employees handling actual cash disbursements, check issuers and signers, are separate from those handling journal entries for the recording of purchase transactions, i.e., those who issue purchase orders, those who receive the ordered goods, and those who enter the purchase, receipt, and disbursement into the company's account books. Accountability for *possessing* the goods or articles so purchased is separated from accountability for the *recording* of such transactions. One person should not have the duties of handling, or possessing, the goods and making journal entries. Further, a trail of documents showing signed authorizations or other authentication measures should flow through the whole purchase transaction, i.e., purchase requisition, purchase order, receiving report, original vendor invoice, check voucher request, and the disbursement check itself.

Other accounting controls that are also built into the process are:

1. The use of serially prenumbered purchase requisitions, purchase orders, receiving reports, and check voucher requests

2. Cosignatures on purchase orders and checks exceeding certain predefined dollar amounts
3. Maintenance of an ''open'' purchase order file
4. Automatic reorder points in the inventory accounting system
5. Maintenance of a current list of preapproved vendors

Audit procedures for accounts payable would then include:

1. Verifying that individual accounts payable (subsidiary ledger details) agree with the control balance in the general ledger
2. Verifying that open balances in the accounts payable detail (subsidiary ledger) are periodically aged in thirty-day increments
3. Verifying that purchase discounts are taken and that full credit is received on returned goods
4. Verifying that accounts payable do not contain debit balances (vendors owe the company) except when authorized advance payments are made
5. Verifying that no variance exists between receiving reports, purchase orders, and vendor invoices regarding quantity, quality, and pricing of goods
6. Verifying that goods are received before payment is made
7. Verifying that disputes overpayments are routed to personnel outside the accounts payable section
8. Verifying that purchases are charged to the proper accounting period

Rarely has this author not seen the accounting and audit controls in place in firms that were victimized by accounts payable frauds. So the question of accounts payable fraud cannot be resolved solely by adding more and more controls, although good controls probably reduce 80% of the risk of fraud. Good controls are intended to minimize the risk of fraud. They are prophylactic in nature, but except in a few of the more obvious cases, they are not useful in ferreting out and detecting fraud.

Internal and accounting controls are designed to facilitate the analysis of accounting systems not accounting, purchasing, receiving, or warehousing personnel, who are the usual culprits in accounts payable frauds. The assessment and analysis of these personnel are separate from the analysis of the accounting system itself. Fraud can be committed in almost any accounting system. None is foolproof. People with fraudulent intentions or motives can always find weaknesses in controls or utilize a ruse to override or bypass controls.

So the fraud audit imperative, as distinguished from the financial or operational audit imperative, is to determine the state of mind or mental disposition of employees toward fraudulent behavior. Is fraudulent behavior tolerated in the work environment? Does the company demand and command honesty from its employees in their dealings and interactions with one another, with customers, with vendors, with stockholders, and with government regulators? Or is the company loose and casual with the truth? Is it dedicated to quality products, and workmanship or will anything pass inspection? Does it take the easy way out of difficult situations or is it committed to higher ethical principles? These questions can provide better insight into the probability of fraud in any environment than can the best audit checklist, control questionnaire, or audit software package available.

Frauds are committed by people not by computers or accounting systems. Computers and accounting systems can facilitate frauds or be used as the means or instruments by which to commit or cover up frauds. But by themselves they have not potential with which to commit fraud. Only the people who operate, work with, manage, or have access to accounting systems commit accounting frauds.

One would need to do the following to make an accounts payable scam work in a manual accounting system with reasonable good internal controls:

1. Be able to get a phony vendor onto the approved vendor list. (Someone in purchasing, or someone who has the authority to approve new vendors, would have to be compromised; or access to a new vendor authorization form would have to be secured and the authorization forged; or access to the approved vendor master file would have to be obtained and the phony vendor added.)

2. Be able to get access to purchase order requisition forms so as to fabricate a requisition (forge the signature of someone who has authority to issue such forms).

3. Be able to issue a fraudulent purchase order. A surreptitious theft of preserially numbered purchase orders would be required and the authorization to issue the purchase order would have to be faked or forged. (If the purchase orders are not prenumbered, it is easier to accomplish this kind of fraud, and random numbers can be used. In a computerized system with proper programming controls, however, a purchase order whose number is random or out-of-current sequencing would be "flagged" as an exception. This is called a sequence check.)

4. Be able to fabricate a receiving report showing delivery of goods.

5. Be able to fabricate a vendor invoice for the amount of the goods allegedly received.

6. Be able to fabricate an account number or expense category to be charged for the alleged purchase.

7. Be able to issue a fabricated check requisition or check voucher.

After looking at all the steps involved in perpetrating an accounts payable fraud one might assume that successful frauds of this type are rarities. They are not. Disbursement type frauds are rather commonplace and certainly the most frequent of all employee frauds.

The reason why such frauds occur with regularity is that each control and procedure can be compromised or bypassed despite what looks like airtight control procedures. The assumption inherent in all accounting and internal controls is that some order exists in the organization and that time is always available to process items in accordance with good, sound control principles. But controls hinder processing. The payment of bills can be greatly expedited if no controls are present, so trade-offs are continually being made when backlogs develop or emergencies arise. In such circumstances, controls get compromised by momentary exigencies. So when designing accounting and control systems, deviations in normal processing steps are allowed for—deviations that permit compromises or overrides of the control procedures. These exceptions to the general rule are what serve as the inspiration for fraud.

For example, when a critical part is necessary for the completion of a manufactured article, the purchasing department may be instructed to buy it anywhere, from anyone, whether the vendor is an approved one or not. Adding the vendor's name to the approved vendor master file may follow rather than precede actual receipt of the parts. Or a large order from a new customer may be so vital to the company's cash flow that normal credit-checking procedures are bypassed.

Other exceptions may include a large firm demanding immediate shipment of goods, even before an invoice is properly prepared or inventory control records that are so far behind in postings that requisitions are issued for goods which are in large supply already.

As previously stated, these deviations or exceptions are what the criminal attempts to exploit. Chaos is his stock-in-trade. Instead of fabricating six or seven documents, an *emergency* event is fabricated to justify the overriding or bypassing of controls. For example, expenditure controls for routine purchases may be quite effective because the charge is to the current year's budget. But capital expenditures come from another budgetary control—the long-range plan or budget. Here the signature of one person, the controller or financial vice president, may be the only requirement for check issuance. A fabricated invoice presented to that one person may be all it takes to get an ''off-line'' check issued to a spurious provider of corporate services if the story accompanying the request is that of a feigned emergency, i.e., the vendor needs an advance to buy materials, or to expedite construction, or to acquire vital equipment. The only other control might be that the amount of the check is within the check requester's capital budget and that its alleged purpose lies in an area of the business for which the check requester has responsibility, i.e., maintenance, construction, office equipment, etc.

THE MEATPACKER PAYABLES SCAM

Companies of substantial size normally have purchasing departments whose role is to secure the best goods, materials, supplies, merchandise, and services at the best prices available. In order to fulfill that role properly a number of controls are built into the purchasing process:

1.   Lists of approved vendors are kept and maintained.

2. Procedures are designed to ensure:
    a. That on very large purchases, bids are solicited from at least three approved vendors.
    b. That purchase orders are issued only on the basis of a signed requisition from an authorized department head.
    c. That purchase order blank forms are preserially numbered, kept under the control of one person, and stored safely.
    d. That buyers (purchasing agents) are periodically rotated so that relationships between them and their vendors do not get too "cozy," which can compromise objectivity as well as integrity over a period of time.
    e. That purchase orders are signed by a purchasing agent or other responsible purchasing official.
    f. That copies of the purchase order are distributed to the vendor, the receiving, accounts payable, and order-originating departments.
    g. That purchasing department personnel are prohibited from acknowledging receipt of goods or authorizing payment for goods received (the separation of duties principle).

When the goods are received, the receiving department matches the purchase order with the goods delivered to verify counts, weight, and other product specifications, and the physical condition of the contents. At this time, quality control may also selectively inspect the goods to verify grade, quality, standard specifications as to compositions, and to update the vendor's quality control file—timely delivery, correct counts and weights, correct grade or quality.

The receiving department then acknowledges receipt and distributes copies of its report to the purchasing department to relieve the open purchase order file, to accounts payable for invoice and check processing, to the stores department for further handling and storage, and/or to the inventory control department to update its stock records.

In smaller companies, these tasks are not always separate. Occasionally, one or more employees may have dual responsibilities, i.e., have physical access to both assets and accounting records. This may create a serious internal control problem. If you add to that the movement by small companies toward utilizing minicomputers and the consequent loss of paper trail documents, you have a ripe situation for employee skulduggery. The following case* has elements of the above. Your goal in analyzing the problem is to identify as many weaknesses in the company's control practices, policies, and procedures as yout can.

On January 12, 1980 a phone call came in at 8:40 A.M. to the Police Fraud Unit. The caller identified himself as the president of a meat wholesaler. His name was William Caruthers. The caller explained that his bank had called the previous day and told him that a check to a vendor had been returned to the vendor's bank for

*This case was designed by Bruce Goldstein, President, Executect Services, Burlingame, California and reprinted with his permission.

insufficient funds. Caruthers was certain that there was enough money to cover the check until he tallied all the deposits and all the payouts for that month. They did not balance, and there was a $40,000 shortage.

As you question Mr. Caruthers, he reveals the following information. The meat wholesale company, the Ampark Meat Co., used a computerized batch-oriented system for all its work. The computer was housed in a segregated area of the office. Security seemed excellent. There was computer room access control by magnetic badge and a log was kept of all personnel entering and leaving. The computer equipment was kept in that one room, i.e., the computer itself, the tape drives, disc drives, and the console. (The data entry terminals, as well as the tape library, were separate.) It was a nondistributed system. Six months before, however, there were several remote sites with terminals in field offices where salesmen could enter billing data and retrieve inventory information.

In the last five years Samuel French, the accountant, William Caruthers, the president, Irwin Davis, the data processing manager, and Philip Berk, the computer operator were the only people who were allowed legitimate access to the computer room. The tape library, which held applications programs, vendor master file listings, and the customer master file, was only open to Davis, Berk, and French. All accounts payable items were monitored by French, and he authorized payment to the vendors. As the accountant, he also approved all new accounts for addition to the file.

The meat wholesale business, like so many other businesses, has fluctuations in product pricing, so Davis, the data processing manager, would have to correct or amend the selling prices on a monthly basis. He had access to all the files in the library but only needed access to some.

The computer operator, Berk, had to mount the tapes on the disk drives for processing and had access to them for that purpose. He also had access to the company's checks, which were computerized forms.

The computer center had a full-time librarian named Margaret Johnson, who had no legitimate access to the computer room. Mrs. Johnson was very efficient and kept thorough records of the tapes taken from the library, when they were taken, and for what job.

You interview the bank officers about Ampark's account and you discover that their average monthly deposits are $700,000 and that their officers have excellent credit. As a matter of fact, accountant, French, has a $65,000 home mortgage loan with the bank, and Caruthers has a boat loan for $30,000.

Realizing that your are faced with a possible fraud, embezzlement, or theft, you begin a paperwork check against computer listings. You discover that there are forty-two different companies selling to Ampark, but there are fifty-seven companies on the vendor listing. You discover further that the company has paid out more for bulk meat than it has sold in the past three months. As these and other facts come to light, you are sure that the thief works for Ampark.

A review of documents discloses the following peculiarities:

- The invoices of the unknown vendors, while different in name, all show the same post office box number and have the same print type and style.
- The canceled checks issued by Ampark for these alleged purposes were endorsed not by rubber stamp or printed endorsement but by pen-and-ink endorsements.

1. Identify as many weaknesses in accounting controls as you can.
2. Who would you suspect?
3. How was the crime committed?
4. What documents could be used in evidence against the culprit?

THE GRANDMA MASON CASE

You are the branch manager of a thriving bank and you take great pride in your branch's growth record and the high caliber of your personnel. One day an elderly customer comes in (Grandma Mason, age 82) and says that she wants to renew her one-year $10,000 certificate of deposit. She says she was not advised that it had come up for renewal but recalled that it was exactly one year ago that she purchased it. She also recalled that it was a very busy day at the bank and that the teller had told her the certificate would be mailed to her when her check for the $10,000 cleared. However, she never received the certificate. Her personal check did clear so she assumed everything was all right. Besides it was January, and she hated to go out into the cold.

You make a quick search of the certificate of deposit files on your branch's terminal, but there is no such account in Grandma Mason's name. You ask Grandma who the teller was. She cannot recall specifically. She thinks the teller was a middle-aged woman. There are several tellers who match that description. Grandma looks them over and says none of them look familiar. Your branch personnel turnover rate is the best in the bank but it still runs around 25% per year. Furthermore, because of the bank's volume and good management your branch is used for training, and three or four tellers a month come through the branch to be trained and are later assigned to other branches.

A year ago, there were eight regular tellers and four trainees employed on the day Grandma said she bought the certificate of deposit. Two of the tellers worked the drive-in window with one trainee under their supervision. The other nine (six regulars, three trainees) worked the lobby windows. Two of the nine regular tellers have since left the bank, but the trainees are still with the bank, working at different branches.

1. What preliminary steps would you take?
2. Would you verify the fraud first or begin to search for suspects?
3. How might you go about verifying the fraud?

4.   What documents would you secure? Who would you interview? When would you call the bank's internal auditor? The FBI?

5.   Would you take handwriting samples from all the tellers who were there a year ago?

THE RETAILER TAX SCAM CASE

You are still a branch manager of a thriving suburban bank. Today, one of your retail customers comes in and says the IRS has accused him of not paying the taxes he withheld from his employees for the last two quarters. He has a book-keeper who handles his payroll manually and once a month she calculates the sum due the IRS and makes out a check for him to sign and take to the bank with the employer's federal depositary card. The check (under IRS regulations) is made payable to the bank. The teller(s) date stamps his employer's federal depository card and makes out a teller machine receipt for him. He has retained the receipts, totaling $8,250, and shows them to you.

What would you do? Rank your choices of the following options:

_____ Call the IRS and tell them to lay off the pressure they are putting on the customer because he is a nice guy and known for his honesty.

_____ Call the FBI.

_____ Call the bank's auditor.

_____ Call all your tellers together and tell them what has happened.

_____ Check the machine numbers on the receipts to see which teller(s) were assigned which machines on the dates in question.

_____ Get out the tellers' tally sheets for the dates in question to see what happened.

_____ Ask the customer to bring in his canceled checks for the payments in question.

_____ Ask the IRS to supply copies of the federal depository receipts in question.

_____ Find out if any tellers have quit the bank since the customer's last tax deposit.

_____ Tell the customer his bookkeeper may be a crook.

Develop an investigative plan. Outline the steps you would take to document the fraud, i.e., the witnesses you would interview and the documents you would review, and explain why.

THE INVENTORY SCAM

You are the supervisor of the inventory control section of a large pharmaceutical manufacturing concern. Your company has a computerized on-line perpetual inventory accounting system that functions to (1) record the receipt of raw materials for manufacturing, (2) release those raw materials for further processing into finished goods, and (3) record the sale or other disposition of the finished goods.

Among the finished goods inventory, there are a number of stimulant drugs, amphetamines, which have easy resale in the underworld market. The internal controls for these substances tend to be somewhat tighter than for non-abuse drugs because of Drug Enforcement Administration (DEA) regulations. However, you were advised today by a DEA agent that a recent arrest of an underworld trafficker and a raid on his premises disclosed a horde of drugs (worth $1,000,000 at street value) manufactured by your company. The agent asks you how such a situation could have occurred with your present accounting system.

You attempt to explain that a diversion of the drug could have been effected by the drug trafficker as a purchase or theft from a legitimate source, i.e., a drug wholesaler, a doctor, or a retail pharmacist. The agent agrees that such could have been the case but asks that you review your own internal controls because an underworld source has alleged that there are gaps in your system's security controls that led to the drug trafficker's acquisition of your products.

You begin your own investigation and discover that the system has a number of vulnerabilities:

- Finished goods, upon release by the manufacturing department, are transferred to the warehouse for storage until a sale is made. Drugs that can be abused are segregated and kept in an enclosed area.
- A journal entry is then made relieving the manufacturing department of the goods and adding them to present stocks of merchandise available for sale.
- Periodic calls or formal requests to remove stocks of drugs and repackage them into samples for use by salesmen (called detailmen) are made by the sales department to the warehouse.
- The salesmen then use the items as freebie samples for doctors and hospitals to introduce them to the drugs.
- A journal entry is made which reclassifies those stock items from inventory available for sale to sample merchandise. As sample merchandise, the drugs are not treated with the same degree of security they formerly had, i.e., sequestered separately from nondangerous drugs in a caged enclosure.

1. What weaknesses in security or accounting procedures do you see here?
2. Would you suspect a conspiracy or a single culprit?

3. What other data or information would you seek?
4. Whom would you interview?
5. What is the most likely scenario of the crime? (How could it have been accomplished within the system of internal controls?)

THE FRAUDULENT CLAIMS BENEFITS CASE

You are a claims benefit senior supervisor for a government agency in Washington, D.C., which dispenses checks to the elderly and indigent for medical care. A telephone call comes in from a Doctor Jones in Muscatine, Iowa who says he got a year-end statement from your organization indicating that he received $118,000 from your agency for medical services he allegedly provided to elderly and indigent patients. He states that his own records show he received only $68,000 from your agency last year and that he has no intention of paying income tax on funds he never received.

You aks him for his full name, address, social security number, and his "provider" number.

You run his pertinent biographical and provider information through your computer terminal and ask for a display of his claims benefit total for 1981. The computer flashes back $118,000.

You search for the individual claims benefit paid and a complete listing of payments is shown that also adds up to $118,000. You then ask for a complete hard-copy account transcription of Doctor Jones's account.

The next morning the report is on your desk when you come in. You examine the account in depth but find no apparent flaws or inaccuracies. Everything looks correct. Patient names are listed along with the dates when the services are provided. Each transaction is coded by a claims benefit number presumably assigned by a data entry supervisor in your department. However, you notice that certain claims benefit numbers are not within the series usually assigned to medical providers in Iowa. The claim numbers run in the series for the state of Maryland. The individuals for whom the services were allegedly provided, which were assigned the Maryland numbers, never appear on Iowa numbered claims. There are six such individuals. Their total claims for 1981 equal $50,000—the difference between what Doctor Jones says he actually received and what his annual statement reflects.

1. What internal control procedures would you review as the next step in your investigation?
    a. Controls over blank claims benefit forms? YES_____ NO_____
    b. Controls over claims benefit check vouchers? YES_____ NO_____
    c. The medical provider's computer listing? YES_____ NO_____
    d. Alternatives and amendments made to the medical provider's individual files? YES_____ NO_____
2. What is your theory about this case? Is there possible fraud? How did it work? Who is the likely culprit—or culprits? What evidence supports your

theory? What other evidence would you like to review before you turn the matter over to the EDP auditors or law enforcement authorities?

3.   What if you knew that Doctor Jones was suspected by your own auditors of submitting fraudulent claims (double billings on real patients and the billing of nonexistent patients) in the past? Would that change your assessment of the situation? How? What would you then do? What records would you want to examine? Whom would you interview?

TRENT'S LAPSED CASE

Your retail customer (Mr. Trent) is back in the bank today and says he has another problem. He was called by the assistant branch manager yesterday, while you were out playing golf, and told that his account was overdrawn that morning. The retailer says an overdraft in his account is impossible because he never has less than a $10,000 balance. His bookkeeper regularly advises him when the balance is getting close to that level and he immediately makes a deposit.

You go to your branch terminal again and ask the computer to display his account's activity for the current month. Sure enough, until three days ago there had always been a minimum balance of at least $10,000. There is no indication that any of the checks he recently deposited were returned for non-sufficient funds. Three days ago, however, the retailer claims he deposited a $15,000 check from his account at another bank into his main account. That deposit does not show up on your screen. You ask him to whom the check was made payable and he states that it was made payable to "cash." To add to the mystery, there is indeed a $15,000 deposit (which would take care of the overdraft), but it is recorded on the statement as having been made yesterday.

1.   What do you do?
   a. Tell him not to worry. The computer probably fouled up. His account balance is okay now.
   b. Begin an immediate investigation.
      a. What do you suspect has happened?
2.   When the bank's savings accounting system was being designed, the internal auditor demanded that provision be made for a monthly report on inactive savings accounts—no deposits or withdrawals for one year or more. Historically, thieving tellers have used such accounts to "borrow" from.
   a. Do you think such a precaution is worthwhile? Why?
   b. Does such a precaution introduce any new problems?

THE LITTLE WELLS CARGO BANK CASE

The Little Wells Cargo Bank does business in a southwestern state. It takes great pride in its one hundred year history of service to business, in its competent management, and in its operational controls.

Two years ago, Sam Succotash, an oil well promoter and wildcat explorer, opened a checking account at the main office with a check for $500,000 from the Interhemispheric Petroleum Corporation. The branch manager, Fonzi Taggert, was ecstatic. The new account fulfilled his deposit goal for three months. Fonzi took Sam to lunch that afternoon, and after two martinis and a Benedictine & Brandy they relaxed over Havana cigars (provided by Sam) and talked about the oil business. Fonzi was intrigued by the stories of sudden wealth and heartaches in wildcatting that were told by Sam with great relish. A social friendship ensured with Sam and Fonzi playing golf together and entertaining each other at home on weekends with their wives.

About six months after their relationship had begun, Sam invited Fonzi to join him for a weekend of skiing at this chalet-condominium in the Rocky Mountains of Colorado. Fonzi and his wife were overjoyed. All in all, it was a marvelous weekend. The ski slopes were fast and cold; the evenings at the chalet were warm and cozy.

A week later Sam came into the bank and seemed troubled. Fonzi asked what the problem was and Sam said that he was expecting another $500,000 check from the Interhemispheric Petroleum Corporation for royalties on wells he had leased to them but they were slow in paying him. An option on some new lands for oil exploration was coming due the next day and he had to have $500,000 to complete the closing. A loan was out of the question because there was not enough time to complete the application, update his financial statements, and wait for the loan committee's approval. Sam said he regretted that he ever believed Interhemispheric's controller, who had assured him the money would be transmitted in enough time to complete the closing. He was convinced the new oil lands would be a "mother lode"—the biggest strike since the East Texas fields were discovered.

Fonzi commiserated with his friend for a minute and then asked what his current bank balance was. Sam told him that there was probably close to a half million dollars but he added that checks for that amount were issued by his accountant the day before, "So in all honesty, I can't say I have anything now."

"Don't worry," said Fonzi. "It'll probably take a few days for those checks to clear anyway. If they come through sooner, I'll cover them temporarily until your check from IPC comes in."

"Oh, can you do that?" asked Sam.

"Well, it's not strictly kosher, but under circumstances like this—you being a good customer and all—we can accommodate you."

"Thanks a lot, Fonzi—you won't regret it. I'll make it up to you. I owe you one."

Sam left with a pleased look and Fonzi authorized an overdraft waiver for Sam's account. Two days later the bank's operations department called Fonzi and told him that Sam's account was overdrawn by $750,000 and asked whether he wanted to increase the overdraft waiver to that amount. Fonzi agreed, explaining that it was only temporary.

Fonzi then dialed up the bank's main computer on the branch's terminal and asked for a display of Sam's account activity for the current month. He was amazed to see the volume of activity in the account—millions of dollars seemed to be floating in and out on a daily basis. There were several large overdrafts even before Sam's conversation with him, but they were always covered within a day or two, sometimes with large sums of cash.

These oil men, thought Fonzi, are really something. Everything is boom and bust. How they keep things straight is beyond me.

A day later the operations department called again to say that Sam's account overdraft was up to $900,000. Would Fonzi authorize the waiver to that amount? (His waiver authority was limited to $900,000.) Fonzi agreed to authorize the waiver, but he then called Sam and asked him to have lunch.

Sam was animated and happy at lunch and presented Fonzi with a gift for his wife—a diamond broach. Fonzi appreciated his generosity. As the lunch wore on, Fonzi approached the subject of Sam's overdraft. Sam reassured him that all would be well in a day or two. But Fonzi insisted he had to know what was going on—his job was at stake.

Sam laughed at that. "Fonzi, my boy," he said, "you're working your behind off for a lousy $20,000 a year. How would you like to make a million a year?"

Stunned by Sam's comment, Fonzi said nothing but was delighted. He finally asked, "Doing what?"

"Get into the oil business with me," answered Sam. "I'll make you rich."

"But I don't know anything about it," said Fonzi.

"What's to know—you buy cheap and sell high. I'll show you the ropes."

"But what about the bank—my career?"

"The bank? Hell, you won't even need to leave. Stay there. I'll give you a piece of my company—a cut of the action. All you have to do is keep my books on weekends."

The offer sounded intriguing to Fonzi. There was no question that Sam lived well. He had several homes, apartments in Denver and New York, a yacht, and he traveled all over the world.

"What do I have to do?" asked Fonzi.

"Nothing. Just do what you're doing now—a favor now and then when my cash flow is a little out of line. You know this business is crazy with ups and downs."

"But what do I get? When can I go to work full-time for you?"

"Look," said Sam, "I'm coming into some leases in the next six months which are going to make me $60,000,000—$60,000,000! How would you like say 10% of that action? A cool $6,000,000."

"But what do I have to do?"

"Fonzi, do I have to draw pictures? You're the banker, you know that one needs cash to buy up good leases and they can't be financed with bank loans. Bankers don't loan money on an "if it comes in" basis. But I know enough lease buyers in the big companies to sell everything I can get my hands on. They're in and out transactions. Buy one week, sell the next. It's all short-term profit. The secret is in knowing how and when to buy. Selling is a snap. And Fonzi, my boy, I really know how to buy. But I need cash. I'll leave that up to you. Let me do what I do best—buying and selling. It's as simple as that.''

A bargain was struck by the two and each left overjoyed with the prospect of quick riches.

However, since he was the more cautious of the two, Fonzi the next day decided to see what had been going on in Sam's account and with Sam's finances. He ordered a credit history and a transcription of his account. The information in the credit history was sketchy. Very little was known about his past—he had come to town two years before from New York, where he said he was self-employed as a petroleum geologist and technical consultant on drilling. His income was estimated to be $150,000 a year. A college degree in engineering was alleged to have been received by Sam from a small and unknown technical institute in southwest Louisiana. He was fifty years old and married to a wife who was considerably younger. They owned no property except the chalet-condominium but maintained several apartments.

The transcription of Sam's account showed many transactions. Money flowed in and out at a frenetic pace. Some days there were as many as four separate deposits made.

Aha, thought Fonzi. He's a real amateur when it comes to running a kiting scheme. Doing it through *one* account.

Fonzi called Sam and asked to meet him for dinner so that he could outline a better plan. Fonzi proposed a scheme whereby a series of accounts would be opened in two different branches. For safety, an account would be opened at another bank as well, preferably a bank in another federal reserve district so that a float factor could be built into the scheme.

The original amount proposed to finance the scheme was $1,000,000 in cash. Sam was to deposit this amount in a New York City bank. Such a handsome deposit would really make a ''splash'' with bank officials and Sam's business would be valued. Thereafter, they could whipsaw funds between Fonzi's bank and the other federal reserve district bank and also within the branch system of Fonzi's bank. The plan Fonzi outlined is illustrated in Figure 7-1.

- What internal control defenses would you build in to thwart or detect such a scheme?

Fonzi's scheme was detected when he attempted to make a deposit in Account B to cover an overdraft, but inadvertently filled out the deposit slip for Account D. Account B therefore went over the $900,000 limit on overdrafts and was flagged for analysis by a bank auditor. It is the inadvertent error that usually causes such schemes to surface.

Fonzi kept his account manipulation records manually. If he had used a home computer . . . Ah, but that's another story—a story for the future.

DAY NO.				WEEK #1 FLOAT	WEEK #2 FLOAT
1	ACCOUNT A NEW YORK	Balance	$1,000,000		
		Withdraw	1,000,000		
1	ACCOUNT B LOS ANGELES Branch #1	Deposit	$1,000,000		
		Withdraw	1,900,000		
		Overdraft*	$ 900,000	$ 900,000	$5,400,000
2	ACCOUNT C LOS ANGELES Branch #2	Deposit	$1,900,000		
		Withdraw	2,800,000		
		Overdraft*	$ 900,000	$1,800,000	$6,300,000
3	ACCOUNT D LOS ANGELES Branch #1	Deposit	$2,800,000		
		Withdraw	3,700,000		
		Overdraft*	$ 900,000	$2,700,000	$7,200,000
4	ACCOUNT E LOS ANGELES Branch #2	Deposit	$3,700,000		
		Withdraw	4,600,000		
		Overdraft*	$ 900,000	$3,600,000	$8,100,000
5	ACCOUNT A NEW YORK	Deposit	$4,600,000		
		Withdraw	5,500,000		
		Overdraft*	$ 900,000	$4,500,000	$9,000,000

REPEAT THE CYCLE

Figure 7-1 A Bank Kiting Scheme. Assume computer limit check on overdrafts for this customer is $900,000 and that the Los Angeles bank reconciles overdrafts by branch only.

THE RANSOMED INFORMATION CASE

You are the vice president for strategic planning for a large multinational corporation in the petroleum exploration, transportation, refining, and retailing business. You have been using an independent computer service bureau for storage and retrieval of highly critical and sensitive data about the company's future growth and development plans. You have on-line access to the service bureau's computer and your market research, competitor analyses, and product development data files are stored there. Access to your data is protected by a user identification number, a password code, and a chain of authoritative commands.

Despite these precautions, someone either in your firm, in the service bureau, or an outside industrial espionage agent has penetrated your files. The culprit now has in his possession highly sensitive documents disclosing all the sites where your firm intends to drill for oil in the next five years, the current status and strategy of negotiations with a foreign government for leasing concessions, and the company's intended bids on future off-shore U.S. government-owned potential oil-producing areas.

The computer log at the service bureau shows the data were accessed two days ago. The reports were transmitted to a terminal site that must have been an approved site, but the reference number of the terminal has been obliterated on the log.

You ask for the assistance of your data processing and security departments. Their investigation discloses that it is highly unlikely the data request originated from a company terminal. They also learn that three competing firms also use the service bureau's computer for strategic planning purposes. A common program is shared by all four firms for venture analyses and other forms of business risk analysis, along with the common use of a software model for forecasting petroleum consumption and production patterns worldwide.

That same afternoon the president of your firm receives a call from a competitor's chief executive officer who tells him he has been approached by a foreign national in Vienna who claims he can deliver some very important information about your company for $5,000,000. The chief executive officer refused to negotiate but felt he should advise your president. The president of the competitor's firm has no idea who the caller was. He shrugs off the situation as a crackpot call.

- What would you do at this point? Who would you call and why? What are the likely consequences of your actions?

The next morning your president receives a call from a man in Vienna who claims he can recover your data for $10,000,000. He alleges he can effect a transfer in Zurich, Switzerland in two days, but your firm must deposit the $10,000,000 in a numbered bank account in Zurich first. Later the account number can be exchanged for a locker key in the Zurich airport, which contains the purloined data. Your president refuses the offer as stated but suggests that the intermediary accompany one of your firm's people to the locker to ensure honesty. The caller agrees but only if a company person is held as a hostage until the contents of the numbered bank account have been confirmed. Your president does not agree but says the man should call him back in an hour for further discussion.

- How would you advise your president at this point? Why?
  What are the likely consequences if he agrees to the latest plan?

The caller reaches your president again and says his client is growing nervous and is threatening to disclose your firm's strategy to the oil country from whom it hopes to win drilling concessions. He adds that if the money is not forthcoming by Friday, two days from now, he will in fact make such a disclosure. The caller does not wait for a response and hangs up.

- What do you do now? What are the likely consequences?
- What did you learn from this experience?
- What will you not do in the future in a situation like this?

THE DRUG HIGHJACKING CASE

You are a vice president and director of international marketing for a large, ethical pharmaceutical manufacturer on the East Coast. You receive a telephone call from the director of sales at your Paris office. He tells you he has just received a call from an unidentified person who claims to be representing an underworld gang responsible for highjacking a truckload of the company's antibiotics after the drugs were unloaded from a ship at a Marseilles pier. The caller offered to sell the drugs back to the company for $1,000,000. (The company's investment in the drugs, at cost, is $500,000.) If the offer is not accepted, the underworld gang threatens to store the drugs under extreme heat in a warehouse and then distribute them through retail pharmacies at bargain prices. (Such storage would cause the drugs to lose their potency, and if administered to a person in need of antibiotics to ward off serious infection could result in death.)

As a further threat, if the police are called in the underworld group is prepared to replace the content of the bottles with poisoned pills and to surreptitiously place them in hospital pharmacies throughout France.

Discuss the following options and their possible consequences:

1. Buy back the drugs for the asking price
2. Negotiate price
3. Refuse to do anything (You are fully insured for loss of the drugs by theft or destruction.)
4. Call the police

5. Buy more product liability insurance
6. Set up a meeting to determine whether the gang in fact does have the drugs
7. Select an underworld intermediary to negotiate for you
8. Determine who are the most likely culprits and what are their previous criminal histories
9. Turn the entire matter over to your legal department
10. Turn the entire matter over to your security director
11. What would you personally recommend as the most feasible alternative?
12. What did you learn from this experience?
13. How would you protect yourself from such events in the future?

HIGH PERFORMANCE FAKERY: CASE 1

While there are few fixed relationships in accounting data, there are some to which fraud auditors should pay particular attention—for example, the past relationship of sales to cost of sales, of sales to accounts receivable and accounts payable, and of sales to bank deposits. Here, evidence is sought of receivables lapping, of inventory overstatement, of check kiting, and of phony invoices for merchandise and services. A fraud audit should contain a trend analysis of these items and their relationships as well as analysis of the relationships of sales to freight out, sales to purchases, and purchases to freight in. These are dollar comparisons and trends. Volume measurements might also make interesting studies, i.e., sales in terms of unit volume, pounds of raw materials in versus pounds of finished goods out, and volume relationships between sales, purchases and inventory.

Because most businesses are seasonal, a month-to-month comparison may not be too useful from a fraud audit perspective. Variances may be spread out. But a consistent buildup of accounts receivable or accounts payable balances discovered through a month-to-month aging process may sometimes highlight a current fraud. An inventory buildup inconsistent with sales volume may also be symptomatic of fraud or mismanagement.

While short-term trend analysis is not always profitable from a fraud audit perspective, long-term trends may be significant.

A long-term buildup of inventory that is inconsistent with sales increases is a "badge of fraud" or "red flag." The same is true with respect to accounts receivable buildups, accounts payable buildups, and deposit volume decreases. These items should be plotted on a year-to-year basis to ensure reasonableness for testing purposes.

For example, XYZ Corporation has established a corporate-wide goal to increase sales by 20% per year. Its executive compensation plan calls for profit center managers to increase unit sales by 20% per year and to increase unit profits by 25% per year to qualify for the maximum bonus. X Unit provides you with the following data regarding its past operations.

- What do you suspect may have happened?
- Were sales inflated?
- What leads you to believe so?
- Was inventory inflated?
- What leads you to believe so?
- Were purchases understated?

	Past Year 4	Past Year 3	Past Year 2	Past Year 1	Current Year
Sales	$12,000,000	$14,400,000	$17,280,000	$20,736,000	$24,883,200
Freight out	240,000	288,000	345,600	414,720	497,664
Cost of sales	6,000,000	7,200,000	8,640,000	10,368,000	12,441,600
Purchases	4,800,000	5,760,000	6,912,000	8,289,600	9,953,280
Freight in	120,000	144,000	172,800	207,360	248,832
Inventory	1,200,000	1,500,000	1,825,000	2,283,250	2,854,062
Accounts receivable	1,000,000	1,200,000	1,440,000	1,826,000	2,273,000
Accounts payable	400,000	480,000	576,000	690,800	829,440
Net income	1,200,000	1,500,000	1,825,000	2,283,250	2,854,062

	Past Year 4	Past Year 3	Past Year 2	Past Year 1	Current Year
Ratios					
Cost of sales/Sales	50.0%	50.0%	50.0%	50.0%	50.0%
Inventory/Sales	10.0%	10.5%	10.5%	11.0%	11.5%
Receivables/Sales	8.3%	8.3%	8.3%	8.9%	9.2%
Payables/Sales	3.3%	3.3%	3.3%	3.3%	3.3%
Purchases/Sales	40.0%	40.0%	40.0%	40.0%	40.0%
Net income/Sales	10.0%	10.5%	10.5%	11.0%	11.5%
Trends					
Sales		+20%	+20%	+20%	+20%
Net income		+25%	+25%	+25%	+25%

A word of caution may be in order to internal auditors. The proliferation of microcomputers being used by executives, particularly for spread sheet applications, has created an opportunity for data diddling by those managers whose ethics are questionable. So be prepared. The clever enemy is now equipped with the latest state-of-the-art for "fudging numbers."

HIGH PERFORMANCE FAKERY: CASE 2

X Unit is a wholly owned subsidiary of XYZ Corporation, a multinational corporation whose primary business is manufacturing paper products, i.e., shipping cartons, packaging material, stationery, and fine paper for printing. X Unit manufactures fine paper and distributes its product to printing houses in a large midwestern metropolitan area. Its raw stocks of paper are purchased mainly from another subsidiary of the parent company, Y Unit, which supplies about two-thirds of its needs; but X Unit buys paper stock from other manufacturers as well.

X Unit's profits have been spotty over the past five years. Competition is keen and price cutting is commonplace in the industry. Two years ago, X Unit's general manager retired after thirty years with the company. He was highly respected by his colleagues and was thought to be an effective manager; however, profits had been sliding downward the last three years of his employment.

In the hands of Clark Adams, the new general manager, X Unit is making great strides in its quest for improved profits. Clark Adams is a bright, energetic, articulate, and ambitious man with an MBA from an Ivy League school. He worked his way up through the finance group in corporate headquarters and his promotion to line management did not surprise anyone. In 1981, however, he met with a number of personal and business setbacks. An avid investor in commodities futures, he sustained a personal loss of $50,000 in his dealings. His wife grew despondent over all the hours he put into his work and outside hobbies (antique car restoration, coin and gun collecting) and ran off with a used car salesman, leaving him with their three children. But under his direction, X Unit's profits in 1982 increased 100% on a 20% sales rise, and Adams qualified for a full bonus of $25,000.

Operating data for X unit for the past five years, as reported to corporate headquarters, are as follows:

	1978	1979	1980	1981	1982
Sales	$15,000,000	$14,000,000	$13,000,000	$15,000,000	$18,000,000
Cost of sales	8,00,000	9,000,000	10,000,000	9,000,000	10,000,000
Gross profit	7,000,000	5,000,000	3,000,000	6,000,000	8,000,000
G&A expense	6,000,000	7,000,000	6,000,000	5,000,000	6,000,000
Net income	1,000,000	(2,000,000)	(3,000,000)	1,000,000	2,000,000
Inventory	1,000,000	1,000,000	1,500,000	2,000,000	2,500,000
Purchases	7,000,000	6,000,000	5,500,000	7,000,000	8,000,000
Payables	700,000	600,000	650,000	700,000	800,000
Receivables	1,500,000	1,400,000	1,300,000	1,800,000	2,400,000
Freight in	50,000	40,000	35,000	50,000	60,000
Freight out	100,000	80,000	70,000	100,000	110,000
Pounds in	70,000,000	60,000,000	55,000,000	70,000,000	80,000,000
Pounds out	66,500,000	57,000,000	52,700,000	65,100,000	75,200,000

	1978	1979	1980	1981	1982
Conversion loss	5%	5%	6%	7%	6%
Scrap Sales	$35,000	$35,000	$23,000	$49,000	$48,000

Paying particular attention to the 1982 data and its relationships with past years, what accounts would you analyze for possible over- or under-statement? Why?

CHAPTER 8

Personal Reflections on Fraud Cases

After thirty years of fraud auditing and investigation, I sometimes wonder why I got into the field and why I even continue. What is it about ferreting out fraud that seems like such a challenge to me and to others who suffer from my "disease"? Are we nonbelievers in human decency and honesty? Do we have a perverted sense of reality? Are we witch-hunters by nature or disposition?

I found these questions difficult to answer on the basis of my own experience—it is always more difficult to be objective about yourself than it is to be objective about others. So one day I began to catalog the names of the fraud auditors/investigators for whom I had the greatest professional respect and I reflected for some time on their personalities, beliefs, values, talents, and attitudes. My analysis led me to an amazing insight. Most of these men and women were ordinary people. Few could be classified as brilliant but none could be called stupid; they possessed ordinary intelligence. Few were biased or hostile toward their prey, i.e., financial criminals. They did not classify themselves as "knights of the round table" either. They just seemed to go about their work in a low-key, no fanfare way. They saw their job as enjoyable and did it the best way they could. They all seemed to have a well-developed sense of humor and a lot of faith and pride in themselves. They were often at odds with their own organizations, whether working for federal, state, or local law enforcement or for regulatory authorities. Their methods were unconventional and their thinking patterns were unconventional. They had a great deal of drive and strong intuitive powers. And they did not mistrust all people, only a selected few. They seemed to be, for the most part, highly motivated, dedicated, fair-minded, honest, and simple people. But they could make sense out of chaos—their one common gift. They could look at complex schemes and mountains of data and neither be threatened by the complexity of what they saw nor lose sight of the significance of it all. They took complexity in stride and saw it as an opportunity to muddle through long enough to make some meaningful observations and to draw some reasonable conclusions.

They were neither afraid to close a case when the available evidence was inadequate nor to vigorously follow a case through to prosecution when the evidence warranted such action. You could say they were "professionals," but that hardly describes their contributions to society. By and large, they were unsung heros and heroines. You have probably never heard of any of the people on my most-admired list. They would not stand out in a crowd. If anything, as a group they are nondescript. Hollywood would never portray them as the nation's defense against corporate and commercial fraud. Efrem Zimbalist, Jr. would feel as uncomfortable in their presence as they would in his.

It is these most-admired people to whom I wish to dedicate this chapter: those who toiled with me through the long and arduous journey of auditing and investigating corporate frauds and without whose advice, counsel, and insight the following cases could never have been made.

CASE ONE: THE GREAT WHISKEY SAMPLE GIVEAWAY

In 1956, while working as a Special Agent of the IRS in Detroit, a collateral inquiry was assigned to me from our office in Montgomery, Alabama. They were conducting a tax evasion investigation of the former head of the state's Alcoholic Beverage Control Board, the so-called ABC Board. The state of Alabama at that time did not permit governors to succeed themselves, and if a governor intended to become rich from public office he had but one term in which to sell favors, state contracts, and pardons. That rule applied to his political appointees as well; they had to "make hay while the sun shone" too, and the ABC Board chairman found a unique way to do that.

Our Montgomery office had received information from a confidential source who alleged that more than $200,000 worth of liquor was stored in a local warehouse for the former ABC Board chairman. How it initially got there was unknown but there was no doubt it belonged to the ex-chairman. His possession of the liquor technically was not a crime but an offer to sell it to someone in Alabama could be a crime because the state had a monopoly on all liquor sales within its borders. To possess $200,000 of liquor may not be a crime for anyone if the proper taxes have been paid, but when a government official shows up with such a stash shortly after his term of office expired, and especially when the job he held paid only $8,000 a year, the IRS tends to get curious.

An agent in Montgomery opened an investigation and issued a subpoena for the records of the warehouse regarding its dealings with the ex-chairman. These records disclosed that a large quantity of booze began to accumulate shortly after his accession to office and continued to grow until the end of his term. Occasional withdrawals from stock were made during that two-year period, and the agent realized through a "flash of insight" that the withdrawal dates coincided with political fund-raising rallies sponsored by the Democratic party. In fact, a total of $300,000 worth of liquor had come to the warehouse during the ex-chairman's term. The agent also noted that there were periodic withdrawals of small quantities—two or three bottles—approved by the warehouse's customer, but consigned to the state chemist for analysis and verification of the proof rating on the label.

The liquor came from a host of distillers, both domestic and international. Bourbon, Rye, Scotch, and the blends of most makes and manufacture were represented as well as afterdinner liqueurs. But the agent detected some rather gaping holes in the array of liquors. Some national best-sellers were not represented. A large Canadian distiller, for example, was not represented by two of its most important lines. Its Scotch brands were there in abundance but not its premier Canadian whiskeys. So the agent's inquiry asked that we determine why the Canadian distiller did not sell these brands to Alabama, what volume of business the Canadian distiller did with the state during the chairman's tenure, and what knowledge the distiller might have about how its liquors came into the chairman's possession.

In 1956 when this inquiry was assigned to me I had less than a year of experience with the IRS and had done very little investigative work on major corporations. I had expected the distiller to be helpful and polite and certainly inclined to cooperate with governmental authorities. Much to my chagrin, such was not the case, and the distiller, located across the Detroit River in Canada, was not inclined to help at all. The in-house attorney suggested that my territorial powers ended in the middle of the river and that I should therefore retreat to where I had come from.

I returned in failure and disgrace to Detroit, where I conferred with my supervisor: he offered some sage advice. "Go back and talk to the Canada Department of Revenue guys in Windsor. See if they won't help you." So I drove across the river again and spoke with the head of the Windsor office of our Canadian counterparts. He listened sympathetically and then said "I think I should tell you we're in there right now doing an audit." What a break, I thought. But then he added, "They haven't been much inclined to cooperate with us either. There is something going on, on both sides of the border, that they don't want us to know about."

"What do you think happened?" I asked.

"Well, if I had to make a guess," he said, "I'd say they're either being shaken down by liquor control authorities or hoods or they are willingly compromising the authorities. Our auditors are finding some strange expense accounts being submitted by their Canadian sales representatives. They seem ungodly high to me. I have a feeling they're building a slush fund of some sort."

"What would they use it for?" I asked.

"Probably to get favored positioning on the shelves of provincial liquor stores." (Canada also operates on a monopoly basis. Liquor by the bottle for consumers and by the case for pubs is sold through stores managed by the provinces. There are severe restrictions on distiller sales and promotion practices, one of which limits the featuring of a brand in a prominent place on the shelf unless its sales are high. Yet without featured billing, a new label can never really get off the ground. So a practice of bribing store managers began to develop.

Sales representatives for distillers would visit a provincial store and bribe the manager to provide a more visible spot on his shelf for new brands, which had no sales history, or for brands that were not doing well in sales and were therefore hidden from public view.)

The situation was a catch-22 for distillers. The impetus for the regulation came from the old-line liquor manufacturers who did not want upstarts competing with them on an equal footing. But when they, in turn, wanted to introduce a new line or label they were caught in the same trap they had set for others. If they elected to remain honest and comply with their own legal handiwork, they would have to accept lower sales for new brands or a long period of sales development. Of course, neither option was what they wanted. So bribing store managers became a common practice.

In any event, since the distiller was a Canadian corporation, my U.S. powers were rather limited. But the company's U.S. subsidiary was a Michigan corporation, which operated as a holding company for all the firm's distilleries and other business assets in the United States and also served as the U.S. importer of its Canadian manufactured liquor products. My research led me to another anomaly. One of the U.S. distilleries shipped its output in bulk back to Canada where it was bottled and then "imported" into the United States as though it had been made in Canada. A neat game that was intended to deceive the U.S. consumer into thinking that he or she was drinking imported Canadian whiskey when it was really made in the corn belt. The word "Imported" on the bottle gave the product a foreign and premium image.

With all this legal and quasi-legal wheeling and dealing across the two borders, I thought I could develop good cause for serving a subpoena on the Michigan corporation. As it turned out, the shipments to Alabama came via the importing company—the Michigan corporation. I served the subpoena on the president of the Michigan corporation in his high-rise office in Detroit around Christmastime. The sales staff were busy wrapping and boxing bottles of booze for holiday distribution to favored customers and political leaders. The president offered to send a case to my house if I gave him my address, but I told him I could not accept gifts.

After the holidays, I received a phone call from a prominent lawyer in Detroit who said that he represented the distiller and wanted to talk to me about the records requested in the subpoena I had served. The meeting was cordial and he explained the intricacies of international corporate legalities, which was that the Michigan corporation was only a conduit used for marketing, customs, and other legal purposes and that all records were in fact kept in Canada. I attempted to clarify to him that my intention at this point was to determine how and why shipments of liquor were made to the Alabama official. He speculated that the official may simply have bought the liquor from wholesalers in nonmonopoly states and that his intentions after that were anybody's guess. "Well," I said, "he surely isn't going to sell it to the state of Alabama. They buy direct. And if he sells it to anyone else in Alabama, he may be committing a crime."

"Sonny," said the lawyer, "you're kind of young and naive. Liquor is like gold. It can be sold anywhere at any time. It's a tough business. It fought gangsters in the '20s and politicians in the '30s. Forget about it. Why should the government give a damn, as long as the tax is paid.''

"The excise tax may have been paid," I said, "but the question is whether Mr. _____ has paid all his income tax.''

"You'll have a long and hard way to go on that one," opined the lawyer. "Those southern politicians are pretty slick and they're well wired. They wouldn't do anything really stupid.''

"Thanks for the advice. Now what are we going to do about the records. When can I get them?''

"I'll call the controller and tell him to dig up whatever he can still find and turn them over to you.''

A week or so later the controller called and asked that I come over to review the records. When I arrived, I found my Canadian Revenue Department counterparts in the controller's office. He had asked them to prepare a Queen's Writ for the same records, and following international protocol the Canadian authorities would then release to me the records I had subpoenaed. The arrangement was agreeable to me, so we were given the records and a room in which we could review them.

I discovered while going through the material that all we had were documents attesting to shipments and customs clearances by the distiller to the state of Alabama for a two-year period. There were no invoices, no purchase orders from the state, and no correspondence. The shipments were all made through a bonded warehouse in Detroit from which the liquor stocks had been removed and to which all shipments from Canada to the United States were made. That did not tell us very much so I approached the controller again and registered my displeasure.

"Oh," he said, "you can reach those records with an American subpoena. We just process the orders from Canada. The details are kept in the States.''

"Why didn't you tell me that before," I asked. "I've already served your Michigan subsidiary and they said the records were over here.''

"You must have misunderstood," he said.

"Well, I'm beginning to understand *now*," I said.

On my return to Detroit I called the attorney and asked him what was going on. I had been back and forth across the border for a month and had seen nothing of the records I wanted. He said he had been misinformed too. He thought what I needed would be in Canada. He apologized and said he would settle the problem.

Feeling somewhat frustrated about the time delay, I called the Special Agent in Montgomery who had the case and explained my situation. He told me not to worry. The ex-chairman was beginning to squirm. He had engaged an expensive tax lawyer from Washington, D.C. and the lawyer was making loud noises about the way the agent got the warehouse documents, so he felt we were on the right track. He also said his confidential source disclosed a network of confederates in the scheme and that the ex-governor could be involved too.

He outlined the scheme as follows:

1. Whenever the ABC chairman wanted liquor for a political rally or party, he would tell the salesmen for the various distilleries who did business with the state to ship "samples" to the state chemist, purportedly to verify proof ratings on the label.
2. The distilleries would then ship the desired number of cases to the state chemist, who in turn would remove one or two bottles for sampling, for appearance sake, and have the remainder sent to the ABC chairman's warehouse.
3. The chairman would later remove whatever was needed for the party or rally and the balance was left for his account.
4. By the end of his term, the chairman had grown so greedy that he demanded that shipments of "samples" be sent directly to his warehouse; his demands became so numerous that when the chemist really wanted to run test samples, he drew his stocks from the chairman's supply rather than request them from the distiller's representative in Alabama.

The Special Agent in Montgomery had also learned of similar situations in other monopoly states from a disgruntled liquor salesman who had worked for the Canadian distiller but was terminated to make way for the chairman's brother-in-law when the chairman took office. The brother-in-law was later fired by the Canadian firm when his relative's term expired.

With that bit of new information, I called the distiller's lawyer and told him we had to have a serious conversation about his client's problem, that the issue no longer involved one lowly state official but many, and that the corporation's own executives, at least those who were U.S. citizens and residents, might be involved. He asked that I see him the next morning.

I opened my conversation the next morning with the observation that I hoped I would be accorded a higher level of cooperation from the company and that it was in the company's best interest to do so. He laughed and said "Jesus Christ, you *are* naive." He said the liquor industry was accustomed to these periodic forays by muckraking journalists, public-spirited citizens groups, and police agencies. He said "We've fought everyone from Carry Nation to Al Capone. What are you trying to do, scare me?"

"No," I said, "I'm not trying to scare you. I'm asking for your help in cleaning up the corruption that your industry either spawned or aided or abetted in."

"Look," he said, "you're a nice kid. What the hell do you want to kick up such a fuss for. We know how to protect ourselves from these leeches and parasites. But we've got to run a business. Everybody's after us, including ourselves. We don't need the federal government to help us."

"Well, where do we go from here?" I asked.

"I'll see that you get your records on that idiot in Alabama. He's a jerk anyway. That greedy bastard belongs in jail. But don't expect me to do you any other favors.

True to his word, the records were delivered and they corroborated what the source in Alabama told the Agent there. Shipments of "samples" were sent directly to the Board chairman's warehouse but were made only after a letter was received by the distiller from the state chemist. No freebies were sent without direct solicitation. The distiller allowed me to make copies of all the documents, shipping manifests, no-charge billings, customs clearances, and the correspondence from the chemist who incidentally became a government witness at the chairman's trial.

The offshoots of the case are interesting as well. The Canadian tax authorities developed cases against the errant liquor store managers, against the distiller's salesmen who bribed them with money derived from their phony expense accounts, and against the distiller as well for aiding and abetting the bribery scheme. There was a major shake up in management of the distiller shortly after that.

On the American side of the border, the IRS determined that the shipments back and forth across the border of whiskey made in the United States were not only a marketing gimmick but a clever way to shortchange the Treasury on excise taxes for liquor made in the United States. After years of litigation, the distiller was forced to pay more than $20,000,000 in additional income and excise tax.

CASE TWO: "SKIMMING" ON GROSS RECEIPTS

In another case, a mobster owned a vending machine business, in which we found a glaring weakness in internal controls. Routemen loaded up each morning, visited their locations, emptied the cash boxes, and restocked the machines with candy, cigarettes, and hot and cold drink materials. Upon their return they supplied both the cash and the listings of each machine's cash take to the bookkeeper–cashier for reconciliation. It was alleged that the machines did not have either product or cash counting devices so the driver's word had to be taken for granted. Since the mobster's reputation for violence was well known, one might have assumed that his drivers would not dare shortchange him for fear of losing their lives, not just their jobs.

But criminals tend to have very little personal trust, even among themselves. I persisted in asking questions of the bookkeeper–cashier about how the firm could be certain that it was not being shortchanged by its drivers. She said that there were some controls—some ballpark estimates to keep the drivers honest. For example, she said, the drivers' loads each morning were recorded and at week's end the load sheets were tabulated at retail prices and matched against each driver's weekly receipts. While the system was not foolproof, the drivers could not steal too much, she added, or the boss would get wise.

It still bothered me because with forty drivers even a weekly knockdown rate of $50.00 per driver was still possible to go undetected within the system and would produce an annual loss of more than $100,000. Something else that disturbed me was the fact that after each weekend's matching of load sheets and receipts the documents were allegedly destroyed. Daily journal entries for each day's sales were made, but without supporting documentation or breakdown. A lump figure was used. Load sheets and location receipt sheets were also destroyed, or so she said. The excuse that was given for destroying all of the documents was that the firm would have drowned in a sea of paper if it had retained them.

An analysis of bank deposits showed that recorded sales found their way into the bank. But how much cash did not get recorded and how could we reconstruct actual sales without any corroborating records? The mobster's net worth did not seem out of line with his reported income. He lived frugally, at least while in Detroit, and he was not noted for being a lavish spender in Florida, where he had a winter home. Yet one thing seemed to stand out in the accounting records. Travel, entertainment, and business promotion accounts were very ordinary for the volume of business done by the firm. There were no unusual amounts spent for anything. And that is what finally brought the point home for me.

The vending machine business in Detroit in the late 1950s was owned and operated mainly by people of nefarious backgrounds. To maintain peace and harmony within the fold, the locally owned companies were members of a trade association and had entered into a sweetheart arrangement with a labor organization which, exempt from the antitrust laws, policed the industry by keeping out interlopers. This was accomplished by not allowing them membership in either the association or the union. If a union location was taken over by a nonunion vending machine company, the location was picketed for being antilabor and allowing a "scab" company to service its employees, who in turn were strongly prolabor and union members themselves. There was a modest amount of competition among the union vending machine companies. Locations could be bought from a rival firm or an employee in a potential customer firm could be bribed to win it away. Someone in management with responsibility for food service or a union leader who was given the right to select the vending machine company was the person to bribe.

The firm in question had been growing rapidly but there was nothing in its account books that showed either the purchase of locations or sub rosa payments to customer management or union personnel. That was the clincher. Where did the money come from to buy or bribe new locations? The books were clean of any evidence.

My questioning of the bookkeeper persisted along that line, and I noticed she was growing terribly uncomfortable. She said she knew nothing about that side of the business. The mobster and sales manager took care of selling to new customers and what they did and how they did it was beyond her knowledge and responsibility. She said I should take it up with the owner.

Interviewing mobsters is like dancing with an eel. They are very "slippery" when they talk at all. The mobster refused to talk to me without his lawyer and CPA, and when they arrived, they informed him to say nothing. However, since the business was a corporation and at that time not able to assert its Fifth Amendment rights, we issued a subpoena for all of the firm's accounting records for the three previous years. The subpoena was served on the mobster the next day in an environment that was, to say the least, hostile. He flared at me and accused me of harassment, unconventional, inappropriate, and unconstitutional behavior. But the records were delivered—a ton of them, which we in turn tagged, receipted for, and brought back to the office for further examination.

After two weeks of further review, we found the records to be so clean we could not believe it. So I took the liberty of telephoning the bookkeeper at home one evening. She seemed greatly troubled and said she did not want to speak on the phone. She asked that we meet her at her mother's home the next evening and we did.

What she told us was a marvel of simplicity. She was ordered by the mobster to withdraw $500 from each day's receipts and set it aside in a separate night depository bag to be placed in the company safe. The daily receipts would be minus that amount on the books of the company. His reason for the procedure, he alleged to her, was that it allowed him to deposit it into another company account, for which he would do all the accounting. (But he laughed when he told her that.) She noted that the bag was always empty in the morning and that when he went to Florida the sales manager took over the responsibility of "making the deposit."

Now our suspicions were confirmed, but beyond her testimony there was no way to corroborate the shortage. We still had to reconstruct actual sales to make a tax evasion case. So I pointedly asked her, "Where is the other set of books?" She said we had taken them all. I said "I mean the records which show what daily sales actually are." (I couldn't believe that a nontrusting racketeer would place any faith in his drivers' honesty.) She said haltingly, "There are some machine cards I was told to destroy which are in the loft above the office in the warehouse."

"What are machine cards?" I asked. She said that machine cards were a subsidiary record of what each machine was stocked with and the cash amount that was taken out each time a route driver serviced the machine. Once a month the cards were pulled and replaced with new ones. The old cards were returned so that a monthly reconciliation could be made with the driver's reported gross receipts from his locations, as a further control on the weekly summaries that were destroyed. An added purpose was to calculate the commission due the location owner, who was paid on a monthly basis by company check. The machine cards were signed by someone in authority at the location who apprized the firm of the commission amount due the firm. They were used to demonstrate an honest accounting of commissions due. (There must be some honor, even among thieves!)

We now had a method to reconstruct actual sales and could corroborate her allegations. However, the job of reconstructing sales was no easy chore. We had to manually review more than 12,000 machine cards to document the skimming operation because it was still a circumstantial case—we could not take a representative sample and project from that basis because courts are not prone to accept criminal cases built on probability theories. But we did win a conviction in the trial court and were sustained on appeal. Both the bookkeeper and sales manager testified on the government's behalf—the bookkeeper out of a sense of shame and guilt, and the sales manager to preserve his freedom.

CASE THREE: THE QUININE CARTEL

Two of my most interesting and exciting years of investigative experience were spent with the U.S. Senate Antitrust and Monopoly Subcommittee, for which I served as Chief Investigator.

The antitrust field is one in which an investigator must pit his skills against the very best in legal talent. Since they serve the interests of the country's largest and most sophisticated corporations, antitrust lawyers tend to be a rather crafty group and what they do not know about antitrust law, which is not much, is countervailed by an understanding of the political processes of the land and the people who man those political processes. So you are normally up against the most prestigious law firms in New York and Washington, firms such as Hogan and Hartson; Arnold & Porter; Covington & Burling; Steptoe & Johnson; Williams and Connolly; Wilmer, Cutler and Pickering; Rogers & Wells; Cadwalader, Wickersham & Taft; Cravath, Swaine and Moore; Dewey Ballantine; Mudge, Rose, Guthrie and Alexander; Paul, Weiss, Rifkind, Wharton & Garrison; Philips, Nizer, Benjamin, Krim & Balloon; and Sullivan and Cromwell. These firms have produced more attorneys general, Supreme Court justices, U.S. senators and cabinet members than all the other law firms combined in the United States. So it is really kind of fun to match wits with them. They are probably the best legal minds in the country, if not in the world.

I was involved in a number of antitrust investigations during 1964, 1965, and 1966—everything from the high cost of dying (the funeral home industry) to the high cost of children's books (children's book publishers). Interspersed with those investigations we also probed television advertising pricing practices, doctor-owned clinical labs and pharmacies, and the pricing of brewer's yeast, movie film rentals, and quinidine, a drug compound that certain heart patients must use to avoid fibrillation and arythmia. The latter was particularly interesting because it showed me how long lasting, convoluted, and insidious some price fixing schemes can be.

Our interest in the pricing of quinidine began when Senator Philip Hart (the Subcommittee chairman) began getting letters from elderly citizens in his home state of Michigan who were complaining about the fact that their prescriptions for quinidine had doubled or tripled in cost from 1964 to 1965. The letters were passed on to the staff, and we began to gather data on the world production and consumption of quinine, from which quinidine is extracted.

Two theories were advanced by the pharmaceutical manufacturers who made and distributed quinidine. The first one was that quinine water had recently become a popular beverage for mixing gin (gin and tonic). The new drink had depleted the world's stocks of quinine and price increases resulted from this surge in demand. The second one was that a new strain of malaria was affecting our servicemen in Vietnam and was not responding to the chemical synthetics of quinine developed in World War II. Quinine in its natural form, extracted from the bark of cinchona trees grown in Indonesia, the Congo, and some areas of South and Central America, was the only treatment that seemed to work on the new and more virulent malaria strain. The growing political instability of the nations producing the cinchona trees was another possible dimension of the problem. There were allegations that cinchona plantations in Indonesia, expropriated by the government when it won its freedom from the Netherlands after World War II, were untended and fell into disrepair; therefore, its production of the bark from which quinine was extracted was substantially down. New fields of trees had been planted elsewhere—Africa and South America—but their crop was insignificant because full production was still some years off and the expected yield from their trees were lower than that from Indonesian trees.

These allegations at first seemed very logical, and if we had been persuaded by logic alone we probably would have concluded our investigation after interviews with the pharmaceutical manufacturers. But we decided to seek confirmation of the "facts" before backing off, and a host of anomalies began to develop:

1. While one group of Defense Department officials were clamoring for more quinine for soldiers in Vietnam, another group was preparing and approving the sale of quinine from a government stockpile held by the GSA (General Services Administration).

2. Previous sales of quinine from the government stockpile had been made in earlier years and the most consistent successful bidder was a Dutch firm, the world's largest supplier and manufacturer of quinine. That firm and two West German chemical manufacturers were the world's major producers of quinine and quinine-related drug compounds. From 1961 through 1964, the Dutch firm had purchased 8.5 million ounces of quinine from the U.S. government's stockpile. The average price they paid was 20 cents an ounce but in 1965 the firm was selling quinine to U.S. drugmakers for an average of $2.00 an ounce—a substantial profit to say the least—about 1,000%.

3. The remaining government stockpile of quinine, inclusive of the malarial incident rate in Vietnam in 1964, was still enough to last one hundred years or more.

4. In researching the Dutch firm in the archives of the Library of Congress, we found in a *Fortune* magazine article that the firm and the two West German chemical companies were indicted and convicted of price fixing charges in New York City in 1928. The article recounted how these firms had controlled the world supply of quinine through a cartel arrangement that involved the Dutch government, Javanese cinchona plantation owners, and certain import firms in New York City and other international trade centers. As part of the legal settlement of the case, the court ordered a permanent injunction against the firms prohibiting price fixing practices and other antitrust law violations.

5.   The Dutch firm's latest bid (1964) for 4.5 million ounces from the GSA stockpile was more than the world price for quinine and thus more than its own production and distribution costs in the same year. (If they were not going to be able to manipulate world prices in the future, the transaction would have made no economic sense. A smart businessman does not pay $1.00 for something that has an immediate resale value of 80 cents, or at least not unless he knows for certain that the price will go up shortly. And the only one who can be assured of that is someone who controls the supply.)

These anomalies were enough for the senator to give us the green light to pursue the investigation more vigorously. What we discovered was shocking, to say the least.

1.   GSA, with prodding from the U.S. State Department, set the terms and conditions of sale of the quinine stockpile in such a way that only the Dutch firm could qualify as a responsible bidder. Even though a small amount of the quinine was supposed to be reserved for domestic (U.S.) manufacturers who could qualify as small businesses, their bids were rejected because they could not finance the purchases under the terms of sale, i.e., large cash deposits on bids and long periods for delivery, during which the original cash deposit would be held by the GSA.

2.   The allegation that servicemen in Vietnam were subject to a new strain of malaria was true; however, they were responding well to treatment with synthetics except in perhaps 20% of the cases.

3.   The cinchona plantations in Indonesia were not in disrepair, and while they had been taken over by the government they were still being managed by Dutch colonials. In fact, the government of Indonesia was cooperating with the Dutch and German combine in not overproducing the cinchona bark.

4.   The Dutch government, through its Kina (Quinine) Bureau, was actively involved in protecting the interests of its quinine manufacturer, N.V. Nederlandsche Kininefabriek, by seeking aid for its GSA purchases from the American embassy in Holland. The trading bait for these U.S. concessions was continued Dutch support for the North Atlantic Treaty Organization (NATO).

5.   Media stories in the United States about the need for quinine for servicemen in Vietnam, the state of disrepair of Indonesian plantations, the low yield from Congolese bark, and the political instability in countries producing cinchona bark were inspired, if not planted, by the Dutch and West German interests.

Despite the fact that the Dutch and German firms were bound by an injunction issued by a U.S. court to refrain from price fixing, we were powerless to issue subpoenas for their records since we had no authority overseas. We did have authority over their New York importing agencies, however, because they were

U.S. corporations, and we served them subpoenas. The documents we gathered from these agencies showed a clear case of control over supply and market price manipulation.

After having acquired a lion's share of the U.S. stockpile, which was the only thing that could have broken their stranglehold on the world's quinine supply, the Dutch and German combine began a consistent practice of price increase announcements that had as its basis the spurious stories which it either planted or inspired in the U.S. media. Another tactic was a "rationing" of quinine products when the world supply was sufficient for many years, which produced psychological shock waves in both the beverage and pharmaceutical industries as firms scampered for higher positions on the priority lists of the New York importing firms—their only source for quinine.

While we could not subpoena the Dutch and two West German firms to testify before the Subcommittee, the data we gathered from their importing agents in New York provided tangible proofs that a price fix did exist. The most damaging evidence came out of the files of the U.S. State Department. Our embassy in Holland was not only well aware of the existence of the quinine cartel but was prepared to support its efforts to acquire the GSA stockpile in order to maintain cordial relations with both the Dutch and Indonesian governments. For example, one "hot" letter from the State Department files reads as follows:

Department of State
August 23, 1956

BACKGROUND OF CARTEL DEVELOPMENTS IN
THE QUININE INDUSTRY
Quinine is derived from cinchona bark which is found primarily in Indonesia and in Latin America. The Indonesian product is of much higher quality. Quinine is manufactured in Europe and the United States as well as Indonesia.

EARLY CARTEL ARRANGEMENTS
Although trade restrictions in this industry date back to 1892, the first effective international cartel was organized in 1913. In that year, European and Indonesian manufacturers entered into an agreement with Indonesian planters[1] to protect their mutual interests. Under the agreement they organized a "Kina Bureau" to supervise its operation and settle any controversies which might arise. The Bureau was delegated the function of establishing bark delivery quotas among the various planters and fixing minimum prices for such deliveries. Under the agreement manufacturers were required to buy certain minimum supplies each year. If any manufacturer needed bark in excess of this minimum, the Bureau determined the extra amount that could be acquired. It also fixed sale prices which could be charged by manufacturers for quinine. All bark was required to be shipped to the Bureau's agency at Amsterdam so that all world manufacturers, whether or not parties to the agreement, had to buy Java bark from the Bureau through this centralized source. Indonesian producers were allowed to purchase bark directly in Java provided its use was confined to Indonesia.

[1] Indonesian manufacturers are in Bandoeng; cinchona is grown in Java.

The Bureau was made up of representatives of planters and manufacturers in equal numbers, the latter consisting of members of Netherlands, England, France, and Germany. Because of the inability of the French, British and German manufacturers to participate in negotiations during World War I, the Netherlands and Indonesian manufacturers represented the others in renewing the accord with the planters when it expired in 1918. It is known that they recognized the manufacturers exclusive representatives in negotiating the agreement's renewal in 1923 and again in 1928, the latter for a ten-year period. Although the American manufacturers do not appear to have been parties to this cartel, they were dependent upon the Kina Bureau for cinchona bark. As a result of the cartel's restrictions, only three American firms produced quinine prior to and during World War II.[2]

U.S. ANTRITRUST ACTION

The effects of the cartel arrangements between 1913 and 1928 led to U.S. Federal Grand Jury investigation of the quinine market in the latter year. The Grand Jury brought an indictment which in itself described the effect of the prevalent cartel practices on U.S. availability. The charges cited a conspiracy among European manufacturers designed to deprive the U.S. market of the benefits of competition. They were specifically charged with price-fixing of cinchona bark and its derivatives, restrictions on quinine production, and attempts to coerce American manufacturers into becoming parties to restrictive agreements. There was further evidence that the Kina Bureau and its New York selling agency were enforcing a market-sharing arrangement for bark and its derivatives in the United States.

Although the Government claimed legal jurisdiction over the cartel in view of its effect upon the American market, it was clear that effective action would be difficult since the principal defendants remained outside the United States. However, a consent decree was negotiated with the principal defendants in 1928, whereby they refrained from fixing retail prices in the United States of cinchona bark or derivatives, dividing the profits or territory within the United States, discriminating in price among purchasers within the United States or maintaining in force any contracts which would deny purchasers the right to deal in the products sold by a competitor.

Throughout the 1930's American quinine manufacturers attempted to obtain permission from the Netherlands manufacturers to carry larger stocks in the United States but such requests were invariably refused. During the Antitrust investigation, in order to provide a method of collecting fines in the event of a criminal conviction the Government had seized stocks in the United States belonging to Netherlands manufacturers. Therefore, the Dutch were reluctant to maintain stocks in the United States on their account. On the other hand, they refused to permit American manufacturers to maintain large stocks. Accordingly, American manufacturers attempted to develop a source of supply in Java independent of the cartel, but the Java planters refused to enter into any commercial relations which might antagonize the cartel participants.

Between the middle of 1940 and the end of 1941, American manufacturers and the Government made repeated efforts to increase substantially the cinchona stockpile in the United States. All such attempts, however, were resisted by the Kina Bureau and supplies were obtained only after lengthy negotiations. Following the Japanese attack on Pearl Harbor and the conquest of Java, the United States Government was forced to rely on the inferior Latin American Bark.

[2]Merck, New York Chemical, and Quinine Graves.

PRESENT SITUATION REGARDING INTERNATIONAL
CARTEL ACTIVITIES

The latest report in our files on the quinine cartel is a dispatch (No. 1953, dated April 27, 1951) from The Hague. It gives no information on the specific international membership of the Kina Bureau but does indicate that, as of 1951, the Bureau was actively functioning. According to the dispatch, " . . . the Kina Bureau is operating at this time in much the same manner as in previous years. The transfer of sovereignty of the Netherlands East Indies to the Indonesian Government has not affected their operations to any degree. The Kina Bureau has an agreement with the Indonesian Government whereby manufacturing and sales of quinine and related products are recognized to be a part of the Indonesian economic structure, and the Indonesian Government has delegated full responsibility and authority to the Kina Bureau to act as its agent in all matters concerning production and sales of quinine and related products. The Kina Bureau has long-term contracts with cinchona producers which, in practice, cover practically 100 percent of the production. Under the new Indonesian Government there are no restrictions on cinchona sales to non-members of the cartel, but, as long as the Government (Indonesia) honors the present Kina Bureau contracts, there is, in practice, little or no cinchona bark available for sales to non-members of the cartel.

The quinine cartel case is important from an investigative point of view because it demonstrates a major principle: confirm and corroborate facts. While a congressional committee is not bound by the rules of evidence, it is still important to distinguish fact from hearsay, fact from opinion, and fact from press releases. Had we accepted the pharmaceutical industries impressions of the causes for quinine and quinidine price escalations as the gospel truth, we never would have discovered the underlying facts.

A selection of the media reports on the quinine situation as taken from the Subcommittee's Hearings Report, which could have easily led us astray, is as follows:

EXHIBIT 45
MILITARY DEMAND FOR QUININE
(Extracts from News Stories)

"With a rapidly escalating war in a tropical area like Vietnam it probably was inevitable that U.S. troops would run into an old enemy—malaria. But few persons—medical or otherwise—predicted the dilemma that now faces U.S. medical authorities. At midweek, Army officials admitted the possibility of an epidemic among troops in Vietnam. Many types of malaria are found in Southeast Asia."

"A Vietnam jungle mosquito that breeds 'upside down' is giving Defense Department doctors almost as much worry as wounds inflicted by Communist Viet Cong guerrillas."

* * * * * *

"The new kind of malaria also has played an important role in drastic increases in quinine and quinidine prices."

* * * * * *

"Some Pentagon planners were described as having an 'absolute shaking fit' over the idea of a large number of troops being infected where they cannot be treated effectively." (*United Press International,* January 27, 1966)

"The resistant malaria has been so serious in Vietnam that by last November, American military doctors there feared they would soon be evacuating more sick than wounded soldiers." (*The New York Times,* March 16, 1966)

At the conclusion of our hearings, we referred the matter to the Antitrust Division of the Justice Department and they in turn took legal action against the cartel by invoking the permanent injunction features of the 1928 conviction of the cartel members. The price of quinine and quinidine shortly thereafter was lowered substantially and no further sales of government-owned quinine were made to the Dutch combine.

CASE FOUR: SAMMY G.—THE MAN WHO LIVED DOWN HIS PAST

The late 1950s was a marvelous time for the IRS Special Agents with a penchant for organized crime cases. The celebrated meeting of Mafia dons at Apalachin, New York in 1957 had finally convinced the general public that a sinister organization existed that had tentacles in every major city. It was something that many law enforcement agencies had been seriously concerned about but that had not yet fired the public's imagination. The crime bosses were seen as aged men practicing old world traditions that ordinary citizens did not need to fear. "They only kill their own and good riddance" seemed to be the public's attitude.

But with stepped-up intelligence and surveillance activity by law enforcement agencies even the hardliners on organized crime were surprised at the extent of the crime and corruption that followed in the wake of these tired, "old" men. In major cities across America it was found that the syndicate's people had managed to corrupt the criminal justice and political systems, the labor movement, and legitimate businesses. Politicians, police and judicial authorities, and labor and business leaders were all content to do their bidding in exchange for their largesse or support.

For me, personally, this sudden awareness of the sinister aspects of organized crime was a vindication. My agency, which knew better, was not inclined to do much about organized crime. The tax evasion cases on organized crime members were complex and protracted, and the hoods were able to buy the best legal and tax accounting services available. They were experts in "masking" their illegal financial transactions through foreign launderings, fronts, and legitimate businesses. Some were even able to bury their pasts. So police agencies preferred taking on the routine crimes and petty criminals; these cases were easier to make and the probability of conviction was greater.

But Apalachin changed all of that. No longer could law enforcement officials deny that a national syndicate existed, that it was rich and politically powerful, and that it was at the center of most of the crime in the United States. Organized crime was no revelation to me as I am the son of a Sicilian immigrant. I knew that it existed by the time I was twelve, perhaps before, when I saw the evidence around me in my ethnic neighborhood. I saw it in my father's fruit and produce business, where he had been its victim. Whether my superiors believed in its existence or not, I knew better.

My penchant for mob cases led to a nickname early in my career. My fellow agents referred to me as Rocky Kane, a television private-eye of fame in the mid-fifties. But by 1957, that had changed. There was a growing professional respect for my preoccupation with mob figures and I too had mellowed a bit from my moralizing and preaching ways. The Apalachin meeting convinced my superiors that perhaps more energy should be directed toward organized crime. An intelligence report I had written some months before was resurrected by my chief and sent to the National Office. The report showed a series of blood relationships and intermarriages among a number of the more prominent "families" of the East Coast, Midwest, and Southwest. The agency's new concern about organized crime led to a number of nationally coordinated programs, one dealing with the gambling activities of organized crime members and the other with a more concentrated effort at gathering organized crime intelligence.

By the middle of 1958 some interesting things were beginning to develop from the intelligence effort. Connections were found among the numbers operators and bookmakers of one region and those of other regions. Long-distance telephone call analyses showed that gamblers all over the country were in contact with one another on a daily or weekly basis. These we attributed to layoff betting, horse racing and sporting results communications, debt settling among the various gamblers, and transmissions of prerace or pregame odds. Patterns began to emerge from all these calls indicating that layoff centers existed for horse racing and sporting events and that the layoff centers also were responsible for setting pregame and prerace odds. For example, the line (odds) for professional basketball came out from Boston; for football, the line was set by a group in New York; for hockey, Minneapolis; for horse racing, Covington, Kentucky, etc. From reviewing toll call volumes, it seemed that every major gambler in America was in regular contact with his cronies all over the country. Thousands of calls a day were being made—the mob must have been the Bell's System's best customer, if it paid its bill, and often did not as we later learned. With a network of underworld figures in daily communication with one another, there was hardly any doubt left in my Intelligence Chief's mind that a national syndicate did exist, if not for all crimes at least for those involving gambling.

In the midst of this data gathering, we received an innocuous request from our Denver office. A toll analysis of phone calls made by a Colorado gambling group headed by the Smaldone brothers (Checkers and Flip-Flop Smaldone) showed several calls to a subscriber in a small central Michigan town—an odd place for gamblers to call, I thought, since it was 175 miles northwest of Detroit and in an area noted neither for gambling nor for any other kind of vice. The town was a junction point where old U.S. 27 and U.S. 10 converged, a midpoint between Detroit and the Straits of Mackinac, which divides the upper and lower Michigan peninsulas. I could not imagine what or who in central Michigan would have any reason to be in contact with gamblers in Colorado. So I did not give the inquiry much time and attention. I did learn the subscriber's name by issuing a subpoena to the Michigan Bell Telephone Company. Their records showed the subscriber to be one Samuel G. _____. His credit file indicated he was a petroleum explorer. I assumed the Smaldone's were taking some of their gambling profits and reinvesting them into oil properties.

Several months later another inquiry was received from our Newark, New Jersey office asking that we determine who the holder of a phone number in central Michigan was. By some quirk of fate that lead was assigned to me also. This time the calling number was the residence of a New Jersey hood—big in everything from gambling to loansharking to labor racketeering, and the number two man in a New York City family. He was also an Apalachin attendee.

I thought it might be sheer coincidence, but I nevertheless retrieved my earlier report and found the phone number was the same—Sammy G (Who is this guy, I thought. I've never heard of him before—nor have any of my agent colleagues. Why would a geologist in Michigan be in contact with gamblers in Colorado and New Jersey. I assumed he was some sort of "high roller" who did his betting out of state because the locals were too small to handle all his action.)

But it troubled me. I felt a little guilty about not pursuing the Colorado lead in more depth, so I decided to do a little background investigating on Mr. G. despite the protestations of my supervisor, who felt I had too much other work to do. I reassured him that I would not spend too much time on the lead but that I just could not let the matter rest with a carbon copy of my earlier report.

My first research effort was to review the IRS tax and intelligence files. The current intelligence files showed no references at all. The files of newspaper clippings and the Kefauver hearing reports on organized crime did not show anything either. His tax returns looked clean—no income from mysterious sources. In fact, he showed a substantial amount of income from what appeared to be legitimate sources, i.e., royalties, capital gains, rents, commissions, etc. The commissions concerned me because mob members tended to use that method of reporting income. Their other favorite method was "speculation." (One hood near Detroit habitually reported income from speculation, some years as much as $150,000.)

The only other aspect of his filing record that seemed peculiar was the fact that his returns were prepared by a Detroit accountant who was a former IRS Revenue Agent and a very good one at that, whose expertise as an Agent was in tax fraud. But that seemed strange too. Why would a taxpayer so far up north use a CPA in Detroit? He seemed to have no business interests in Detroit. There must have been good accountants closer to home, or at least in Flint, Bay City, or Saginaw, somewhat closer than Detroit.

My next visit was to the morgue files of a large Detroit newspaper, whose name indexes tended to be much better than ours. There I began to have some luck. While there was nothing current on Sammy G., there were several references to him going back to the late 1920s and mid-1930s, with no references from about 1929 to 1934.

The clippings for the 1920s were references to Sammy G.'s arrests, mostly for gambling, suspicion of bootlegging, disorderly person, etc. Nothing big—no murders, no robberies, nothing of a serious criminal nature. The stories linked Sammy G. with two different criminal groups; a Jewish group and an Irish group (the Purple Gang and the Sullivan-Fitzgerald Gang.) His alleged occupation was bookmaker.

In the mid-1930s clipping files, which were fewer, Sammy G. was shown as attending the funeral of and serving as pallbearer of, a notorious criminal lawyer who had left New York City under a cloud in the early 1930s and moved to Michigan where he became quite rich in the oil business. The lawyer was killed during an argument over a business deal in a hotel in Clare, Michigan. Since Clare did not have a Jewish cemetery or a synagogue, his remains were sent to Detroit for burial. The newspaper article indicated that a number of well-known Detroit business leaders and politicians attended the funeral along with some Prohibition-era bootleggers, among them the Goldstein brothers. (The Goldsteins were later indicted during the rackets-busting grand jury headed by Judge Homer Ferguson, who was elected to the U.S. Senate for his fearless cleanup of political corruption in Detroit—corruption of police and city officials by gamblers, notably the Goldsteins and several other groups of Italian and Irish heritage.)

Well, that seemed enough for me to convince my supervisor that Mr. G. warranted a little more probing and perhaps even a case file opening. He disagreed, but he did allow me to serve a subpoena on Michigan Bell for the toll call records of Mr. G. A few days later an official of Bell called and said the toll call records were available but that I should plan to spend a few days there because there were hundreds of them. Bingo! I thought I could hardly contain myself. I practically ran from the Federal Building to the Bell offices, only two blocks away.

I scheduled all the calls on columnar pads for about two days and then sent requests to the appropriate IRS offices around the country for determination of who the recipients of Sammy's calls were. Through the Royal Canadian Mounted Police (RCMP) I was able to get the Canadian subscribers.

The responses, which began to return in a month, read like a rogue's gallery. Sammy G. was in contact with practically every mob family in the United States and Canada. But there was more. He had been in contact with at least a dozen stockbrokers in both countries, bankers in New York, Miami, Toronto, London, Paris, and Rome, Las Vegas casinos, oil and motor company executives, lawyers, accountants, and politicians. Yet I still had to ask myself who is this guy and what the hell does he do for a living? The mountain of information I had accumulated still did not provide any sort of clear picture. The toll calls also showed he traveled a great deal because a large number of calls were made by him from Denver, New York, Las Vegas, Miami, Los Angeles, and other cities across the United States to his wife in Michigan. She apparently did not travel with him very much.

After studying and analyzing the data for some time, I saw some patterns begin to emerge. For example, almost every call he made to a certain number in Toronto, a broker, was followed immediately by a call to a New York City broker and then to a New Jersey number, which was the headquarters for a large corporation, in whose stock his return for the previous year showed he had made a great deal of money.

The broker in Toronto had a reputation for being "shady," a peddler of penny stocks in questionable mining ventures in Canada. He was regarded by the Mounties as a front for Canadian and U.S. hoodlums. He had a reputation for laundering money as far back as Prohibition and was a close personal friend of the financial wizard of organized crime in the United States, a resident of Miami, but at that time was known more as the czar of casino gambling in Havana. (These two principals were later the architects of the mob's move into casinos in the Bahamas.)

Because of the social, political, and underworld prominence of Sammy G.'s callers, his case file was made a matter of National Office interest. The new classification gave me some investigative advantage. It got my boss off my back for awhile, but better yet, my leads to other offices got expeditious handling and the agents assigned to cover the leads were senior types with some experience in organized crime matters. Another advantage was that information to which I might never become privy became available; information from sources I never knew and never met nor asked any questions about.

One such tidbit, reported through international channels, was that Sammy G. was in trouble with certain syndicate leaders of Italian ancestry on the East Coast. They were late arrivers on the Havana gambling casino scene and by the time their casino was about to be opened, Fidel Castro took everything over and sent them packing for home with their investment totally lost. Someone had to account for their money and since Sammy had been their contact, sponsor and coinvestor, they looked to him for recoupment of their losses. There was some evidence showing that Sammy's investment colleagues were concerned, shortly after construction of the casino had started, that Castro might come to power and that Sammy's contacts with the Batista regime would not do them any good. Sammy allayed their fears by suggesting he could take care of Castro, that Castro "owed" his group for arms and ammunition. He was taking no chances. But then Castro reneged, and in the code of the underworld, Sammy had to make good for his investors—or else.

Sammy's answer was to cut them in on his stock promotion schemes, which turned out to be his major preoccupation and chief source of income. He also supplied money laundering services and phony tax shelters. In his prime he probably moved $1,000,000 a month for various mobsters. (Who would suspect a geologist from a small town in central Michigan? A guy who looked more like a professor than someone who would be cast in a Hollywood gangster movie?)

The IRS National Office, realizing that in Sammy G.'s active travels around the world he had at one time or another consorted with every major syndicate boss and swindlers of all descriptions, political leaders, and business tycoons, authorized me to conduct a more intensive background investigation.

One of my first steps was visiting Sammy's hometown. Since Sammy was the leading citizen of a small town, it was difficult to make inquiries without arousing his suspicions. An outsider who asks too many questions will soon "blow his cover." So I approached this part of my work with great care. I used, as a pretense, a story that I was in town as a magazine writer who was digging into the twenty-year-old shooting of the New York Lawyer mentioned previously. Much to my surprise, everyone alive at the time of the shooting wanted to talk about it. Each had his own version too. But there was enough repetition to reconstruct a scenario of what had happened, and better yet, some of those interviewed talked about Sammy's activities in that era as well.

The story I pieced together went something like this. The lawyer showed up in town about 1933 or 1934, allegedly to acquire some oil leases for clients in New York City. A year or so before an oil discovery brought sudden wealth to the area. Farmers who had been eking out their existence on submarginal land during the midst of the Depression were suddenly flush with money or being vigorously courted by oil company lease buyers. It was a heady experience for most of them. They had rarely earned more than $1,000 a year from their farms and now they were being offered $25,000 to $50,000 for the mineral rights alone. That suddenness of wealth has a way of corrupting even the most conservative dirt farmer. With little else to do with their new-found wealth, many of them began to drift into town for a little Saturday night fun. There were only a few attractions in town—a movie theater, a few general stores, a couple of restaurants, two bars, and a hotel. The hotel became the favorite drinking spot for the local gentry, the visiting farmers and the oil company surveyors, geologists, roustabouts, and lease buyers. There was joy and great happiness at the hotel on weekends as news spread of the latest oil strike. Farmers who a few months before were setting their dinner tables with nothing but pig hocks and turnips were now ordering steaks and drinks for the house.

Such good news travels fast and the word got back to the Goldstein brothers in Detroit. Joe, being the brighter of the two, saw great opportunity in the lifestyle of the nouveau riche and in the profits to be made in the oil business. He had an old friend and comrade-in-arms there—Sammy G. Sammy had been laying low as a result of a disagreement he had in the late 1920s with his then partners in gambling, the Sullivan-Fitzgerald gang. They claimed Sammy short-changed them $10,000 on a gambling venture of some kind and were eagerly pursuing him in an effort to collect. He could not pay up and could not enlist the support of either the Italian or Jewish groups, who also had serious doubts about his integrity in the matter. Since he could not buy his way out of the dilemma with cash or influence, he left Detroit and got lost in the north woods in 1929.

Central Michigan at that time had nothing of interest to bootleggers and gamblers in Detroit, so Sammy chose to settle down there. He soon won respectability by marrying a local schoolteacher who was highly esteemed in the community and he became a real estate salesman. Unknown to Sammy was the fact that what lay under the ground was much more valuable than the scrubby potatoes and hearty root vegetables that popped up through the ground in late summer.

When the black gold began oozing from the ground, Sammy decided to come out of his "deep cover." He suggested to Goldstein that millions could be made in the oil business, that he knew many of the farmers in the area, and that they trusted him more than the city slicker oil company leasemen. He would buy their mineral rights and in turn sell them to the oil companies at a substantial markup because he knew how to bargain and negotiate. The idea sounded attractive to Goldstein so he and Sammy incorporated with Sammy supplying the buying and selling expertise.

They found however, that the major oil companies and wildcatters were a crafty lot too. Bidding wars broke out between Sammy and his competitors for the choice farm lands and more capital was needed. Beyond that, a bidding war with the same people you ultimately had to sell to did not make much economic sense. If you would not sell them your 1,000-acre rights they could always buy around you, and since they had the capital to drill the oil before you could, your investment was not likely to appreciate very much.

Since Prohibition had ended, the Goldstein crowd had to rely more on its profits from gambling and prostitution to maintain itself, and gambling was becoming very competitive as other bootleggers, caught with declining profits, also entered the business. Short of cash with which to compete with the major oil companies, Goldstein enlisted the aid of New York City hoodlums. They were intrigued by the promise of rich and quick profits in oil to supplement their declining profits from liquor, but to protect their investment they sent one of their favorite lawyers, who was courting disbarment, to make certain that Sammy G. and Goldstein lived up to their part of the bargain.

Sammy G. and the lawyer made a great combination in central Michigan. Both were highly creative, glib, and personable. But even with their natural talents, competing with the "haves" of the oil industry was no mean challenge. They were really neophytes—the Davids versus the Goliaths. One thing they knew more about than their big competitors, however, was gambling. The lawyer particularly was a "cool hand" at poker.

Sammy arranged for Saturday night poker games at the hotel, in which he cut into the pots as a houseman and his lawyer-confederate displayed his virtues with a deck of cards. Leases, which could not be bought at any price during the week, were turned over as collateral for the right to draw an inside straight. Fortunately not too many straights were ever drawn so Sammy and the lawyer began to flourish. The friendly poker games continued with Sammy supplying the facilities and social amenities, and things were going well. The Goldstein Oil Company prospered and not only owned leases but began to drill some of its own wells.

The lawyer added a local resident as a partner to win more credibility. After all, New Yorkers in central Michigan are not the most acceptable companions, particularly when they are of a different faith, have a funny accent, and seem overly aggressive. Unfortunately for the lawyer, the man he selected as a partner tended to be a hothead and easily aroused to anger. One Saturday night he joined his lawyer-partner in the poker game at the hotel. After losing heavily and drinking much, an argument ensued with the lawyer, who had won most of his money, and he shot and killed him.

Life must have been cheap in central Michigan in those days or the local folks did not like outsiders, because the lawyer's killer was only sentenced to a short term in the county jail—less than a year.

Sammy continued for a while, but after the death of his lawyer–colleague, things did not go as well. However, he learned a great lesson in human behavior: folks with new-found wealth and nothing to do with it are real suckers for games of almost any kind. Gold mine fever is not listed as a disease in any of the medical textbooks but every conman in the world can quickly diagnose it: pious hopes and dreams of glory, coupled with a large measure of greed and carelessness. What a formula for success.

So Sammy's next stop in the mid-1930s was in southern Illinois and Indiana, where another oil strike had occurred. Using the same modus operandi, Sammy placed himself in a local hotel with a deck of cards and a green felt table. But this time he was on his own. Goldstein had been paid off completely, still owned many leases, and had also bought off the Sullivan-Fitzgerald gang for Sammy. Peace had been made. Sammy had a track record of faithful and profitable service for the mob bosses, and he could set out on his own. Sammy did have a few problems, however. His card games were raided on several occasions by the local sheriffs but the only penalties were small fines.

Sammy's contacts with syndicate layoff centers added to his stature with clients whose gambling interests were in games other than poker and craps. He was able to steer their business to friends in the big cities. And of course they appreciated such high-class customers as oil industry executives, wildcatters who struck black gold, and local politicos whose pockets had been enriched during the frenetic days of a new strike by doing favors on zoning and land use and special permits. Sammy continued to prosper throughout World War II and learned enough about the oil business to be retained as a consultant by several large firms for purchasing oil properties.

His next stop was Colorado where he joined with a Western wildcatter in a drilling venture. Now he was acquiring leases for his own account and drilling for oil. But his contact with gamblers was still an important part of business life. He enjoyed a little action on his own on sporting events, such as hockey, football, and prize fights. One of his arrests in Indiana occurred in a hockey layoff center that was run by a former Detroit gambler who was later indicted for attempting to fix hockey games. Sammy claimed he was only visiting the establishment at the time of the raid. He was charged with being a disorderly person and released after a small fine and after he presented a business card stating he was a field representative for a large Cleveland oil company.

With the introduction of casino gambling in Las Vegas after World War II he was able to steer many of his friends in the oil business to "Bugsy" Siegel's

Flamingo Hotel and thereafter to the Desert Inn, which was owned by an old Detroit friend and several of his cronies from Cleveland's Mayfield Road Gang.

Sometime in the early 1950s, Sammy met a high stakes roller, land developer, and stock swindle artist whose background was as mysterious as Sammy's own. A recent immigrant from the Philippines, the developer hit the financial community with great style and verve. He was the original conglomerate, slapping together an admixture of manufacturing, land development, and other assorted enterprises into a company he called Shawano Development. The original money in Shawano came from a group of rich Filipinos who entrusted their fortunes with him for American investment. The stock swindler went about seeking investment opportunities and along the way picked up Shawano Development, which owned some land in Florida that was expected to rise rapidly in value as people from all over America's northern states sought a little winter solace from the cold.

Sammy traded some oil leases and stock in one of his own enterprises for stock in Shawano Development. Within a short time Shawano's stock price soared upward and Sammy made a small fortune, but not before cutting in some of his Desert Inn buddies for a piece of the pie. Unfortunately, many other investors also bought Shawano because of its meteoric rise but they were not as lucky. The stock swindler's lifestyle and gambling debts were too much for the corporation to afford and before long the Securities and Exchange Commission began to look into Shawano. What they found did not impress them and action was brought against him, Sammy, and several of his friends in the high command of the Desert Inn. They were later convicted of stock fraud.

Sammy's star was beginning to fade in the late 1950s. He had brought one group of investors in a Havana gambling venture to financial ruin. To make good, he provided them with investment opportunities in "hyped" stocks that allowed them to recoup some of their losses but there was still some bitterness by them toward Sam. He then allied himself with the Las Vegas group but they too found themselves in a financial mess and facing criminal prosecution.

Sammy's last scam was selling phony tax shelters to rich people, who for the most part had shady backgrounds. It was a simple kind of scam, a paper scam. Sammy merely purported to sell fractional interests in nonexisting or depleted oil wells which then were used by the taxpayers as a basis for deducting alleged intangible drilling costs and depletion allowances from their other income. The legitimate businessmen among his clients were unaware that nothing, no real or tangible property, backed up the paper Sammy was selling. But since they were rich and in the highest tax brackets, their losses were underwritten by the smaller taxpayers, by those who did not know about or could not afford such tax-saving schemes.

The final word on Sammy (who has since died) is that among these well-heeled citizens who were joint adventurers with him, whose "markers" he backed at Las Vegas casinos and whose gambling advice they sought, are some of the most prominent industrialists in America; leaders and executives of Fortune 500 companies. They never knew of Sammy's criminal history until later in his career and never knew that their partners in some of Sammy's oil ventures were the mob leaders of every major city in America.

Appendix 1

Incidents of Corporate Fraud

1. "High Performance Fakery" by executives is on the rise! This fraud mainly involves overstating sales or understating costs. Three recent incidents were reported in the *Wall Street Journal:* JWT Group, Inc. (3/30/82), DATA-POINT (5/27/82), and McCORMICK & CO. (6/1/82). Undue pressures by top management on subordinates for performance was apparently involved in each case.

2. PENTRON INDUSTRIES, INC. Two former executives (president and vice president of Sales) were sued by the company for using $500,000 of PENTRON's funds for unauthorized purposes, i.e., specious sales commissions. (*Wall Street Journal,* 6/1/82)

3. BANKERS TRUST COMPANY. Six persons (including four former employees) were indicted in New York City on charges of conspiring to embezzle $1.2 million from the bank. The scheme involved the conversion of funds from inactive accounts that were about to be escheated to the State of New York. A routine audit uncovered the fraud. (*Wall Street Journal,* 5/27/82)

4. CHROMALLOY AMERICAN CORPORATION. A class action suit was filed against CHROMALLOY and its outside auditors, Peat, Marwick and Mitchell, which alleged that because the firm understated its insurance reserves, CHROMALLOY's assets and earnings were materially overstated and inflated. The suit followed a company announcement that a computation error relating to reserves for losses and loss adjustment expenses would lower its previous four years earnings by $15.2 million! (*Wall Street Journal,* 5/26/82)

5. CHASE MANHATTAN BANK. Two former commercial lending officers of the bank were indicted for fraudulently funneling $18 million in unsecured loans to a Florida land developer, who diverted the funds for his own use and for use by the two lending officers. (*Wall Street Journal* 5/21/82)

6. Criminal charges were brought against employees of the UNIVERSITY of MARYLAND HOSPITAL. A computer operator at the hospital was

charged with embezzling $40,000 by submitting false invoices, which were processed through the hospital's computer. A former assistant data processing manager accepted a $41,000 bribe from one data processing consultant and conspired with another consultant to steal $126,000 from the hospital by submitting false invoices for software services. Both the computer operator and the assistant data processing manager had previous convictions for data processing related crimes! The hospital did not, as a matter of course, conduct background investigations on data processing employment applicants. (*Computer World*, 5/31/82)

7. MAGNETIC PERIPHERALS, INC., a subsidiary of CONTROL DATA CORPORATION, was another victim of computer crime. An accounts payable terminal operator of MAGNETIC PERIPHERALS and her boyfriend conspired to defraud the company by fabricating invoices from a fictitious vendor, a firm which they had formed earlier. Five checks totaling $155,000 were issued to the phony vendor after which the terminal operator and her boyfriend left for sunnier climates. The operator finally turned herself in to the police and disclosed the fraud after her boyfriend tried to reconcile with his estranged wife and began to physically abuse the operator. The investigating police officer alleged that MAGNETIC PERIPHERALS was too busy conducting business to build in any safeguards for its computer! (*Computerworld*, 5/3/82)

8. DATA TERMINAL SYSTEMS, INC. of Boston was sued by a shareholder who alleged the firm misled stock purchasers by "recklessly issuing bullish news." The company's executives predicted better sales and earnings in the spring of 1980, but reported a sharp earnings drop in the third quarter, which ended October 31, 1980. The shareholder criticized the company for failing to disclose slowing sales and earnings growth, rising parts costs, and overstated inventory values. The company has denied the charges. (*Wall Street Journal*, 6/7/82)

9. DATAPOINT CORPORATION, a San Antonio computer maker, was also the subject of a stockholder's suit claiming the firm misrepresented its financial data by engaging in a "warehousing and brokerage scheme" to inflate sales. Customer orders were booked as sales in advance by certain DATAPOINT marketing representatives to achieve sales goals. This later resulted in an "unusually high level of returned products" according to the firm's CEO. The company is contesting the charges alleged by its shareholders. (MIS *Week*, 8/18/82)

10. A former vice president of the MIDLOTHIAN STATE BANK (Illinois) pleaded guilty in a case involving the embezzlement of $1,250,000. The embezzlement scheme went on for about nine years before it was uncovered. (*Wall Street Journal*, 6/7/82)

11. The Securities Exchange Commission (SEC) penalized a small CPA firm located in Waltham, Massachusetts for failing to report properly a $235,000 embezzlement from a client firm, HERMITITE CORP. The SEC charged the firm conducted audits of HERMITITE "with a marked disregard for

generally accepted accounting principles.'' (SEC actions against accountants have declined during the past few years. Critics say the Commission is growing soft on the auditing profession, but the SEC defends its position by claiming that auditing is improving.) (*Wall Street Journal,* 8/20/82)

12. A Boston federal grand jury indicted a former supervisor in the BANK of NEW ENGLAND's proof and control department for embezzling $30,000. The bank provided custodial and record keeping services for a number of investment companies, over which the accused had some responsibility. The indictment charged that he substituted his own name or account number for those of the actual buyers of shares in the funds. He then used the computerized record keeping and correction system to conceal the imbalances and avoid detection. (This is another example of an input scam, i.e., altering or fabricating computer input, or deceiving the computer.) One possible defense against bank employee scams of this type might be to keep employee accounts (loans and deposits) segregated from customer accounts. Any intergroup transfer (customer to employee or vice versa) could then be flagged for audit or exception-to-the-rule reporting purposes). (*Computerworld,* 8/23/82)

13. The head of GOULD's INC.'s development laboratory was indicted in St. Louis for allegedly stealing a total of $300,000 in cash and computer equipment. Phony invoices were apparently used to deceive GOULD. (*Computerworld,* 8/16/82)

14. VALLEY INDUSTRIES, INC., a St. Louis maker of steel products, fired a vice president after its internal audit staff discovered a diversion of about $2.6 million in corporate funds. The funds were diverted through phony invoices for paving work and machinery designs. The phony invoices showed no street address or phone number for the vendors who allegedly supplied the services. VALLEY has recovered $700,000 through restitution and has $500,000 more in insurance coverage.(The FBI is investigating the case.) (*Wall Street Journal,* 9/20/82)

15. The former CEO of RUSCO INDUSTRIES, INC. was alleged to have cost the company $2.7 million by making "nondisclosed insider transactions" according to a report by the firm's internal audit committee. The allegations included the use of corporate funds for loans to the CEO and his friends and relatives, with little effort made to collect on the loans. (*Wall Street Journal,* 9/24/82)

16. SAXON INDUSTRIES, INC. and three former executives were cited by the SEC for falsifying company records. The SEC charged that the officials created fictional inventories worth $75 million by listing additional inventory after the physical count was taken, by programming the company's computers to automatically add inventory, and by transferring fake inventories from one division to another. SAXON is now under court protection (Chapter 11). (*Wall Street Journal,* 9/10/82)

17. PENN SQUARE BANK was in the news again. The Oklahoma City bank, which collapsed under the weight of questionable loans made to oil and gas

interests in the Southwest, was the victim of kickbacks, misapplications of funds, bank fraud, concealment, wire fraud, falsified books, and interstate transportation of stolen property, or so says a congressional committee. Federal banking authorities have referred thirty fraud-related cases to the U.S. Department of Justice for investigation, with more expected soon. (*The New York Times,* 9/28/82)

18. A former EDP employee of TEXACO, INC. and his wife were indicted for stealing $18,000 from the company in an accounts payable-type scam. The employee instructed TEXACO's computer to pay his wife the rent for land she allegedly leased to TEXACO by assigning her an alphanumerical code as a lessor and then ordering that payments be made. (The lesson here is simple: *never* let a data entry clerk in accounts payable, who processes payment claims, also have access to the approved vendor master file for additions or deletions. Doing so violates the separation of duties principle of internal control.) (*Computerworld,* 6/28/82)

19. A federal grand jury in Washington, D.C. returned an indictment on conspiracy and tax charges against the BANK of NOVA SCOTIA and seven promoters of a coal and methanol Research and Development tax shelter. The charges involve the sale of interests in the tax shelter, which provided $122.5 million in questionable tax deductions for the investors. (While the SEC is moving strongly against "insider" trading, the IRS is vigorously pursuing questionable tax shelters.) (*Wall Street Journal,* 10/1/82)

20. An ARA SERVICES, INC. employee was indicted by a Philadelphia grand jury for defrauding his employer of more than $250,000. The employee was the director of the company's fleet services and used the units' checking account for personal expenses, i.e., fifteen cars, two speedboats, and his daughter's wedding. (*Wall Street Journal,* 10/21/82)

21. A former procurement manager of RAYTHEON CO was found guilty by a Washington, D.C. jury of accepting bribes from a company contractor who provided freight forwarding services. More than $1.0 million was allegedly paid to the procurement manager and RAYTHEON's senior manager in Saudi Arabia, who had secured the services of the freight forwarder to ship modular housing units from the United States to Saudi Arabia. The bribe payments were allegedly added to freight charges. (*Wall Street Journal,* 10/20/82)

Offshore bank secrecy policies are coming under more attack by U.S. courts. Countries such as Switzerland, Panama, and the Cayman islands, which have been havens for dope peddlers, tax evaders, and inside traders, are being ordered to make disclosures about account holders in situations where tax, securities, and other federal violations are suspected. (See the *Wall Street Journal,* 10/14/82)

22. JWT GROUP, INC. (J. Walter Thompson) said that its outside audit firm will provide $1.0 million in services and $1.3 million in cash. This spring JWT discovered "irregularities" in its television barter syndication unit,

which resulted in recasting its profits downward by some $30 million for several previous years. Fictitious computer entries were allegedly made to inflate gross revenues of the unit. JWT said the "contributions" by its audit firm will help pay some of the costs incurred in investigating the matter. (*Wall Street Journal,* 10/22/82)

Speaking of accounting firms, DELOITTE, HASKINS and SELLS is conducting research to determine whether the communication of financial information to external users (shareholders, creditors) can be improved. Footnotes and supplementary material added to annual reports have become so complex that only accountants and attorneys can comprehend them. A "summary reporting" of these data might perhaps be more meaningful. (See *Director's Monthly,* October 1982, a publication of the National Association of Corporate Directors, Washington, DC)

23. The SEC, in an administrative proceeding, took action against RONSON CORPORATION concerning the accounting practices followed by a former RONSON subsidiary in California (RONSON HYDRAULIC UNITS CORPORATION—RHUCOR). For a period of five years prior to its sale in 1980, RHUCOR understated its expenses and recorded as sales products that had not been completed. These tactics resulted in an overstatement of profits by the subsidiary and were allegedly committed to meet the unit's profit goals. Arbitrary increases were also allegedly made to the unit's monthly ending inventory to overstate profits for the period.

RONSON settled the charges with the SEC by neither admitting nor denying them, and agreed to report accurately in the future. (*Wall Street Journal,* 11/5/82; *Legal Times,* 11/8/82)

24. The cost accounting manager of NABISCO BRANDS INC.'s office in Burlingame, California was accused of defrauding the company of $2.1 million. The cost accounting manager allegedly opened a post office box and bank account in the name of a fictitious company, which then was used to bill NABISCO for services never performed. The defalcation was discovered by the firm itself, who enlisted the aid of the FBI in its investigation. (*Wall Street Journal,* 11/5/82)

25. The Justice Department charged a former vice president of the NATIONAL ASSOCIATION OF SECURITIES DEALERS with mail fraud. The official allegedly billed the NASD $45,000 for nonexistent software services through a phony company he set up. The NASD official was a senior manager in the Association's data processing department. (*Wall Street Journal,* 11/3/82)

26. PEPSICO, INC. was sued by two shareholders who alleged that it filed false and misleading financial statements because of irregularities in its overseas operations. The irregularities resulted in $92.1 million in overstated earnings over a five-year period and overstated assets of $79.4 million. Also joined in the shareholder class action suit were fifteen of PEPSICO's current and past directors and its outside auditors. PEPSICO itself

made the irregularities known after it conducted its own investigation into the matter. Internal controls have since been tightened and a dozen employees of its foreign subsidiary have been terminated. (*Wall Street Journal,* 12/20/82)

27. BANK OF AMERICA and MERRILL LYNCH were the joint victims of a computer fraud engineered by insiders at both firms which involved the unauthorized reprogramming of the BANK of AMERICA computer in a scheme to defraud it and MERRILL LYNCH of $200,000. A computer operator for the BANK OF AMERICA has been arrested and named as a coconspirator with a MERRILL LYNCH insider, who has not yet been arrested. The scheme involved the BANK OF AMERICA computer operator gaining access to a terminal and inflating the balances of three accounts held by a MERRILL LYNCH customer, the coconspirator. The MERRILL LYNCH insider then modified records at that firm to show that funds in the customer's account were disbursable (though based on bogus checks issued on the BANK OF AMERICA inflated accounts). The scheme did not accomplish its desired results because the BANK OF AMERICA's programming controls were tight enough to identify the terminal and the operator who was making programming changes. Only $17,000 was stolen before the plot was discovered. (*Computerworld,* 12/20/82)

28. In another allegation of computer tapping, a federal grand jury in Washington, D.C. is investigating whether a former Federal Reserve economist tried to access the Reserve's computer for sensitive and confidential information. The economist, who had left the Federal Reserve and was now working on Wall Street as a "Fed Watcher," was required by his new employer to analyze "Fed" credit policies for investment recommendation purposes. The Reserve discovered something was amiss when a caller from New York attempted to gain access to its money supply data base by use of a canceled password. The call was traced back to a Wall Street brokerage firm. (*Wall Street Journal,* 12/10/82)

29. Four ex-employees of the FEDERAL RESERVE BANK OF NEW YORK's Bulk Verification Section were sued by the bank to recover $93,000, allegedly stolen by them and converted to their personal use. (*Wall Street Journal,* 1/26/82)

30. CROCKER NATIONAL BANK of Los Angeles filed a suit accusing eleven people, including seven officials of a Las Vegas, Nevada bank, of operating a check-kiting scheme which cost CROCKER about $2.4 million. (*Wall Street Journal,* 1/7/82)

31. In another bank check-kiting scheme, a federal jury in St. Paul, Minnesota convicted an independent banker (DEIL O. GUSTAFSON) of covering overdrafts on accounts. The overdrafts involved the TROPICANA HOTEL in Las Vegas, in which Gustafson was part owner at the time. The overdrafts were intended to help the TROPICANA overcome its cash-flow problems. A codefendant of Gustafson, JOSEPH V. AGOSTO, was convicted also. Agosto is one of the defendants in the CROCKER suit men-

tioned above and also faces trial this spring in Kansas City for his alleged involvement in "skimming" casino proceeds from the TROPICANA before it was acquired by RAMADA INNS. (*Wall Street Journal,* 1/25/83)

32. The former CEO of DATA ACCESS SYSTEMS, INC. (GERALD R. CICCONI) was sentenced to four years in prison and fined $20,000 for transporting checks fraudulently obtained across state lines. The alleged crime took place before Cicconi became CEO of DATA ACCESS, a computer distributor in Blackwood, New Jersey. The SEC, in a report filed with the federal court, accuses Cicconi of using a company in which he was a principal partner to divert DATA ACCESS's funds for his personal use. More than $9.0 million is involved in the fund diversions. (*Wall Street Journal,* 1/26/83)

33. The former marketing vice president of CRAWFORD ENTERPRISES, INC. pleaded guilty to making subrosa payments to an official of PEMEX, the Mexican state oil company, to secure contracts for oil- and gas-field equipment. CRAWFORD fired the vice president in 1979 and has pleaded innocent to charges that it was involved in a scheme to pay $10 million to Mexican oil officials to secure orders for natural gas compression machinery. (*Wall Street Journal,* 1/7/83)

34. In an alleged domestic cash laundering operation, a grand jury in Newark, New Jersey is looking into charges that a municipal bond house provided unregistered, easily negotiable bearer bonds to certain customers for cash, without reporting the sales transactions to the IRS as required by federal law. (Cash transactions over $10,000 at banks and brokerage houses must be reported.) Some of the bond purchasers were alleged to be members of organized crime. (*Wall Street Journal,* 1/5/83)

35. Who is most prone to unethical practices in gathering competitive intelligence? The defense and aerospace industries says William F. Glueck of the University of Georgia. (See *Business Policy and Strategic Management.* New York: McGraw-Hill, 1980, pp. 147–152) Professor Glueck's book is good reading for those subscribers interested in strategic planning and protecting trade secrets. Other findings in his research on those most prone to unethical competitive spying: (1) younger executives; (2) marketing executives; (3) executives in advertising, media, and publishing; and (4) small firms.

36. A former principal with ERNST & WHINNEY's New York City office was sentenced to thirty-nine weekend stays in prison for using information to trade in the stock of DRUG FAIR, INC., a firm with whom an E&W client (Gray Drug Stores, Inc., of Cleveland, Ohio) was considering a merger or acquisition. As an "insider" with E&W, the principal learned of the plans and that the offering price for DRUG FAIR's stock would be about double its then market price. He netted about $46,000 on the transaction and has since repaid that amount. (*Wall Street Journal,* 2/4/83)

37. FOOTE, CONE and BELDING, the ad agency, reported it is investigating a possible embezzlement at its Philadelphia subsidiary. It was discovered in

a routine internal audit that an unknown amount was diverted by an employee or employees to his/their own use. The subsidiary, AITKIN-KYNETT & CO., does about $30,000,000 a year in billings. (*Wall Street Journal,* 2/1/83)

38. A California CPA was barred by a federal judge in San Francisco from auditing financial statements of public companies. Charges were brought against the accountant by the SEC, which alleged that he signed an unqualified opinion of the accuracy of OLYMPIC GAS & OIL, INC.'s financial statements for the six months ending 8/31/78 without conducting an examination. The Commission also claimed that the accountant had not properly tested the sales account for the year ending 2/28/79 and that sales were materially overstated. (*Wall Street Journal,* 2/18/83)

39. Sixteen banks sued FOX & CO., former auditors of SAXON INDUSTRIES, INC. and SAXON's former top officers and directors. The suit stems from SAXON's alleged inflation of inventories. The suit claims FOX & CO.'s audits for the years 1976 through 1980 were "highly unreasonable and deficient in the circumstances" and an "extreme departure from the standard of care expected of independent accountants." The complaint charged that SAXON's reported inventory of $120.6 million for the year ending 12/31/81 was overstated by $67 million. (*Wall Street Journal,* 3/2/83)

40. A shareholder of CHASE MANHATTAN CORP. has brought suit against certain officers and directors of the bank and its auditors, PEAT, MARWICK AND MITCHELL. The suit alleges poor bank lending practices, which led to inferior loans involving DRYSDALE GOVERNMENT SECURITIES, PENN SQUARE BANK, and the governments of Poland and Mexico. PEAT, MARWICK and MITCHELL is charged with "breaching its contractual duty" by rendering an unqualified opinion on the bank's financial statements. PMM's response is that accountants are not responsible for assessing what loan risks a bank should take. CHASE MANHATTAN took losses of $117 million on the DRYSDALE loans and $75 million on the PENN SQUARE loans in 1982. But it posted total profits of $332.5 million for the year (down about 25% from 1981). (*Wall Street Journal,* 3/21/83)

41. TOUCHE ROSS was sued by SEAGRAVE CORP., which claimed it relied on misleading assurances regarding its acquisition of the assets of SEAGRAVE's predecessor. (*Wall Street Journal,* 3/9/83)

42. ERNST & WHINNEY was the subject of critical comment in a *Wall Street Journal* feature piece (3/4/83), which referred to ERNST & WHINNEY's audit opinion of the UNITED AMERICAN BANK of Knoxville, Tennessee. The bank collapsed three weeks after E&W rendered an unqualified opinion of its financial statements. FDIC auditors, in the bank at the same time E&W's staff was engaged in its review, were not consulted on their (FDIC) findings. (The bank was ordered closed by the FDIC because of large possible loan losses.) E&W defended its audit on the grounds that it did not have access to the same data that the FDIC auditors had. (See *The*

New York Times, 3/17/83, for E&W's defense.) FDIC auditors did not discover the loan problems until they conducted a concurrent examination of all eleven banks in the UNITED AMERICAN BANK chain.

43.   A former lending officer of AMERICAN BANK & TRUST CO. of Reading, Pennsylvania is suspected of attempting to defraud the bank of about $9.5 million by false loans and other unauthorized transactions. A routine review of the lending officer's loans uncovered the problem. An investigation is now under way. The FDIC, the FBI, and the bank's fidelity bond insurer have been notified. (*Wall Street Journal,* 3/21/83)

44.   A Rotterdam bank, SLAVENBURG BANK, has reported an embezzlement scheme which may have cost the bank $65 million. The bank's foreign transfer department head was arrested by Dutch police authorities, who say that the bank employee broke the computer code and transferred funds to outside accounts. The alleged fraud was discovered through an audit. (*Wall Street Journal,* 3/22/83)

45.   A Cleveland, Ohio UNITED WAY accounting supervisor was indicted for embezzling $63,000 from the agency. Checks were issued for specious building and remodeling projects and then endorsed and cashed by her; or they were deposited to accounts she had created for the fictitious contractors. (*Cleveland Plain Dealer,* 3/9/83)

46.   A cashier in the Ohio State Treasurer's office pleaded guilty to embezzling $1.15 million. The funds were used partly to finance the musical ambitions of her boyfriend, a bandleader. The cashier had access to public funds in a state vault and could make entries in the state's accounting journals. At audit time when the cash was counted, the cashier made up shortages by replacing missing funds with fictitious checks. (*Cleveland Plain Dealer,* 3/9/83)

47.   The U.S. Government continues its efforts to put a clamp on criminals who use financial and other institutions to launder their loot. The IRS is tightening its efforts to have banks and brokers report unusual cuurency transactions, i.e., those involving large amounts of cash. MERRILL LYNCH was alleged to have reported about one hundred currency transactions involving about $1.5 million in 1981, when it should have reported about five hundred of these transactions involving about $10 million. A New York City federal grand jury is also investigating the matter and has asked MERRILL LYNCH to supply a large number of documents. (MERRILL LYNCH says that it may take three months to gather all the requested information.) (*Wall Street Journal,* 3/4/83 and 3/7/83)

48.   Gaming casinos are also being studied as sources or conduits for the laundering of funds. Casinos are not bound by IRS regulations on unusual currency transactions, so they are prime candidates for servicing the cash laundering needs of drug traffickers and other underworld figures. The IRS claims the ROYAL CASINO in Las Vegas was so used. Two principals at the casino were indicted by a Tampa, Florida grand jury for conspiracy to defraud the IRS. (*Wall Street Journal,* 3/17/83)

49.   Bank secrecy laws in the Bahamas make that country a safe refuge for the

laundering of funds by drug traffickers, organized crime figures, stock swindlers, tax evaders, and other white collar criminals. One such bank, COLUMBUS TRUST CO. of Nassau, was the subject of intensive comment by the *Wall Street Journal* (3/8/83). The *Journal* article recounted some interesting facts about COLUMBUS TRUST CO: (1) fugitive financier ROBERT VESCO was once a part owner of the bank, (2) it is now partly owned by Bahamian Prime Minister LYNDEN PINDLING, (3) it was used by a group of conspirators to defraud more than two hundred investors in a fraudulent coal mining tax shelter, (4) it offers clients a number of preexisting "shell" corporations which can be used as secrecy shields, and (5) it was used by a Houston oil promoter to launder unreported oil revenues and by a Pittsburgh dope dealer to finance the purchase of airplanes and boats.

50. SECURITY AMERICA CORP., a casualty underwriter taken public by JOHN MUIR & CO., a brokerage house that collapsed in 1981, is the subject of SEC scrutiny. The Commission filed a complaint against SECURITY AMERICA's former president and a former vice president alleging they falsified company records and caused the company's prospectus to contain untrue financial results for 1979. Insurance loss reserves were understated by $40 million, resulting in inflated estimates of earnings and net worth. (*Wall Street Journal,* 3/18/83)

51. FEDERAL EXPRESS CORP. was the recent victim of a plot to rig bids on its construction projects by a contractor whose scheme involved compromising FEDERAL EXPRESS employees through payoffs and kickbacks. The employees were fired and the contracts terminated. The contractor now stands charged with offering to pay $20,000 for a "hit" on "anybody who talked." (*Wall Street Journal,* 3/30/83)

52. RICHARD FIRESTONE and MILTON DORISON were convicted of promoting fraudulent coal mine tax shelters. Hundreds of investors were victimized in the scheme, which involved eastern Kentucky mining ventures. Investors were told they could put up $25,000 in cash and borrow $75,000 (from COLUMBUS TRUST CO. of Nassau) and thus have a $100,000 tax deduction. There was some question as to whether the promoters ever intended to mine any coal. (*Wall Street Journal,* 4/21/83)

53. MARSHALL CLINARD, in a recent study conducted for the U.S. Department of Justice, found that among sixty-four retired corporate middle managers of Fortune 500 companies ratings of the ethics of their former companies were relatively high: 25%, very good; 44%, good; and 33%, fair. The largest share of fair ratings came from former employees of motor vehicle and aerospace companies. The retired managers showed a strong support for governmental regulation, a surprise to CLINARD. There was, however, far more concern about health and safety regulations than about price fixing and illegal rebating. Slightly more than half of the respondents felt top management is responsible for setting the ethical tone of a firm. (*Wall Street Journal,* 5/16/83)

54. For an example of the danger from absence of controls, SOUTHERN

ILLINOIS UNIVERSITY was the recent victim of fraud allegedly perpetrated by its former data processing department head and eight others. The university filed a civil suit to recover $400,000 in damages it alleged had been incurred through the purchasing and leasing of computer equipment at inflated prices from bogus companies. The university was not required to submit the purchases to competitive bidding. (It does now.) The fraud did not surface for several years. A successor asked for an internal audit and "certain questions" then arose. (*Computerworld,* 5/9/83)

55. A former executive vice president of GENERAL DYNAMICS CORP. was sued by the bankruptcy trustee of FRIGITEMP CORP. for taking bribes and kickbacks from FRIGITEMP on a subcontract for the construction of liquified natural gas tankers. The trustee alleges in the civil suit for $4.5 million that 10% of the contract award given by GENERAL DYNAMICS to FRIGITEMP was paid over or kicked back to the executive vice president, a subordinate, and several former FRIGITEMP executives through a number of sham corporations, phony invoices, and Swiss bank accounts. GENERAL DYNAMICS was also listed as a defendant. No criminal charges have been filed and the defendants have denied the allegations. (*Wall Street Journal,* 5/20/83)

56. AM INTERNATIONAL was charged by the SEC with illegally inflating its profits by $23 million in its 1980 and 1981 fiscal years. (AM INTERNATIONAL is involved in Chapter 11 proceedings.) The Commission charges AM INTERNATIONAL recorded as "sold" products that were being rented by customers or that had not even been shipped. Inventory overstatements were also reported. (*Wall Street Journal,* 5/3/83)

57. The president of NORTH BROWARD INDUSTRIES, INC. of Coral Gables, Florida was convicted by a federal court in Philadelphia for rigging $13 million in bids on military supply contracts for machine parts, nuts, and bolts. A former purchasing agent for the Defense Department, the president of NORTH BROWARD was alleged to have secretly controlled or represented seven companies who bid on the contracts. A number of Defense employees were also convicted on charges of conflicts of interest and accepting gratuities in the same scheme. (*Wall Street Journal,* 6/9/83)

58. Six of the nation's largest electrical contractors were indicted on bid rigging charges involving the construction of three nuclear power plants. This case is unique in that certain of the contractor's top officers were also indicted in the antitrust criminal action. Executives are rarely made defendants in antitrust cases. The indictment, returned by a federal court in Seattle, Washington, is the first of several expected to be filed against thirty electrical contractors by the Antitrust Division of the U.S. Justice Department. (*Wall Street Journal,* 6/9/83)

59. A former executive of MR. COFFEE (made by NORTH AMERICAN SYSTEMS, INC. of Bedford Heights, Ohio) was indicted for diverting about $884,000 of corporate funds to his own use. (*Wall Street Journal,* 6/9/83)

60. The former office manager of WALTER E. HELLER INTERNATIONAL's Phoenix, Arizona office was indicted by a state court for divert-

ing $1.9 million. The proceeds were used to acquire real estate holdings. (*Wall Street Journal,* 6/8/83)

61. DEAN WITTER REYNOLDS, INC. did not expect its new twenty-four-hour commodities trading desk to be compromised so soon. In January the trading desk was offered as a new service to customers who wanted to trade around the clock by entering commodity orders in London and Hong Kong as well as New York; the desk was soon tapped for $14 million by two DEAN WITTER brokers. The scheme, which began in February 1983, involved the creation of a fictitious account through which both brokers executed their own orders. Profits were transferred by wire by the duo to a Swiss bank. Losses were concealed by rolling forward the loss positions, a form of lapping or delay-of-loss reporting. The loss will have no material impact on DEAN WITTER. A suit may be instituted against the discharged brokers for the profits they accumulated in Switzerland. Insurance may cover the balance. (*Wall Street Journal,* 6/9/83)

62. The good news is that bank, savings and loans, and credit union embezzlement and fraud incidents are down says the FBI. The bad news is that total losses from these crimes are up. Losses more than *doubled,* from just under $200 million in 1981 to about $450 million in 1982. Eighty-three percent of these banks frauds were internally caused and seventeen percent were externally caused.

63. PEAT, MARWICK and MITCHELL is ecstatic over a ruling by a Federal District Court judge in Hawaii. The judge absolved PMM from any responsibility for audit shortcomings in an action brought against it by a bankruptcy trustee for a former audit client. PMM fought the charges at a cost of $5 million but thought that the fight was worth the expense. (Traditionally, Big 8 firms have settled such nuisance suits out of court because of possible embarrassment.) Victor Earle, PMM's general counsel, says the suit should never have been brought in the first place. (See *Goss* v. *Crossley,* No. 79–0037, D. Hawaii, April 4, 1983.)

64. FSLIC charged two officers of FIRST FINANCIAL S&L, Downers Grove, Illinois with embezzling $2.5 million. The FSLIC says that false entries were made to cover up the defalcation. (*Wall Street Journal,* 4/29/83)

65. FSLIC also charged in several lawsuits that officers of MANNING SAVINGS AND LOAN, a Chicago thrift institution, paid excessive salaries and illegal dividends to themselves during the institution's dying days. (*Wall Street Journal,* 5/3/83)

66. The annual study of inventory shrinkage at retail establishments, which is conducted by Arthur Young & Co. for the NATIONAL MASS RETAILING INSTITUTE, had some unusual results reported last year. Security expenditures by retailers rose 14% in 1981 but shrinkage remained at 2% of sales, or about $1.7 billion.

In order of priority, strategies suggested for reducing inventory shrinkage were:

- Employee education
- Better paperwork methods
- Improved screening of new employees
- Increased controls at cash registers
- Increased security forces

Shrinkage was attributed to the following causative factors:

- Employee theft, 50%
- Customer shoplifting, 30%
- Paperwork (Sloppy accounting), 20%

(*Security World,* March 1983)

Appendix 2

Corporate Fraud Environment Checklist

	YES	NO	RATING		
			HIGH	MED	LOW

I. Planning Skills Inventory

  A. Strategic Planning

    1. Does the organization have a long-range plan (three to five years)?

      a) Does the plan contain a clear and concise statement of organizational purpose or mission?

      b) Does it contain clear and concise policies toward the organization's human resources, shareholders, vendors, and suppliers, and the communities in which it does business (social responsibilities)?

  B. Operational Planning

    1. Does the organization have an operational master plan (one year)?

    2. Does the operational plan integrate and convert long-range goals and strategies into immediate objectives?

    3. Are objectives clear, concise, measureable, challenging, and realistic?

	YES	NO	RATING		
			HIGH	MED	LOW

4. Have accountabilities for their accomplishment been established?

5. Have resources been pledged toward their accomplishment?

6. Have time lines for their accomplishment been established?

7. Overall, how well does the organization practice operational planning?

C. Budgeting

1. Does the organization have an annual budget?

2. Does the budget integrate and convert operational objectives into dollar projections of expense and revenue?

3. Is net operating profit forecasted?

4. Are expected ratios and relationships between revenues and expenses established?

5. Are variances between budgeted amounts and actual amounts of revenues and expense provided for in the budget report format?

6. Are parameters of acceptable financial performance provided for, so that management by exception may be practiced? (Pessimistic, realistic, and optimistic forecasts of revenue and expense)

7. Are overhead costs (general and administrative) allocated by profit center, cost center, department, or operating division?

8. Overall, how well does the organization practice budgeting?

	YES	NO	RATING		
			HIGH	MED	LOW

II. Organizing Skills Inventory

  A. Operational Structures

    1. Does the firm have an organization plan which establishes the chain of command?

    2. Does the firm have a *current* and *coherent* organizational chart specifying by hierarchical level the functional relationship between each major component of the firm?

    3. Does the organization have job descriptions for all major positions detailing the current responsibilities, duties, areas of accountability, and authority of the persons holding such positions?

    4. Is the firm's organizational structure appropriate for its size, degree of complexity of operations, geographical dispersion, product diversity, and nature of business?

    5. Does its structure hinder internal communications?

    6. Overall, how would you rate the appropriateness of the organization's structure?

  B. Delegation Skills

    1. Is delegating of authority practiced by senior management?

      a) To what degree?

    2. Is delegation perceived as a developmental experience for subordinates by top management?

      a) To what degree?

	YES	NO	RATING		
			HIGH	MED	LOW

3. Are acts of delegation planned in advance with predefined objectives established, time frames set for completion, and evaluation points?

   a) Does coaching and counseling of the subordinate follow after a task has been delegated?

   (1) To what extent?

4. Are the tasks that are delegated only those which the manager/delegator does not wish to do personally?

   a) If yes, to what extent does this form of delegation exist in the firm?

5. Overall, how well do the organization's top managers delegate authority in a positive or developmental way?

III. Coordination Skills Inventory

  A. Communication Skills

   1. Are job roles clear and unambiguous?

      a) To what degree?

   2. Are performance expectations clear and unambiguous?

      a) To what degree?

   3. To what degree do managers know the job roles of their peer group colleagues?

   4. To what degree do managers know the job roles of their subordinates?

   5. Do communication gaps or bottlenecks exist?

	YES	NO	HIGH	MED	LOW

a) Between top management and middle management?

b) Between middle management and first line supervision?

c) Between peer groups?

6. Do communication gaps or bottlenecks adversely affect the accomplishment of goals and objectives?

7. To what degree are operational problems suppressed?

a) Openly discussed?

8. To what degree are interpersonal conflicts or disagreements suppressed?

a) Openly discussed?

9. To what degree is internal communication

a) Free-flowing between superiors and subordinates?

10. To what degree is internal communication stylized?

a) Formal and stiff?

b. Informal and friendly?

11. Is information flow predominately

a) Topdown?

b) Bottom up?

c) Lateral?

d) Flowing equally in all directions?

12. Are regular staff meetings held to facilitate internal communication?

a) To what degree do these meetings enhance internal communication?

	YES	NO	RATING		
			HIGH	MED	LOW
13. What are the main means and instruments used to facilitate internal communication?					
a) Formal staff meetings held on a regular basis?					
b) Informal meetings held sporadically as needs dictate?					
c) Written bulletins, memos?					
d) Telephone?					
e) Oral instruction?					
14. Is the predominant communication style of managers					
a) Directive, formal, and authoritarian?					
b) Collaborative, informal, and participative?					
c) Noncommunicative, guarded, and defensive?					
15. To what degree can lower level managers influence decisions at higher levels?					
16. Overall, how effective is lateral communication? (between peer groups)					
17. Overall, how effective is interpersonal communication between superiors and subordinates?					
IV. Motivational Climate Inventory					
A. Reward System					
1. Are salaries, wages, and fringe benefits competitive and comparable to other organizations in the same industry and same market areas?					
2. Are recognition awards and bonuses provided for outstanding performance?					

	YES	NO	RATING		
			HIGH	MED	LOW
3. To what degree is performance appraised on the basis of					
a) Objective criteria, i.e., achievement of job-related goals and objectives?					
b) Subjective criteria, i.e., personality, style, education, experience, and technical skills possessed?					
4. To what degree are promotional opportunities possible for outstanding performance?					
5. To what degree are the following criteria used to evaluate candidates for promotion?					
a) Length of service?					
b) Education?					
c) Work experience?					
d) Past job-related achievements?					
e) Technical skills possessed?					
f) Managerial style?					
g) Old school ties and other social alliances?					
h) Political influence within the firm?					
i) Assessed potential for growth within the organization?					
j) Ability to work well with others, willingness to accept responsibility, ability to cope with change, determination to excel and succeed?					
6. Is the organization in a major expansion mode?					
7. Will more employment opportunities and promotions exist in the future than existed in the past?					

	YES	NO	RATING		
			HIGH	MED	LOW

8. Will employment be more secure in the future than in the past?

9. Is the company profitable now?

10. Is future profitability threatened or challenged by outdated technologies used by the firm?

11. Is the company unionized?

12. How good are labor/management relations?

13. Are tardiness, absences, and turnover higher than those of competitors?

14. Are employee grievances higher than those of competititors?

15. Is the grievance backlog growing?

16. Does the organization have an equal opportunity employment plan?

17. Are the recruitment and staffing goals of such a plan being met?

18. To what extent are skilled job categories unstaffed?

19. To what extent are nonskilled job categories unstaffed?

20. Is recruitment of skilled and non-skilled employees a major concern of management?

21. Is the average length of service growing longer?

    a) Growing shorter?

22. Are routine and repetitive jobs being automated?

23. Has the organization ever utilized job enrichment or job enlargement programs?

24. Does the organization have a human resource development plan?

	YES	NO	RATING		
			HIGH	MED	LOW
a) Is management succession a component of the plan?					
b) Are criteria for promotion specified?					
c) Are training and development needs specified?					
d) Are recruitment needs specified?					
e) Is an inventory of available talents within the firm specified and maintained?					
f) Are future talent needs specified?					
25. Overall, how good is the motivational climate of the firm?					

V. Management Information System Inventory

A. Performance Data Gathering

1. Are all jobs specified with norms or standards of expected performance, i.e., quantitative, qualitative, time or cost measurements?

2. Is there a feedback mechanism provided for all jobs on a continual or regular basis? (A performance reporting system on a real-time basis)

3. Are variances highlighted so that correctional measures may be taken when performance levels are below expectations or standards?

4. Are variance reports submitted by subordinates to superiors?

	YES	NO	RATING		
			HIGH	MED	LOW
5. Are the actions taken by subordinates to correct variances reported to superiors?					
6. Are additional resources pledged to subordinates when variances become chronic, i.e., advice, counsel, coaching, more time, manpower, etc.?					
B. Performance Evaluation					
1. To what use is performance data applied?					
a) Performance evaluations?					
b) Modification of standards?					
c) Establishment of problem-solving objectives for the next planning cycle?					
d) Reinforcement of subordinates when performance is high?					
e) Coaching and counseling of subordinates when performance is below expectation?					
f) Establishment of points for cash bonuses or other financial incentives?					
2. Does the performance data gathered measure results (outputs and impacts) rather than activities (thruputs)?					
a) Work volume versus quality of work?					
b) Value added rather than value consumed in the production process?					
3. Overall, how effective is the management information system in providing relevant performance					

	YES	NO	RATING		
			HIGH	MED	LOW

data on a timely basis which can then be used to reinforce subordinates and detect variances from standards or expectations?

VI. Management Environment

  A. Trust Environment

    1. Does management display a real sense of commitment to the growth and development of the firm's human resources?

      a) Are funds committed to the training and development of employees?

      b) Are promotions to senior management jobs mainly from within?

      c) Are promotions to middle management jobs mainly from within?

      d) Are career plans established for all new employees?

      e) Does the company encourage employee education?

      f) Are selection, promotion, bonus, and recruitment policies fair and equitable to all?

    2. Is power diffused, i.e., delegated downward?

    3. Is decision-making power conferred to the lowest level possible?

    4. Are goals and objectives negotiated between superiors and subordinates interacting as peers? (versus being imposed arbitrarily on subordinates)

    5. Overall, what is the level of interpersonal trust in the organization?

	YES	NO	RATING		
			MED	HIGH	LOW
B. Ethical Environment					
1. Does management display a high sense of business ethics toward its varied audiences, i.e., shareholders, employees, vendors, competitors, and the communities in which it does business?					
a) Are company executives involved in community activities which enhance the arts, sciences, education, local economy, and the quality of social and political life?					
b) Are the religious rights and freedoms of employees respected?					
c) Are the rights of personal privacy of employees respected?					
d) Is the information disseminated to shareholders honest, factual, and adequate to make intelligent and informed investment decisions?					
e) Are the demands made on vendors reasonable?					
f) Are competitive tactics adopted by the firm fair and reasonable under the circumstances as compared within the industry?					
g) Are employees treated as individuals?					
2. Is sufficient time provided for employees to enjoy their families, communities, leisure, and personal or professional renewal?					
3. Overall, what is the level of organizational ethics practiced by the firm?					

Appendix 3

Glossary of Computer Fraud Techniques
and Countermeasures

A. COMPUTER FRAUD TECHNIQUES

   1. Input Scams

      a) *Data Diddling.* Changing data before or during their input to the computer, i.e., counterfeiting, forging, altering, or fabricating input documents. (This is the most common computer scam.)

      b) *Piggybacking.* A form of impersonation in which a nonauthorized person gains access to a terminal which has not been deactivated (signed off) and uses it for his own purposes; or the nonauthorized person knows the authorized person's password code and signs on with that password.

      c) *Imposter Terminal.* Using a home computer or an offsite terminal with a telephone modem to gain access to a main computer by fabricating authorization (cracking the password code) and then either intercepting data or using time on the computer free of charge.

      d) *Multiple Data Base Manipulation.* Gaining access to one computer in a network and using that access privilege to break into other computers in the network by use of a common access code; or cracking an access protocol by successive attempts to decipher the access code then stealing time on the computer, converting software, or manipulating data files.

   2. Thruput Scams

      a) *Trojan Horse.* Covert placement of instructions in a computer program so that the computer will perform unauthorized functions.

      b) *Salami Slicing.* Thefts of small amounts of money from a large number of sources, i.e., shaving a penny from each savings account during an interest calculation run or rounding off the mills (one-tenth of a cent) and accumulating them for transfer to your own account.

c) *Trap Doors.* A systems programming design flaw intended to facilitate subsequent modifications or debugging. If not edited out after the program is debugged, an unscrupulous programmer may be able to access the computer (steal time on the computer) or obtain data or programs which he has no authority to have.

d) *Logic Bombs.* Instructions inserted in a computer operating system or program facilitating the perpetration of an unauthorized or malicious act.

3. Output Scams

a) *Pizza Boy Ploy.* Gaining access to the computer room (normally at night or on weekends when security is relaxed) by posing as a pizza deliveryman or serviceman and then stealing output reports or console logs, or sabotaging the computer mainframe.

b) *Software Piracy.* Stealing or copying output reports, computer files, or programs and then using them for your own purposes, selling them to others (competitor firms), or offering to return them to the company for ransom.

c) *Scavenging.* Searching through the computer room's trash (old reports, operations logs, used punch cards and paper tapes, etc.) to learn enough about the system to compromise it.

B. COMPUTER FRAUD COUNTERMEASURES

1. Programming Controls

a) One way to detect thruput scams is periodically to run the current version of a program against the original or backup copy to determine whether any modifications or changes have been made. But if the computer abuser has also modified the backup copy, it is very difficult to determine if a program has been altered.

b) Input and output scams are easiest to detect. Thruput scams, since they take place inside the "black box," are more difficult to detect. They are less visible.

c) Good security controls are transparent—the abuser does not know he is being monitored or observed.

2. Data Transmission Security Controls

a) *Cryptographic Transmission* and data storage. To avoid interception and casual perusal of sensitive information.

b) *Scramblers.* To garble the computer message being transmitted.

3. Computer and Terminal Access Controls

a) *Passwords.* Alpha or numerical.

b) *Compartmentalization.* Restricting users to only those files and programs which they are authorized to use.

c) *Error lockout.* Shutting down the terminals' power after successive incorrect attempts to log on.

d) *Voice print recognition*

e) *Finger print recognition*

f) *Palm geometry*

g) *Magnetic card access*

h) *Automatic shutoff.* Occurs after transmission is completed if operator fails to sign off.

i) *Time lock.* No messages can be received or transmitted at the terminal after normal working hours.

j) *Call back.* Before user gains complete access, a phone call is made to the terminal site to verify the user's identity.

k) *Random personal information.* Before the computer allows access, it will pose random personal questions that are stored in its memory, i.e., "What is your mother-in-law's maiden name or date of birth?" "In what hospital was your oldest child born?" "When will you celebrate your twenty-fifth wedding anniversary?" (This is personal information you would not usually carry in your wallet. If your wallet were stolen, the thief could not use the information therein to impersonate you to gain access to a computer.)

l) *Personal identification number* (PIN). Used in conjunction with a magnetic card which has a coded authorization. You must present or insert both the card and your PIN (a 4- or 5-digit number you commit to memory) as proof of identity.

m) *Personal signature recognition.* After logging on, the terminal operator writes his name with a light pen and the computer matches that signature with an authentic sample in its memory.

Appendix 4

Glossary of Words and Phrases with Fraud Implications

Abuse of Trust
Accounts Payable Fraud
Accounts Receivable Lapping
Actionable Fraud
Active Fraud
Advance Fee Scams
Alteration of Documents
Antique Schemes
Antitrust
Arson for Profit
Art Forgery
Arthritis Cures
Artifice
Asynchronous Attack

Bad Faith
Bait and Switch
Baldness Cures
Bank Fraud
Bankruptcy Fraud
Bankruptcy Sales
Benefit Claims Fraud
Bid Rigging
Body Building
Booby Trap
Breach of Confidence
Breach of Equitable Duty
Breach of Fiduciary Duty
Breach of Legal Duty

Breach of Promise
Browsing
Bunco Game
Business Fraud
Business Opportunity Fraud
Bust Out

Cancer Cures
Cash Lapping
Cemetery Lots
Chain Letters
Charade
Charity and Religious Frauds
Cheating
Check Forgery
Check Kiting
Check Raising
Chimney Repairs
Civil Fraud
Collateral Forgery
Commercial Bribery
Commodity Futures
Computer Fraud
Concealment
Confidence Games
Con Man
Connivance
Constructive Fraud
Consumer Fraud

Contests
Contract Fraud
Contrivance
Conversion
Cookware Scheme
Corporate Fraud
Corruption
Counterfeiting
Credit Card Fraud
Creditor Fraud
Criminal Fraud
Customer Fraud

Dance Studio
Data Diddling
Deceit
Deception
Defalcation
Defraud
Diploma Mill
Discount House
Dishonesty
Distortion of Fact
Double Dealing
Duplicity
Duress

EFTS Fraud
Embezzlement
Employee Fraud
Employer Fraud
Employment Fraud
Encyclopedias
Entrapment
Equitable Fraud
Evasion
Expense Account Fraud

Fabrication
Fake
Fallout Shelters
False Advertising
False and Misleading Statements
False Arrest
False Claim

False Collateral
False Count
False Data
False Document
False Entry
False Gesture
Falsehood
False Identity
False Imprisonment
False Information
False Ownership
False Passport
False Pretenses
False Report
False Representation
False Research
False Statement
False Suggestion
False Token
False Valuation
False Weights and Measures
Falsify
Fast Talker
Fiction
Fictitious Benefit Claimant
Fictitious Person
Fictitious Vendors, Customers, and
   Employees
Financial Fraud
Financial Misrepresentation
Food Supplements
Forged Documents/Signatures
Forgery
Franchising Fraud
Fraud
Fraud in Fact
Fraud in Law
Fraud in the Execution
Fraud in the Inducement
Fraudulent Concealment
Fraudulent Conversion
Fraudulent or Dishonest Act
Fraudulent Financial Statement
Fraudulent Representation
Freezer Schemes

Funeral Frauds
Furnace Cleaning Schemes

Geological Report Fraud
Get Rich Quick Scheme
Going Out of Business
Guile

Health Frauds
Home Repair Fraud
Home Study Courses

Imitation
Impersonation
Imposter
Imposter Terminal
Imposture
Industrial Espionage
Infringement of Patents,
   Copyrights, Trademarks
Infidelity
Innuendo
Input Scam
Insider Trading
Insurance Fraud
Intentional Deception
Intentional Fraud
Intentional Perversion of Truth
Inventory Overstatement
Inventory Reclassification Fraud
Investor Fraud

Kickbacks
Knock-Offs

Land Fraud
Lapping
Larceny
Larceny by Trick
Legal Fraud
Lightning Rods
Loaded Dice
Loan Fraud
Logic Bomb
Lonely Hearts Schemes

Look Alikes
Lost Gold Mine
Lying

Magazine Sales Schemes
Mail Fraud
Mail Order Frauds
Malevolence
Malfeasance
Management Fraud
Marked Deck
Masquerade
Material Misstatement
Medicaid/Medicare Fraud
Medical Fraud
Misapplication
Misappropriation
Misfeasance
Misleading Statement
Misrepresentation
Multiple Data Base Manipulation

Non-Accrued Expenses
Non-Actionable Fraud

Obituary Frauds
Oil and Gas Scams
Output Scam
Overbilling
Overstatement of Assets
Overstatement of Revenue

Padding Expenses
Padding Government Contracts
Patent Schemes
Payables Fraud
Payroll Fraud
Perfidy
Performance Fraud
Photo Studio Schemes
Phony
Pigeon Drop
Piggybacking
Pious Frauds (Phony Charities)
Pizza Boy Ploy

Plagarism
Plot
Price Fixing
Pricing and Extension Fraud
Procurement Fraud
Puffing Wares
Pyramid Schemes

Quacks
Quality Substitution

Raising Plants and Animals
Receivables Fraud
Repair Fraud
Reserves—Over and Under
Restraint of Trade

Salami Slicing
Sales Overstatements
Scam
Scavenging
Scheme
Securities Fraud
Seduction
Self-Improvement Fraud
Sharp Practices
Sleight-of-Hand Trick
Snake Oil
Software Piracy
Spanish Prisoner
Spoofing
Stacked Deck
Statute of Frauds (1677)
Stealing
Stock Fraud
Subterfuge
Sunken Treasure
Superzap
Swindling

Tag Switching
Talent Agency

Tax Evasion
Tax Fraud
Tax Shelter Scam
Technology Theft
Theft of Computer Time
Theft of Proprietary Information
Three Card Monte
Thruput Scam
Time Bomb
Trade Secret Theft
Trap Door
Treachery
Trespass—de Bonis Asportatis
Trespass—on the Case
Trick
Trojan Horse

Undue Advantage
Undue Influence
Understatement of Costs
Understatement of Liabilities
Unjust Enrichment
Unordered Merchandise
Untruth

Vacuum Cleaner Schemes
Valuation Fraud
Vanity Press
Vendor Short Shipment

Water Conditioner Schemes
Watered Stock
Welfare Fraud
White Collar Crime
Wile
Willful Misrepresentation
Wily
Wire Fraud
Wire Transfer Fraud

BIBLIOGRAPHY

1. Akin, Richard H. *The Private Investigator's Basic Manual.* Springfield, IL: Charles C. Thomas, 1976.
2. Allen, Brandt R. "Embezzler's Guide to the Computer." *Harvard Business Review* July–August, 1975. Volume 53, No. 4, page 79.
3. Allen, Brandt R. "Computer Fraud." *Financial Executive* 39: 38–43 May 1971.
4. American Bar Association Section of Litigation. *Litigation Outline Series, No. 2:* "The Role of Experts in Business Litigation." Chicago: American Bar Association, 1977.
5. Awad, Elias M. and Data Processing Management Association. *Automatic Data Processing—Principles and Procedures.* Englewood Cliffs, NJ: Prentice-Hall, 1973.
6. Baruch, Hurd. *Wall Street Security Risk.* Washington, DC.: Acropolis Books, 1971.
7. Becker, Jay, ed. "Computer Crime." A Special Issue of Computer/Law Journal, Vol. II, No. 2., Spring 1980.
8. Becker, Jay. *The Investigation of Computer Crime.* Report prepared for Battelle Law and Justice Study Center, Seattle, WA, 1978.
9. Becker, Robert S. *The Data Processing Security Game.* New York: Pergamon Press, 1977.
10. Bender, David. *Computer Law: Evidence and Procedure.* New York: Matthew Bender, 1978.
11. Bequai, August. *Computer Crime.* Lexington, MA: D. C. Heath, 1978.
12. Bequai, August. *White Collar Crime: A Twentieth Century Crisis.* Lexington, MA: D. C. Heath, 1978.
13. Bequai, August. *Organized Crime: The Fifth Estate.* Lexington, MA: D. C. Heath, 1979.
14. Bequai, August. *The Cashless Society: EFTS of the Crossroads.* New York: John Wiley & Sons, 1980.
15. Bequai, August. "Crooks and Computers." *Trial Magazine* 12: 48–53, August 1976.
16. Bequai, August. "Legal Problems in Prosecuting Computer Crimes." *Security Management* 21: 26–27, July 1977.
17. Bequai, August. "The Forty Billion Dollar Caper." *Police Chief* 44: 68–69 September 1977.
18. Bequai, August. "Computer Fraud: An Analysis for Law Enforcement." *Police Chief* 43: 54–57 September 1976.
19. Bequai, August. "The Cashless Society: An Analysis of the Threat of Crime and the Invasion of Privacy." *University of Utah Journal of Contemporary Law* 3: 46–60 Winter 1976.
20. Bequai, August. "The Electronic Criminal." *Barrister* 4: 8–12 Winter 1977.

21. Blake, Ian F. and Bruce J. Walker. *Computer Security and Protection Structures.* Stroudsburg, PA: Dowden, Hutchinson & Ross, 1977.

22. Block, Dennis J. and Marvin J. Pickholz. *The Internal Corporate Investigation.* New York: Practicing Law Institute, 1980.

23. Bologna, Jack. "Computer Crime: Wave of the Future." *Journal of Assets Protection,* 1981.

24. Burch, John G., Jr. and Joseph L. Sardinas, Jr. *Computer Control and Audit: A Total Systems Approach.* New York: John Wiley & Sons, 1978.

25. Canadian Institute of Chartered Accountants. *Computer Audit Guidelines and Computer Control Guidelines.* Toronto, Canadian Institute of Chartered Accountants, 1970.

26. Carroll, John M. *Computer Security.* Los Angeles: Security World Publishing Co., 1977.

27. Comer, Michael. *Corporate Fraud.* New York: McGraw-Hill, 1977.

28. Comptroller General of the United States. Report to the Congress. *Computer Related Crimes in Federal Programs.* Washington, DC: U.S. General Accounting Office, 1976.

29. Coughran, Edward H. *Computer Abuse and Criminal Law.* San Diego: Computer Center, University of California, 1976.

30. Coughran, Edward H. "Prosecuting Computer Abuse." *Criminal Justice Journal* 1: 1978.

31. Crowley, George and Richard Manning. *Criminal Tax Fraud—Representing the Taxpayer before Trial.* New York: Practicing Law Institute, 1976.

32. Davis, Keagle W., William C. Mair, and Donald R. Wood. *Computer Control and Audit.* Altamonte Springs, FL: Institute of Internal Auditors, Inc., 1976.

33. Dertouzos, Michael L. and Joel Moses, ed., *The Computer Age: A Twenty-Year View.* Cambridge, MA: MIT Press, 1979.

34. Edelhertz, Herbert, Ezra Stotland, Marilyn Walsh, and Milton Weinberg. *The Investigation of White Collar Crime.* Washington, DC, Law Enforcement Assistance Administration, 1977.

35. Elliott, Robert K. and John J. Willingham. *Management Fraud: Detection and Deterrence.* New York: Petrocelli Books, 1980.

36. Finch, James H. "Espionage and Theft Using Computers." *Journal of Assets Protection* Vol. 2, No. 1, 1976.

37. Fitzgerald, Jerry. *Internal Controls for Computerized Systems.* Redwood City, CA: Jerry Fitzgerald and Associates, 1978.

38. Glick, Rush G. and Robert S. Newson. *Fraud Investigation.* Springfield, IL: Charles C. Thomas, 1974.

39. Graham, Michael H. "Impeaching the Professional Expert Witness by a Showing of Financial Interest." *Indiana Law Journal* 53: 35– , 1975.

40. Hagen, Roger E. *The Intelligence Process and White-Collar Crime.* Report prepared for Battelle Law and Justice Study Center, Seattle, WA 1978.

41. Hoffman, Lance J. *Modern Methods for Computer Security and Privacy.* Englewood Cliffs, NJ: Prentice-Hall, 1977.

42. Honeywell Information Systems. Computer Security and Privacy Symposium. *Proceedings 1975, 1976, 1977, 1978, 1979.* Phoenix: Honeywell Information Systems.

43. Hoyt, Douglas. *Computer Security Handbook.* New York: Macmillan Information, Inc., 1973.

44. Hsiao, David, Douglass Kerr, and Stuart Madnick. *Computer Security.* New York: Academic Press, 1979.

45. IBM. *Data Security and Data Processing.* Volume 5. Study Results, IBM, 1973 (No. G320-1375).

46. Inbau, Fred E., Andre A. Moessens, and Louis R. Vitullo. *Scientific Police Investigation.* Philadelphia: Chilton, 1972.

47. Institute of Internal Auditors. *Systems Auditability and Control Study.* A three-part report prepared by Stanford Research Institute under a grant from IBM Corporation. Altamonte Springs, FL: The Institute of Internal Auditors, 1977.

48. Jancura, Elise G. and Arnold H. Berger. *Computers, Auditing and Control.* Philadelphia: Auerbach, 1973.

49. Karchmer, Clifford and Donna Randall, eds. *Compendium of Operational and Planning Guides to White-Collar Crime Enforcement.* Seattle, WA: Battelle, 1978.

50. Kell, William G., and Robert K. Mautz. *Internal Controls in U.S. Corporations.* New York: Financial Executives Institute Research Foundation, 1980.

51. Kirk, Paul L. and John I. Thornton, eds. *Crime Investigation.* 2nd ed. New York: John Wiley & Sons, 1974.

52. Klotter, John C. *Criminal Evidence.* Cincinnati: Anderson Publishing Co., 1980.

53. Koba Associates, Inc. *Expert Witness Manual: Use of Outside Experts in Computer Related Crime Cases.* Washington, DC: U.S. Department of Justice, 1980.

54. Krauss, Leonard I., and Aileen MacGahan. *Computer Fraud and Countermeasures.* Englewood Cliffs, NJ: Prentice-Hall, 1979.

55. Krauss, Leonard I. *SAFE: Security Audit and Field Evaluation for Computer Facilities and Information Systems.* New York: American Management Associations, 1973.

56. Kwitny, Jonathan. *Vicious Circles.* New York: W. W. Norton & Co., 1979.

57. Leininger, Sheryl, ed. *Internal Theft: Investigation and Control: an Anthology.* Los Angeles, Security World Publishing Co., 1975.

58. Liebholz, Stephen and Louis Wilson. *Users Guide to Computer Crime.* Radnor, PA: Chilton, 1974.

59. Lott, Richard W. *Auditing the Data Processing Function.* New York: American Management Associations, 1980.

60. Lykken, David Thoreson. *A Tremor in the Blood: Uses and Abuses of the Lie Detector.* New York: McGraw-Hill, 1981.

61. Martin, James. *Security, Accuracy, and Privacy in Computer Systems.* Englewood Cliffs, NJ: Prentice-Hall, 1973.

62. Mettler, George B. *Criminal Investigation.* Boston: Holbrook Press, Inc., 1977.

63. Miller, Gordon H. *Prosecutor's Manual on Computer Crimes.* Decatur, GA: Prosecuting Attorneys' Council on Georgia, 1978.

64. National Bureau of Standards. *Federal Information Processing Standards Guidelines for Automatic Data Processing.* Washington, DC: Physical Security and Risk Management (FIPS PUB Document No. 31), 1974.

65. National Bureau of Standards. *Federal Information Processing Standards Guidelines for Documentation of Computer Programs and Automated Data Systems.* Washington, DC: Physical Security and Risk Management (FIPS PUB Document No. 38), 1976.

66. National Bureau of Standards. *Approaches to Privacy and Security in Computer Systems.* Washington, DC: (National Bureau of Standards Special Publication 404), 1974.

67. O'Hara, Charles E. *Fundamentals of Criminal Investigation.* 3rd ed. Springfield, IL: Charles C. Thomas, 1978.

68. O'Neill, Robert. *Investigative Planning.* Report prepared for Battelle Law and

Justice Study Center, Seattle, WA, 1978.

69. Osborn, Albert S. *Questioned Document Problems*. Albany, NY: Boyd Printing Co., 1944.

70. Parker, Donn B. *Computer Abuse Assessment*. A Stanford Research Institute report prepared for the National Science Foundation, Washington, DC, 1975.

71. Parker, Donn B. *Crime by Computer*. New York: Charles Scribner's Sons, 1976.

72. Perry, William E. *Selecting EDP Audit Areas*. Altamonte Springs, FL: EDP Auditors Foundation, 1980.

73. Russell, Harold F. *Foozles and Frauds*. Altamonte Springs, FL: The Institute of Internal Auditors, 1977.

74. Ruthberg, Zella G., ed. *Audit and Evaluation of Computer Security*. Washington, DC: U.S. Department of Commerce, National Bureau of Standards (NBS No. 500–19), 1977.

75. Schabeck, Tim. "Computer Crime Investigation Manual." *Journal of Assets Protection,* 1979.

76. Shaw, Paul D. "Investigative Accounting." *Journal of Assets Protection.* Vol. 3, No. 1, Spring 1978.

77. Sokolik, Stanley L. *Computer Crime: Its Setting and the Need for Deterrent Legislation*. Springfield, IL: Data Systems Commission, Illinois General Assembly, 1979.

78. SRI International. *Computer Crime-Criminal Justice Resource Manual*. Produced under contract to the National Criminal Justice Information and Statistics Service, Government Printing Office, 1979.

79. Department of the Treasury. *Financial Investigative Techniques*. Washington, DC: Internal Revenue Service. 1979.

80. United States Senate. Committee on Government Operations. *Problems Associated with Computer Technology in Federal Programs and Private Industry: Computer Abuses*. Washington, DC: Government Printing Office, 1976.

81. United States Senate. Committee on Government Operations. *Staff Study of Computer Security in Federal Programs*. Washington, DC: Government Printing Office, 1977.

82. Vandiver, James V. "Forensic References." *Journal of Assets Protection,* Vol. 2, No. 4, Winter 1977.

83. Van Tassel, Dennis. *Computer Security Management*. Englewood Cliffs, NJ: Prentice-Hall, 1972.

83. Wagner, Charles. *The CPA and Computer Fraud*. Lexington, MA: Lexington Books, 1979.

84. Walker, Bruce J. and Ian F. Blake. *Computer Security and Protection Structures*. Stroudsberg, PA: Dowden, Hutchinson and Ross, Inc., 1977.

85. Whiteside, Thomas. *Computer Capers: Tales of Electronic Thievery, Embezzle-*

COMPUTER FRAUD INFORMATION

Computer Fraud and Security Bulletin. Elsevier Journal Information Center, 52 Vanderbuilt Avenue, New York, NY 10017, $110 per year.

Computer Security Digest. Computer Protection Systems, Inc, 711 W. Ann Arbor Trail, Suite 4, Plymouth, MI 48170, $75 per year.

The Computer Security Newsletter. Computer Security Institute, 5 Kane Industrial Drive, Hudson, MA 01749, $75 per year.

EDPACS. Automation Training Center, Inc., 11250 Roger Bacon Drive, Suite 17, Reston, VA 22090, $48 per year.

INDEX